JOSEPH BRODSKY AND COLLABORATIVE SELF-TRANSLATION

JOSEPH BRODSKY AND COLLABORATIVE SELF-TRANSLATION

Natasha Rulyova

BLOOMSBURY ACADEMIC
NEW YORK • LONDON • OXFORD • NEW DELHI • SYDNEY

BLOOMSBURY ACADEMIC
Bloomsbury Publishing Inc
1385 Broadway, New York, NY 10018, USA
50 Bedford Square, London, WC1B 3DP, UK

BLOOMSBURY, BLOOMSBURY ACADEMIC and the Diana logo are trademarks of
Bloomsbury Publishing Plc

First published in the United States of America 2020
This paperback edition published 2022

Copyright © Nataliya Arbuthnott, 2020

Cover design by Eleanor Rose
Cover images: Portrait: Joseph Brodsky, November 10, 1991, Strasbourg, France
© Ulf Andersen / Getty Images; Additional images © Getty Images

For legal purposes the Acknowledgements on p. xii constitute an extension of this copyright page.

Whilst every effort has been made to locate copyright holders the publishers would be grateful to hear from any person(s) not here acknowledged.

All rights reserved. No part of this publication may be reproduced or transmitted in any form or by any means, electronic or mechanical, including photocopying, recording, or any information storage or retrieval system, without prior permission in writing from the publishers.

Bloomsbury Publishing Inc does not have any control over, or responsibility for, any third-party websites referred to or in this book. All internet addresses given in this book were correct at the time of going to press. The author and publisher regret any inconvenience caused if addresses have changed or sites have ceased to exist, but can accept no responsibility for any such changes.

Library of Congress Cataloging-in-Publication Data

Names: Rulyova, Natalia, author.
Title: Joseph Brodsky and collaborative self-translation / Natasha Rulyova.
Description: New York: Bloomsbury Academic, 2020. | Includes bibliographical references and index. |
Summary: "Uses an archival research method, which has not yet been done in relation to Joseph Brodsky's work, to examine how the Nobel Prize winning Russian poet mastered English as his second language and legacy"– Provided by publisher.
Identifiers: LCCN 2020029911 (print) | LCCN 2020029912 (ebook) | ISBN 9781501363924 (hardback) | ISBN 9781501369797 (paperback) | ISBN 9781501363931 (epub) | ISBN 9781501363948 (pdf)
Subjects: LCSH: Brodsky, Joseph, 1940-1996–Criticism and interpretation. | Brodsky, Joseph, 1940-1996–Authorship–Collaboration. | Translating and interpreting. | Self-translation. | Second language acquisition.
Classification: LCC PS3552.R6229 Z86 2020 (print) | LCC PS3552.R6229 (ebook) | DDC 811/.54–dc23
LC record available at https://lccn.loc.gov/2020029911
LC ebook record available at https://lccn.loc.gov/202002991

ISBN: HB: 978-1-5013-6392-4
PB: 978-1-5013-6979-7
ePDF: 978-1-5013-6394-8
eBook: 978-1-5013-6393-1

Typeset by Deanta Global Publishing Services, Chennai, India

To find out more about our authors and books visit www.bloomsbury.com
and sign up for our newsletters.

For Tom, Mila and Alex Arbuthnott

CONTENTS

List of illustrations	viii
List of abbreviations	x
Note on the text	xi
Acknowledgements	xii
INTRODUCTION	1
Chapter 1 JOSEPH BRODSKY: EXILE AND THE GREAT ENGLISH LANGUAGE	9
Chapter 2 FROM SOLO WRITER IN RUSSIAN TO COLLABORATIVE SELF-TRANSLATOR IN ENGLISH: THEORETICAL FRAMEWORK AND INSIGHTS INTO THE PRACTICE OF SELF-TRANSLATION	37
Chapter 3 WHAT ARE JOSEPH BRODSKY'S COLLABORATIVE SELF-TRANSLATIONS MADE OF?	83
Chapter 4 'MICROHISTORIES' OF JOSEPH BRODSKY'S TRANSLATORS	131
CONCLUSION	177
Bibliography	183
Index	196

ILLUSTRATIONS

Figures

2.1	Stage one of Brodsky's collaborative translation: Brodsky's collaboration with a poet translator (PT)	69
2.2	Stage two of Brodsky's collaborative translation: Brodsky's collaboration with a network of interlinear translators (IT) and poetic translators (PT), editors and publisher	77
2.3	Stage three of Brodsky's collaborative translation: The self-translator's collaboration with a network of translators, editors and publisher	80

Pictures

1.1	'Ia vkhodil vmesto dikogo zveria', English translation by Brodsky: Glossary	35
2.1	FSG's list of interlinear and poetic translators for *A Part of Speech*, page 1 out of 2	71
3.1	'I recognise this wind advancing over the grass' from the sequence 'A Part of Speech' ('Chast' rechi'), English interlinear translation by Stephen White	86
3.2	Stanza 11 'You've forgotten that village lost in the swampland' from the sequence 'A Part of Speech' ('Chast' rechi'), English translation by Alan Myers, draft	87
3.3	'Centaurs I' ('Kentavry I'), English translation by Brodsky, draft, 1989, page 1	115
3.4	'Centaurs I' ('Kentavry I'), English translation by Brodsky, draft, 1989, page 2	116
3.5	'To My Daughter', a draft poem written in English by Brodsky	127
4.1	Interlinear translation of '1972' and translator's notes by Masha Vorobyov	136

Tables

3.1	Five English Translations of 'Near the Ocean, by Candle Light. Scattered Farms' ('Okolo okeana, pri svete svechi; vokrug...') from 'A Part of Speech' ('Chast' rechi') by Joseph Brodsky	91

3.2	Three English Translations of 'I Was Born and Grew Up in the Baltic Marshland' ('Ia rodilsia i vyros v baltiiskikh bolotakh') from 'A Part of Speech' ('Chast' rechi') by Joseph Brodsky	94
3.3	Five English Translations of 'From Nowhere with Love the Nth of Marchember Sir' ('Niotkuda s liubov'iu, nadtsatogo martobria') from 'A Part of Speech' ('Chast' rechi') by Joseph Brodsky	96
3.4	Five English Translations of 'December in Florence' ('Dekabr' vo Florentsii') by Joseph Brodsky, Stanzas I and IX	102
3.5	Two Translations of 'Eclogue IV: Winter' ('Ekloga 4-ia (zimniaia)') by Joseph Brodsky: An Interlinear Translation by Masha Vorobiov and a Self-Translation by the Author, Stanzas I, II and III	107
3.6	A Draft Translation of Joseph Brodsky's 'Eclogue V: Summer' ('Ekloga 5-ia (letniaia)') by G. L. Kline with/and the Author, Stanzas I, II and III	109
3.7	Translation of Joseph Brodsky's 'The Bust of Tiberius' ('Biust Tiberiia') by Alan Myers and/with the Author, Selected Lines	110
3.8	Two Translations of 'Dorogaia, ia vyshel segondnia iz domu pozdno vecherom', Known in English as 'Brise Marine' by Joseph Brodsky	112
3.9	Joseph Brodsky's Draft Translations and a Printed Version of 'Daedalus in Sicily' ('Dedal v Sitsilii'), including Ann Kjellberg's Corrections	118
3.10	Poem 'Anthem': Joseph Brodsky's Drafts in English, Including Corrections by Ann Kjellberg and an Unidentified Reader	125
4.1	Four Translations of 'Lullaby of Cape Cod' ('Kolybel'naia treskogovo mysa') by Joseph Brodsky, Stanzas II.3 and VII.1	144
4.2	Two Translations of 'Lagoon' ('Laguna') by Joseph Brodsky: Masha Vorobiov's Interlinear Translation and Anthony Hecht's Poetic Translation, Stanzas I and II	147

ABBREVIATIONS

Abbreviations used in references to Brodsky Papers held at the Brodsky Archive, Beinecke Rare Book and Manuscript Library, Yale University, New Haven

JBP	Joseph Brodsky Papers, GEN MSS 613
S.I	Series I. Correspondence
GC	General Correspondence
S.II	Series II. Poetry
S. II	Series II. Writings. Poetry
IP	Individual Poems

Abbreviations used in references to George. L. Kline Papers held at Beinecke Rare Book and Manuscript Library, Yale University, New Haven

GLKP   George L. Kline Papers, GEN MSS 650

Abbreviations used in references to Farrar, Straus, & Giroux Papers at The New York Public Library, New York

FSGI	Farrar, Straus, & Giroux, Inc. records.
M&AD	Manuscripts and Archives Division.
NYPL	The New York Public Library. Astor, Lenox and Tilden Foundations.

Other abbreviations

ST	Source text
TT	Target text

NOTE ON THE TEXT

The sources of drafts and printed poems including translations are identified individually for each text. Some Russian poems are presented in Cyrillic. Poems are presented stanza by stanza. When quoting short passages from Russian poems, the Library of Congress romanization system is used, unless they are quoted from manuscripts, in which case the same romanization system is used as in the given manuscript. The rhyme words are presented between slashes for easy comparison. Draft translations presented in tables are coded by using a variety of fonts in bold, italic, grey as well as underlining and a double-underline for comparative analysis of the used lexis. Figures do not refer to the production of particular texts but summarize self-translation and writing practices at each stage. All manuscripts printed in the book are sourced from the Brodsky Archive at Beinecke Rare Book and Manuscript Library, Yale University. The Bibliography follows the Bloomsbury Academic guidelines. Authors' names can be spelt differently if their work appeared in both English and Russian – for example, Brodsky and Brodskii, Losev and Loseff.

ACKNOWLEDGEMENTS

I am grateful to Ann Kjellberg, literary executor of the Brodsky Estate, and the Wylie Agency for kindly giving permission to print the copies of selected manuscripts and quote from Brodsky Papers held in the Brodsky Archive at Beinecke Rare Book and Manuscript Library (Beinecke Library), Yale University, as well as from printed works by Joseph Brodsky: Copyright © 2020, The Estate of Joseph Brodsky, used by permission of the Wylie Agency (UK) Limited. I am also indebted to Kjellberg for reading my manuscript and sharing some valuable insights into her experience of working with Joseph Brodsky.

Special thanks are due to the staff at Beinecke Library and the New York Public Library, Astor, Lenox and Tilden Foundations (NYPB), for being helpful and efficient. I would like to express my gratitude to Valentina Polukhina, Stephen Forcer and John Klapper for reading chapters of my manuscript.

I am grateful to Jonathan Aaron, Laura Anderson, Nancy Berner (Meiselas), Paul Graves, Chris Hanak, Helen Hecht, Mark Hutcheson, Stephanie Viereck Gibbs Kamath, Juliet McKane, Valentina Polukhina, Sam Ramer, Naomi Teplow, Harry Thomas, Ben Weissbort and Stephen White for verifying facts, sharing thoughts on parts of my manuscript and giving permissions to use relevant private correspondence and draft translations by Brodsky's collaborators. Thanks are also due to the Wylie Agency for giving permission to quote from Mark Strand's broadcast interview and to *The New Yorker* for the permission to quote from Howard Moss's correspondence.

I owe a debt of gratitude to the University of Birmingham, UK, for giving me a research leave to complete my book project and for providing financial support to cover the cost of copyright permissions. Thanks are also due to students, colleagues and friends who heard papers based on chapters of this book or read parts of it. They are too numerous to list individually but without their feedback this book would not have come into being. Finally, special thanks go to my family for their support and encouragement while I was writing the book.

INTRODUCTION

In June 2002, I completed my PhD dissertation, *Joseph Brodsky's Auto-Translations*, at the University of Cambridge. It was the first attempt to compare and contrast the Russian and English versions of poems by the Nobel Prize-winning Russian-American poet Brodsky (1940–96). My dissertation was interpretive but, as I was working on it, I became interested in *how* Brodsky mastered the English language in just under twenty years as a grown-up émigré writer, having settled in the United States in 1972. Unlike Vladimir Nabokov, he was not brought up in a multilingual household, with an English nanny. Brodsky grew up in a communal flat in Leningrad, was an autodidact and left school at the age of fifteen. His essays show that his English was still weak when he arrived in America. His rocketing success as a bilingual author was recognized in his being appointed the fifth Poet Laureate of the United States in May 1991. I was intrigued but I could find no clear answers to my questions in his published texts. I had to wait.

In 2004, when the Brodsky Archive opened at Yale University's Beinecke Rare Book and Manuscript Library (Beinecke Library), I rushed there to look at Brodsky Papers. My excitement was dampened by the sheer enormity of the task. The Brodsky Archive contains 116.77 linear feet (248 boxes) of the Joseph Brodsky Papers, which 'document all aspects of Brodsky's professional life, including writings, appearances, readings, lectures, advocacy, and relations with other literary figures' as well as 'much relevant material, including multiple drafts (many corrected) of poems and essays (including translations by Brodsky and others)', as the archive's website (JBP webpage) states. I realized that the one week that I had planned to spend at Beinecke in 2005 would hardly scratch the surface, especially as, at the time, Special Collection readers had to ask for permission for each copy made of a paper that was of interest to them. I ended up going back to the UK with a few copies of draft translations. Reading these and Brodsky's correspondence at Beinecke I was struck by how many collaborators he had worked with on his English poems. I began to ask whether Brodsky actually was a great solo poet in English. I returned to Beinecke three times in the following years.

I discovered that Brodsky commissioned multiple translators to render his work. Sometimes he asked different people to translate the same poem without telling them that other translators were involved. Moreover, he interfered in their translations and changed them as he saw fit without consulting his collaborators. Sometimes he would still feel dissatisfied with several translations of the same poem and would construct his own version from them. I was perplexed by what I saw. One translator was so upset at having his texts 'bowdlerized' by Brodsky and his 'sundry other visitors to his apartment' that he banned him from using his English-language translations without consulting him (see Chapters 2 and 4 for the discussion of Brodsky's collaboration with Daniel Weissbort). Yet I was also amazed at how delighted other translators felt to be co-translating with Brodsky. They volunteered to help with interlinear translations, poetic rendering and editing. Ann Kjellberg, the poet's editor and secretary in the 1990s, described working with Brodsky on his poems as 'one of the great experiences' as an editor. She says that sometimes they 'would sit in cafes and just think up lists of rhymes' (Kjellberg 2020). She describes these sessions as 'brainstorming with him, helping him to think up solutions'. Being in his company was like participating in a creative poetry workshop and many collaborators, including eminent poets, established translators and scholars, felt that it was a great privilege for them, such was his aura and poetic genius.

While I was collecting data and making sense of the archival material, Alexandra Berlina in 2014 published Brodsky Translating Brodsky. Her book provides a comprehensive, nuanced and informative close comparative reading of Brodsky's Russian originals and his self-translations. Her analysis, rooted in comparative literary studies, sheds light on the intricate interplay of meanings between his Russian and English texts. She is interested in self-translation as a tool for 'stereoscopic' reading of bilingual texts. In the introduction, she states that one purpose of her book is to bring attention to Brodsky's English texts among students of English literature and English-language readers. This book offers a completely different approach to the study of self-translation. Instead of focusing on the interpretation of the text, I examine the *process* of self-translation by chronologically applying an archival research method. While Berlina examines published self-translations, I provide insights into the stories behind their production. Brodsky's idiosyncratic approach to self-translation and writing poetry in English has also been examined by Zakhar Ishov in his 2008 PhD dissertation published online. Ishov examines the origins of Brodsky's 'mimetic' approach to translating poetry and aims to emphasize its strengths compared with the methods adopted by other translators.

My objective is to study chronologically *how* Brodsky's collaborative practices of translation and self-translation contributed to the production of his English-language texts in theory and in practice. My approach to the study of self-translation is informed by 'social turn' in translation studies, which encourages the researcher to move from focusing entirely on the text to examining the processes of its production and distribution, the agents and institutions involved, translation practices, the distribution of power between the author and translators, and the construction of translators' identities through the prism of gender, geographical and cultural context.

The resulting book is the first in-depth study to scrutinize Brodsky's translation practices throughout his bilingual career. I examine his translators' and editors' contribution to the production of his English-language texts; I consider *how* Brodsky's distinct English voice shaped; I study translators' networks, their relationships with the poet and each other and assess the role of publishers in the production of the text. The chapters of the book draw on the work of Anthony Pym (2017) who proposed prioritizing the stories of translators over texts, and Rainier Grutman's analysis (2013a, 2013b, 2015) of a gallery of self-translators' portraits and on the notion of translators' 'microhistories' coined by Jeremy Munday (2014).

My analysis is focused on the years of Brodsky's exile (1972–96) and is based on the archival study of the poet's manuscripts in Russian and English, including drafts, published translations and self-translations, notes, comments in the margins, correspondence with his translators, editors and friends. Most of the studied archival material is held at Beinecke. A smaller number of documents, referenced in the book, are located in FSGI, M&AD, NYPL.

My study of Brodsky's self-translation practices is underpinned by recent developments in the area of self-translation as part of translation studies. Encouraged by Grutman's (2013a) call to go beyond Beckett and other symmetrical bilingual writers, I focus on Brodsky as a late bilingual, whose translation practices reveal the struggles of a self-translator who lacks fluency in his second language and has to shift from writing solo in his mother tongue to collaborative co-authorship in English. In Brodsky's bilingual writing, I identify three stages of collaborative translation and writing in addition to five modes of collaboration (Chapters 2 and 3), and this is a completely original contribution to our understanding of bilingual writing, authorship and self-translation. In terms of bilingual writing, the novelty of my work is the examination of writing strategies employed by Brodsky as a late bilingual. My contribution to the concept of authorship is the analysis of Brodsky's collaborative co-authorship in his second language, drawing on Jack Stillinger's work on multiple authorship (1991). In the study of self-translation, the originality of my approach is in showing a collaborative aspect and highlighting the significance of retranslation in the process. This book also contributes to the debate about translations' ownership by considering conversations between Brodsky and his translators, which touch on ethical and aesthetic principles in historical, poetic and cultural contexts. The book brings new light to our understanding of authenticity and 'authentic voice' by demonstrating that the author's authentic writing style in a second language develops in response to and in collaboration with native-speaking translators, peer poets, editors and friends. It is not something given but is achieved and curated in the process of collaborative self-translation.

As a solo writer, Brodsky's ethics and aesthetics were ruled by his servitude to language. His calling as a poet was immense, leading to his well-known defence of his right to be a poet in a Soviet courtroom in 1964 (see Chapter 1). Later, in exile, when he needed to negotiate the translation of his poems with his collaborators, the previously simple and beautiful unity of ethics and aesthetics characteristic of his monolingual period became impossible. His translators came in with their own voices, ideas about poetry and poetic rendering, different values and views on poetic form, varied cultural baggage and professional experiences. They had different demands, limitations and talents. Even when they agreed on the fundamental principles of poetic translation, there were still at times unsurmountable disagreements about detail, the choice of the metre, rhythm schemes, lexical choices and even the use of punctuation. In those cases, Brodsky tended to use his authorial privilege to make the choices that seemed right to him but may have sounded awkward or unidiomatic to his colleagues. Brodsky was accused of writing in *translationese*, of Russifying the English language, insisting on the metre and rhyming schemes that were more characteristic of Russian than English; but he insisted that he was working in the tradition of his beloved English poets, such W. H. Auden and John Donne.

Framing my comparative analysis of drastically opposing reviews – from admiration to sneer – on Brodsky's published self-translations within Georg Simmel's *strangership* theory highlights the complexity of Brodsky's social and linguistic position as a stranger in the United States (see Chapter 2). Brodsky described himself as a 'mongrel' or a 'centaur' to refer to his being in the space that Pym refers to as 'intercultural', that is, the space where cultures 'overlap' and 'intersected' (Pym 2017). As a result of this duality Brodsky could not escape making aesthetic and ethical choices that seemed wrong to those who belonged to one culture only. Unsurprisingly, these choices often had to do with translation. Tensions between Brodsky and his translators often emerged as a result of disagreement about fidelity and accuracy. Brodsky's mimetic approach to translation insisted on the fidelity to the poetic form of the ST and accuracy in rendering the metre and the rhyme scheme. His translators' interpretation of fidelity and accuracy differed from his in various ways, but often native English speakers found it difficult to compromise idiomatic expression for the sake of formal fidelity in the target text.

It is instructive to make a parallel with Nabokov's approach to translating Alexander Pushkin's *Evgeny Onegin*. Nabokov also developed a 'ferocious care for accuracy' (Twirlwell 2010) by adopting a literalist approach. Brodsky and Nabokov have completely different approaches to translation (see Bethea 1995), but yet they share their sharp criticism of existing translations of Russian poets, especially Acmeists, into English. Nabokov fiercely criticized Robert Lowell's 'adaptations' of Mandelshtam's poems (Leitch 2017: 599). Brodsky was equally adamant that there were very few good translations of Russian poetry, especially of Acmeist poems (including Mandelshtam). In a letter to Barry Rubin, he lamented that good translations had become exceptions (see Chapter 2). Both Nabokov and Brodsky rejected most English translations of Russian poetry and were adamant in promoting their differing views on poetic translation despite the criticism both of them received for their unidiomatic and unrecognizable English, as Edmund Wilson, Nabokov's friend of twenty-five years and the editor of *The New Republic*, described Nabokov's translation of *Evgeny Onegin* (see Beam (2016) for further details about their tumultuous relationship). Equally damning accusations were directed at Brodsky by reviewers of poetry in translation (see Chapter 1 and Simic (2000)). Both Russian writers furiously defended their renderings and blamed their critics for being unable 'to comprehend the mechanisms of verse – either Russian or English', as Nabokov put it (Butler 2012). Brodsky, in turn, insisted that his mimetic approach was not an attempt to Russify English but was rooted in the English tradition of formal poetry, which went out of fashion in the late twentieth century. The difference between the two authors is arguably that Nabokov had double standards in his translation approaches: one for his self-translation and bilingual writing, and another when translating other poets' work such as his translation of Pushkin's *Evgeny Onegin*. Brodsky, on the other hand, consistently employed and defended the formal, mimetic method of poetic translation, whether for other poets' work or his own.

Reflecting on Brodsky's collaborative self-translation, I define self-translation broadly to include five different modes of the poet's collaboration with translators, peer poets and editors of Brodsky's texts (see Chapter 3). The archival material that I have analysed in Chapter 4 emphatically reinstates the human, interpersonal, social, psychological and moral aspects of translation. The complexity of human interactions is present in the process of translation, whether they are between co-translators or between a co-translator and the author, or between the critics' reception of a translation and the self-translator. The moral aspect of translation is also manifest in the relationship between the translator and the author, whether the author is alive or dead, between co-translators working either in parallel with each other or together, or between the self-translator and co-translators, varying with whether their relationships are overt or covert.

On top of this, as a scholar writing about Brodsky's self-translation practices, I also have to make moral choices in the ways in which I select archival material, present my analysis and make comments. For example, looking at Brodsky's relationships with male and female collaborators from the position of a twenty-first-century female academic, the differences in the gender make-up of his 'interlinear' translators (two females out of four translators)[1] and poets-translators (all male) have not escaped me. However, there is also plenty of evidence, mostly in the form of personal letters to his translators, that he treated them all equally. If a translation did not look right to Brodsky, whether it was done by an eminent poet (the last two lines in Richard Wilbur's poem – see Chapter 4) or by a scholar (G. L. Kline), he would change it as he saw fit, based on his principles of poetic translation. Despite the tensions caused by these interventions, Brodsky's relationships mostly survived thanks to his deep feeling of camaraderie with his fellow collaborators, his light humour and affectionate way of addressing friends and colleagues.

---

1. Four translators were originally invited to make interlinear translations of *A Part of Speech*.

My main challenges as a researcher undertaking archival study at the Brodsky Archive have been to analyse and interpret documents in a fair and productive way. It turned out to be much harder than I expected. Randall C. Jimerson, the president of The Society of American Archivists, emphasizes three functions of archives, which correspond to three 'changing images of the archives, as sites of power':

> The temple reflects the power of authority and veneration. The prison wields the power of control. The restaurant holds the power of interpretation and mediation. These represent the trinity of archival functions: selection, preservation, and access. The archives is a place of knowledge, memory, nourishment, and power. (Jimerson 2005)

Researchers walk into archives like people enter temples, anticipating to be enlightened. They are treated in archives like prisoners, as their possessions are held in lockers and they are watched by security cameras. Finally, they are treated to the lists of catalogues that they can enjoy like they would food in a restaurant, ordering items that they are salivating to read. The power of archival researchers should not be underestimated, as they can legitimize narratives based on their interpretation of documents. This is particularly relevant when archival documents are not dated or incomplete. In the Brodsky Archive, many draft translations are not dated, so putting them in a chronological order is not always easy. Some draft translations are by unidentified authors. To protect myself from potential accusations of 'fake news' or distorted truths, I have made every effort to share my analysis of manuscript with Brodsky's collaborators or their heirs when possible. In one case, my analysis of an unidentified translation led me to assume that it was by Brodsky himself (see Chapter 4). This assumption is based on a number of observations and a comparative study of several documents, like a piece of detective work. When it comes to notes in the margins, some collaborators' handwriting is recognizable and clear, for example, Kjellberg's, but that is obviously not the case for other examples. In addition, Beinecke archival documents are well organized within two main series: Brodsky's correspondence and individual poems but in some cases the letters discussing draft poems could be found in either of the series or in both (if copied). To fill in some gaps and gain some crucial bits of information to make sense of some documents, I have been in correspondence with Kjellberg, Brodsky's secretary in the 1990s and the literary executor of the Brodsky Estate, who also read the draft of my book and commented on relevant parts of it. Kjellberg's insights have been most valuable. I have been in correspondence to confirm some facts and to gain insights with Jonathan Aaron (Brodsky's translator), Nancy Berner (also known by her maiden name Meiselas who worked at FSG at the time when Brodsky's book *A Part of Speech* was being produced), Paul Graves (Brodsky's translator), Chris Hanak (daughter of Brodsky's translator G. L. Kline), Helen Hecht (widow of the poet Antony

Hecht who translated Brodsky's poems), Mark Hutcheson (a Russian literature scholar), Stephanie Viereck Gibbs Kamath (granddaughter of Brodsky's friend Peter Viereck), Juliet MacKane (daughter of Brodsky's friend Richard McKane), Valentina Polukhina (widow of Daniel Weissbort, Brodsky's translator, and a Brodsky scholar herself), Sam Ramer (Russian historian and a friend of Brodsky), Naomi Teplow (Brodsky's former student), Harry Thomas (translator and Brodsky's friend) and Stephen White (Brodsky's interlinear translator).

The four chapters of my book are loosely structured to flow from the centre to the periphery of Brodsky's collaborative translation networks, from the poet to the stories of his translators. Chapter 1, 'Joseph Brodsky: Exile and the Great English Language', provides an account of the relevant biographical aspects of Brodsky's life in exile in the United States, discusses the poet's literary and aesthetic influences, gives an overview of Brodsky's idiosyncratic view of language and languages, and provides his reflections on exile. Chapter 2, 'From Solo Writer in Russian to Collaborative Self-Translator in English: Theoretical Framework and Insights into the Practice of Self-Translation', engages with recent theories of self-translation, especially in light of the 'social turn' in translation studies. It introduces the notion of linguistic *strangership* to interpret Brodsky's bilingual journey; the chapter makes interventions in the existing knowledge about collaborative translation, self-translation and multiple authorship. In the second part of the chapter, I identify the three main stages of Brodsky's collaborative self-translation, illustrated by three diagrams, each sketching the predominant relationship of the poet with his translators during each period. Chapter 3, 'What Are Joseph Brodsky's Collaborative Self-Translations Made of?', provides a close comparative reading of the English-language drafts of selected Brodsky's poems written in different periods of his bilingual career. It reveals five modes in which the poet approached translation and self-translation. The chapter expands our understanding of retranslation and its role in curating the poet's voice in the second language. Chapter 4, 'Translators' Microhistories', focuses on the stories of Brodsky's translators, interlinear and poetic, overt and covert published and not. The mosaic of different translators' accounts helps us to understand how translators' networks were interlinked and what motivated Brodsky's translators to contribute to the poet's English poems. The Conclusion reiterates the book's contribution to the study of self-translation, collaborative translation, multiple authorship and our understanding of what we mean by an 'authentic' literary voice.

Chapter 1

JOSEPH BRODSKY

EXILE AND THE GREAT ENGLISH LANGUAGE

A writer's biography is in his twists of language. (Brodsky 1986: 3)

Brodsky in Russia: 'Walking out'

Joseph Brodsky, the Nobel Prize winner for literature in 1987, is one of the most revered Russian poets of the twentieth century. He is also the first Russian poet who has mastered the English language to be appointed the fifth Poet Laureate of the United States in May 1991. This book is an inquiry into his extraordinary linguistic journey and the first attempt to understand how he became a bilingual writer.

Joseph Brodsky was born into a Jewish family in St Petersburg in 1940. His father Alexander was a newspaper photographer (Brodsky 1986: 461). He was assigned to the navy and went through the Second World War. In 1950, his 'father was demobilized in accordance with some Politburo ruling that people of Jewish origin should not hold high military rank', as Brodsky recalls in an autobiographical essay (Brodsky 1986: 469). Under Stalin's rule, anti-Semitic persecution turned into a government policy. At the age of seven, Joseph himself experienced the consequences of anti-Semitic Soviet laws when he and his schoolmates had to fill in school library membership application forms, which contained a question about ethnicity (Brodsky 1986: 7). Joseph refused to fill in the form on the grounds that he did not know his 'nationality'[1] and walked out. He concealed the truth to avoid the consequences of his being Jewish that automatically inscribed him into the category of 'outcasts'. Many years later Brodsky justifies his act by saying that he was 'ashamed of the word "Jew" itself – in Russian, "*yevrei*" – regardless of its connotations' (Brodsky 1986: 8). Svetlana

---

1. Nationality (*natsional'nost'*) – race under a different name – played a significant role in defining identity in the Soviet Union. ID papers such as passports contained the rubric 'nationality', which could be entered as, say, 'Russian' or 'Jewish'.

Boym observes the two consequences of this 'walk out': artistic, which led to 'the art of estrangement', and 'political', which was manifested in 'the embarrassment of national identity' (Boym 1998: 259). His first 'free act', a silent rebellion, was prompted by being Jewish in Soviet Russia. By distancing himself from ostracism of Soviet anti-Semitism, Brodsky felt further estrangement, and his first 'walk out' became symptomatic of his life story: 'I've been walking out ever since, with increasing frequency' (Brodsky 1986: 13). Brodsky's act of self-identification through a 'walk out' echoes Ernst Van Alphen's remark on Maurice Blanchot: 'the Jew is someone who relates to the origin, not by dwelling, but by distancing himself from it. Separation and uprooting are the acts in which the truth of origin can be found' (Alphen 1998: 230).

David Bethea makes a parallel between the Polish-Lithuanian origin of Czeslaw Milosz and Brodsky's Jewish Russian roots. He suggests that it is not their ethnicity but the duality of their origin which is the source of their personal alienation. Bethea finds that the two poets have in common their 'metaphysical' passion for ideas, the 'gnomic representation of them', their 'stoic' world view and their repulsion in the face of the 'martyrial-messianic reflex' of their respective cultures as a consequence of their origin (Bethea 1994: 14). Milosz himself points to the 'advantages' of his duality in terms of its power that allows one to estrange oneself from 'the present moment'.

Brodsky grew up in Leningrad (St Petersburg) where his family lived in a 'room and a half' in a communal apartment in Liteinyi street, as described by Brodsky himself (Brodsky 1986: 447–500). He was an autodidact, having left school at the age of fifteen. In 1956, he went to work as milling-machine operator, moving to a job in a morgue and then joining geological expeditions. Between 1956 and 1962 he changed thirteen jobs. In Brodsky's biography, the poet's friend and professor of Russian literature at Dartmouth College Lev Loseff lists thirty jobs that Brodsky held at different times. But he was truly committed only to poetry. He soon became part of the unofficial Leningrad literary scene, being recognized for his exceptional talent by Anna Akhmatova, one of the greatest Russian poets of the twentieth century, and Nadezhda Mandelshtam (1999; 2001) who is known for her powerful memoirs, providing a fearless critique of Stalinist repressions, which led to the death of her husband, the poet Osip Mandelshtam. When Brodsky read his elegy to John Donne to Akhmatova she famously exclaimed, 'You have no idea what you've written!' (Losev 2006). She was so impressed with Brodsky's verse.[2]

---

2. Brodsky's life in Russia and his commitment to poetry have been discussed in many books and articles about the poet and his contemporaries in Russian and English (Shraer-Petrov 1989; Vail' and Genis 1990: 23–8; Ufliand 1991: 108–15; Rein 1994: 186–96; Rein 1997; Naiman 1999; Shrayer 1993: 45–64). Nevzgliadova (1998: 119–23) examines Brodsky's relation to St Petersburg and Moscow schools of poetry.

However, Soviet authorities did not consider 'writing poetry' as a job for someone who neither graduated with an appropriate degree from a university, nor was a member of the Writers' Union. In Brodsky's own words, in the Soviet society a person had to choose between the two roles only: either to be 'a slave with enthusiasm' or 'an enemy' (Polukhina 2000: 295). Brodsky's free views, idiosyncratic behaviour, the refusal to submit to the social norm were intolerable to Soviet bureaucrats and turned him into an 'enemy'. As Brodsky's friend Yakov Gordin recalls, the 'irreconcilability of Leningrad authorities' towards Brodsky was caused not only by his poems which seemed 'difficult to understand' ('maloponiatnye') and did not have any 'political declarations' but by the style of his social behaviour because 'he lived like a free person' (Gordin 2000: 130–1). His freedom was in conflict with the requirements of Soviet society for the poet and citizen, according to which talent was seen as a 'social/public phenomenon', and the goals of poetry were not to please a few but to 'serve millions and to encourage the shaping of a new communist person'. Gordin cites this from the article 'What Is a Real Poet?', which appeared in *Smena* on 23 March 1963 (Golubenskii 1963), and was directed against another freethinking young Leningrad poet and Brodsky's friend, Aleksandr Kushner (Gordin 2000). In the same year, the newspaper *The Evening Leningrad* (*Vechernii Leningrad*) published a feuilleton *A Semi-Literary Drone* exposing Brodsky's 'parasitic' lifestyle (Ionin et al. 1963). The accusation was based on the Soviet government decree on people who led a 'parasitic lifestyle'; that is, they did not hold a job (Iakimchuk 1990: 4). The law was 'On strengthening the fight against individuals who avoid socially useful work and lead anti-social, parasitic lifestyle', which was adopted by the Supreme Soviet of the RSFSR on 4 May 1961 (Article 273).

In 1964, Brodsky was tried for 'social parasitism' and convicted to five years of hard labour in Norenskaia in the Arkhangelsk region. The records of his infamous trial have been preserved and published thanks to the journalist Frida Vigdorova, who took notes of the process. They reproduce the trial in detail. Nadezhda Mandelshtam recalls that those notes mark a new historical threshold because Frida was the first to record a Soviet trial. The judge who allowed Frida to take notes could not imagine that a Soviet journalist would dare to publish the notes of the trial without due censorship or self-censorship and even leak it to be published abroad (Mandel'shtam 2001: 256–7). Efim Etkind adduces ten 'accusations' which the Soviet authorities could have laid against Joseph Brodsky, among them 'selfishness' and 'egotism', 'thinking about death', 'pessimism', 'decadence' and 'modernism', the fact that Brodsky did not complete secondary school and remained 'undereducated' ('nedouchka'), that he did not want to join societies and stayed astray. He was accused of 'Jewish nazism' and castigated for saying that 'reality made him lie' (Etkind 1988: 24–8). The allegations were thus mainly aesthetic and social.

Brodsky's worst memories, nevertheless, were evoked not by his banishment to Norenskaia but by his treatment in the mental hospital where he was incarcerated twice. The two years of his banishment, on the other hand, he described as the best times of his life. It needs pointing out that although he later claimed to have enjoyed physical work, it was damaging for his health. In May 1964, two months into his banishment, he was taken to hospital. Upon his return he was given less hard physical work to do, such as shepherding cows. He spent his free time reading and writing. By the poet's request, his friend Gordin posted him an anthology of contemporary English poetry subtitled *From Browning to Our Days* (Brodsky 1986: 359–60). It was in that book that Brodsky discovered Auden's poem 'In Memory of W. B. Yeats'. Later Brodsky admitted that the lines 'time . . . worships language' had had an extraordinary effect on him and shaped his own relationship with language. Brodsky writes that this poem confirmed his own understanding of language as 'greater, or older, than time, which is in its turn, older and greater than space' (Polukhina 1989: 86) (further discussion of Auden's influence on Brodsky is in a section of this Introduction).

In 1965 Brodsky's prison term was shortened; and he was freed after a campaign by Soviet and foreign writers including Akhmatova, Samuil Marshak, Korneĭ Chukovskii and Jean Paul Sartre. He returned to his hometown Leningrad and tried to settle back into his life. According to Ellendea Proffer Teasley and Carl Proffer, who met the poet on several occasions in the late 1960s and the early 1970s, Brodsky looked for opportunities to leave the former USSR but none of them came to fruition (Teasley 2017). However, the offer to emigrate to Israel, which he received by telephone from the authorities, took him by surprise. He agreed without yet realizing that this was the beginning of his new life in a new 're-incarnation', as he refers to it in the documentary film *Joseph Brodsky: A Maddening Space* (Pitkethly 1999). Brodsky never returned to Russia, even after Gorbachev's perestroika and the collapse of the USSR in 1991.

Brodsky in the west

In June 1972, Brodsky arrived in Vienna, Austria, his first destination in Europe. At the airport, he was met by Carl Proffer, George L. Kline and some other Slavists and émigrés who learnt about Brodsky's arrival (Teasley 2017). Carl Proffer took him to the hotel, in which Proffer had booked a room to share with the poet. According to Teasley, Proffer looked after Brodsky during the first several weeks abroad. He helped him with accommodation, general advice, paperwork, tickets and the bureaucracy needed to be dealt with in order for Brodsky to move to the United States instead of emigrating to Israel.

Proffer also managed to find a teaching position for Brodsky at the University of Michigan where Carl Proffer held the post of the Professor in Russian. His wife and a Slavist herself Ellendea Proffer Teasley describes how confusing and alien Western life appeared to Brodsky upon his arrival, for example, his first encounter with a toaster, a device, which did not exist in Soviet Russia, or opening a bank account (Teasley 2017).

While still in Vienna, Brodsky met his beloved Auden. Teasley recalls that Proffer and Brodsky visited Auden in his residence in Austria. Despite the first lukewarm meeting (according to Teasley), Auden warmed to Brodsky and later in the same year travelled with him to England. Brodsky's recollection of this first meeting with Auden reflects the humility that Brodsky felt at the time, commenting with self-deprecation that his English was weak and he was sure not to make a mistake only in one question: 'Mr. Auden, what do you think about . . .' (Brodsky 1986: 376). Brodsky kept repeating the same question but adding different names of contemporary poets and 'grilled him [Auden] quite extensively on the subject of poetry' (Brodsky 1986: 376). In Brodsky's interpretation of events during those first weeks after banishment, Auden looked after his 'affairs with the diligence of a good mother hen'. Correspondence for Brodsky was sent 'c/o W. H. Auden'. Auden solicited the first financial support of $1,000 from the Academy of American Poets for Brodsky (Brodsky 1986: 377). This money covered Brodsky's expenses until he was paid his first salary at the University of Michigan.

Both poets read each other's poems in translation. In 1973, Auden admits that he 'can do little more than guess about the poems of Joseph Brodsky', but Professor G. L. Kline's translations 'convince him that Brodsky is an excellent craftsman' (Auden and Kline 1973). Once Auden offered to translate some of Brodsky's poems but the Russian poet diverted the conversation because he could not imagine his worshipped Auden 'working on him'. In his turn, Brodsky rendered several of Auden's poems but Auden never found out about them because Brodsky did not think that his translations were good enough. Auden wrote an introduction to Brodsky's *Selected Poems*, translated into English by G. L. Kline (Brodsky 1973a). This was the first approved collection of Brodsky's poems in English, launching his poetic career in the United States. The two poets remained friends until Auden's death in 1973.

Brodsky's poetry travelled to the West prior to the poet himself. His first book of poems in English came out in Nicholas Bethell's translation *Elegy to John Donne and Other Poems* (1967). Brodsky did not authorize this publication, but it played a certain role in introducing Brodsky and his work to Western audiences. For example, it was through this collection and a BBC programme about the Brodsky trial that one of Brodsky's future friends, Richard McKane, found out about the poet and eventually became fascinated with his work (see Chapter 4).

As was mentioned earlier, at the time of his exile, Brodsky's command of the spoken and written English language was fairly poor. His letters in English to the Proffers from Leningrad sent in late 1971 – early 1972, shortly before his exile – provide evidence of his written English. Brodsky's English was sufficient to make himself understood. His tone was witty, playful and light-hearted. He peppered his letters with jokes, puns and even attempted to rhyme in English but yet his letters contained numerous grammatical, lexical and stylistic errors. For example, in his letter to the Proffers from Leningrad on 24 June 1971 he jokes that he writes from the Hotel Syringe (*Otel' Chprits*):

> My dear Carlendear,
> I write you this letter being in the hospital (not mental, rather rudimental) under medical test. Something strange happened with my dirty-thirty bloody blood. Behind one of this [sic] hospital walls (I worked here in the morgue as a corps-man [sic]) – behind one of them is that factory in which I began my first labor steps as metal (not mental) worker. Behind another – our local place for sing-singing where I also sang. Probably it means that I came back 'on my own circles'.³ (JBP, S.I, GC, Proffer, Carl and Ellendea, Outgoing, 1971–2, Box 11, Folder 315)

At the time, Brodsky was well aware of his own insufficient command of the English language, which he comments on in a letter to Proffer from Leningrad dated 12 December 1971:

> Dear Carl,
> I was very glad to receive your last letter with a piece of your fine translation from my science-fiction efforts, because at that time I began to worry about your silence explaining it to myself with two propositions: (1) you are a bit [sic] took offence by with my hospital's letter (although I couldn't believe that you will react seriously on [sic] the opinion of a man who demonstrates his low knowledge of English in the letter itself); (2) you are very busy. Now I see this last one was right. (JBP, S.I, GC, Proffer, Carl and Ellendea, Outgoing, 1971–2, Box 11, Folder 315)

The letter finishes with a humorous poem and a drawing of the poet standing by a chair and a small table, on which a candle is burning and a newly typed up poem is flowing out of the typewriter:

---

3. By 'I came back "on my own circles"', Brodsky meant to say 'back to square one', as his expression in English is a literal translation of the Russian phrase '*vernut'sia na krugi svoia*'.

> There is pretty Lady named Bianca
> Who always prefer vino Bianco.
> The time which she spends
>   among decadents
> Is calling [*sic*] in Russian 'the пьянка'.
>> (JBP, S.I, GC, Proffer, Carl and Ellendea, Outgoing, 1971–2,
>> Box 11, Folder 315)

Brodsky enjoyed writing short humorous verses in English in his letters. He also attempted to translate some short poems from Russian to English. The earliest one that I have come across is Brodsky's translation of his Russian friend Vladimir Ufliand's verses into English in 1969: 'In general, people are beautiful and very fine [*sic*] dressed' (JBP, Box 59 Folder 1197). It the early 1970s, before his exile, Brodsky also began to experiment writing some 'serious' poems in English. On 27 November 1971, Brodsky sent a letter to Proffer containing one of such efforts:

> Or – if you prefer pure poetry I can offer you these eight lines:
> The night which tries to change one season
> into another gives a sense
> that somebody retraines [*sic*] his reason
> from consequence
>
> In wrinkled time whose minutes make an hour
> You who forgets and I who love.
> We no become more beautiful but our
> old photograph. (JBP, S.I, GC, Proffer, Carl and Ellendea, Outgoing, 1971–2,
>   Box 11, Folder 315)

Even though Brodsky's English was not yet good enough to write in English confidently, his rhyming is already characteristic of his future poetic style; it helps deliver emphasis on the rhymed words and bring out their meaning. Brodsky had the ambition to master the language because, as he put it in his other letter to Proffer, the 'destiny' of his poems in English mattered to him. Although he was not yet self-translating, he already expressed strong views on the translations of his poems by others, like he does in a letter to Proffer on 6 November 1971 from Sestroretsk, which is cited below:

> The translations are good, I think so. Especially Mr(s) Fuller's ones. Is he Irishman? Please, pass him my 'gracia', 'spasiboys'. Although George's [G. L. Kline's] variant of 'Stopping' is more closer [*sic*] (I mean: more dear) for me. Because, probably, it was the first. I should like to notice only that there were not frozen-crested waves [. . .]; these waves were 'stopped' as if photographed ones; they were '*ostanovivshimisia*'. (JBP, S.I, GC, Proffer, Carl and Ellendea, Outgoing, 1971–2, Box 11, Folder 315)

From Brodsky's detailed comments on the lexis, rhyme and rhythm of the poem and its translations, it is possible to recognize his future approach to collaborative translation and self-translation (see Chapter 2), as he makes some sharp remarks on the topic, which will soon become a stumbling block in his relationship with some translators because of his profound disagreement with free verse and 'organic' translation, which were popular at the time among poets and the translators of poetry in the United States. Brodsky's strong conviction that poetic form should be retained in the translating language is already unshakable. He writes to Proffer from Sestroretsk on 6 November 1971:

> Necessity of rhymes is more obvious than anywhere. Lack of them is very sad, but, of course, I cannot agitate [sic] you to find the rhymes. Saying the truth, I cannot imagine at all why you got yourself into this uniworse. [...]
>
> You know, Carl, this is very strange and, in the [sic] some time, important for me: english [sic] destiny of my verses. If one man in States or in England will find in my lines at least 1/10th part of all that I did receive reading your native authors, I'll say then I am [sic] lucky person. (JBP, S.I, GC, Proffer, Carl and Ellendea, Outgoing, 1971–2, Box 11, Folder 315)

The letters provided here reveal that Brodsky enjoyed writing in English, and already in the early 1970s he felt that it was important to him to find readers in English largely due to his own deep appreciation of English poetry.

One of the first published poems by Brodsky in English is 'Elegy to W. H. Auden' ('The tree is dark, the tree is tall'), which came out in the collection edited by Stephen Spender *W. H. Auden: A Tribute* (1975). According to Polukhina's chronological account of Brodsky's life and work, Brodsky also wrote a few humorous poems dedicated to Professor Faith Wigzell (Polukhina 2012). Despite these first experiments of writing in English, Brodsky continued to write poetry mostly in Russian and his poems were often translated by the people who admired his work. Many of them were Slavists and for them it was an honour to translate the work of the talented poet, Akhmatova's and Mandelshtam's protégé.

At the University of Michigan, where Brodsky worked in 1972–3 and 1974–80, he taught literature. His lessons were far from being ordinary. As a Russian autodidact poet, he had a sharply different approach to teaching English and American poetry. Having attended one term of his lectures and seminars in 1980, Polukhina shares her admiration of Brodsky as a lecturer in a chapter entitled 'The University of Michigan' (Losev and Vail' 1999). Teasley's account is somewhat different; she recalls that Brodsky did not often take his teaching job seriously. He could show up in the classroom unprepared or hangover, but he always managed to keep students' attention thanks to his unorthodox views and passion for literature. Gloria Glickstein, one of his former students, describes her feelings of awe and fear when she was taught by Brodsky in her letter dated 7 December 1985:

> Dear Joseph,
> [. . .] I wanted simply to convey my great admiration of you and my gratitude for those hours of rapture, so frowned upon by Plato, when even your explications were charged with poetry.
> I must admit that you terrified us, your students, at times. Perhaps it was because the spirit of genius that permeates your poetry now appeared in the flesh. Very intimidating . . . but entirely luscious, too, and I am happy to have been its witness. I will miss your 'monologues, dialogues, and synagogues' on the nature of life, art, poetry, and history: they created a brilliant light which illuminated my week. (JBP, S.I, GC, Glickstein, Gloria, 1985–9, Box 5, Folder 151)

This sentiment is shared by another student of Brodsky, Marty Myers, who writes in a letter dated 7 April 1988 from Boston how pleased he was to attend Brodsky's Lyric poetry class on 5 April 1988. He continues that Brodsky along with Rilke and Montale are 'capable of rendering me [him] absolutely mute'. In the end, he is asking for the opportunity to attend this class again before the end of term if possible (JBP, S.I, GC, Myers, Marty, 1988–95, Box 10, Folder 273). In a letter to Brodsky on 3 October 1973, Bill Jack, another former student and a driving instructor at Ann Arbor, writes how much Brodsky was missed in the Russian department, which felt 'staid' without 'one maverick Iosif Brodsky', comparing the poet's presence with 'something like the presence of Christ in the "Grand Inquisitor"' (JBP, S.I, GC, 'Jac'-'Jer' general, 1972–95, Box 7, Folder 183).

Later Brodsky also worked as professor of literature at Mount Holyoke College, invited to teach there by Professor Peter Viereck. Monica Partridge, one of his former students and a Los Angeles writer, who took his course on Russian Literature and Lyric Poetry at Mt Holyoke in 1989–93, writes: 'Though a half-tyrant autodidact prof, he was an invaluable teacher opening up our minds and exposing us to a vast array of authors not traditionally taught in English Lit departments' (Haven 2013). Retrospectively, she shared the reading list that Brodsky had given his students. The reading contains eighty-three books including ancient Greek and Roman philosophers, Hindu and Christian texts, Russian, German, English, French, Spanish philosophers and writers (Haven 2013). In addition to the breadth of writers discussed by Brodsky, he also made students focus on the detail, as described by Holly A. Case, another student who attended Brodsky's class at Mount Holyoke College. She praises Brodsky's method of teaching students by making them memorize a poem and then write it down from memory in class. Case explains the value of this method, which she learnt to appreciate with time: 'Brodsky's method teaches intimate knowledge, because only what you know intimately can take you beyond what you know' (Case 2016). His remarkable knowledge and eruditeness gave him due confidence in his academic worth, which quickly grew along with his linguistic confidence. He soon came to the conclusion that the quality of his self-education was second to none, stating that he knew 'as much as or even more than 99% of his colleagues' and that it took him three years to feel comfortable as a lecturer' (Polukhina 2000: 201).

During his first several years in the United States, Proffer arranged many talks, appearances, seminars, public lectures and poetry readings for Brodsky. On the poet's behalf, he corresponded with many US universities and colleges: with Albion College,[4] Armstrong State College in Savannah, Georgia,[5] the University of California, Berkley,[6] the University of Iowa,[7] the University of Minnesota,[8] the University of Oregon,[9] the University of Tennessee,[10] the University of Texas at Austin,[11] the University of Virginia,[12] Rockford College,

---

4. A letter from Professor R. V. Bevan to Proffer confirms arrangements and payment for Brodsky's reading, dated 11 October 1972 (JBP, S.1, GC, 'Ak'-'Am' general, 1972–94, Box 1, Folder 3).

5. A letter from John Duncan, program chairman of Poetry Society of Georgia, confirms interest in bringing over Brodsky for a reading, dated 1 August 1972 (JBP, S.1, GC, 'Arb'-'Aro' general, 1972–94, Box 1, Folder 5).

6. A letter from Professor Karlinsky to Proffer finalizes the details of Brodsky's reading, dated 6 October 1972 (JBP, S.1, GC, 'Uel'-'Uni' general, 1072–95, Box 15, Folder 403).

7. A letter from Ray to Proffer confirms plans to arrange a poetry reading in the spring 1973, dated 4 November 1972 (JBP, S.1, GC, 'Uel'-'Uni'general, 1972–95, Box 15, Folder 403).

8. A letter from Chairman Adele K. Donchenko of the Department of Slavic Languages to Proffer confirms their interest in organizing a talk by Brodsky, dated 15 August 1973 (JBP, S.1, GC, 'Uel'-'Uni'general, 1972–95, Box 15, Folder 403).

9. A letter from Professor Albert Leong of the Department of German and Russian to Proffer discusses a series of Brodsky events including a Spring Modern Russian Poetry seminar, a Brodsky symposium and a lecture at the University's Cultural Forum, dated 4 March 1973 (JBP, S.1, GC, 'Uel'-'Uni' general, 1972–95, Box 15, Folder 403).

10. A letter from Professor Martin P. Rice to Proffer confirms arrangements for a poetry reading, dated 10 September 1972 (JBP, S.1, GC, 'Uni'-'Uto' general, 1972–95, Box 15, Folder 404).

11. A letter from Sidney Monas of the Department of Slavic Languages, to Proffer, states that they are delighted at Brodsky's forthcoming visit, dated 9 October 1972 (JBP, S.1, GC, 'Uni'-'Uto' general, 1972–95, Box 15, Folder 404).

12. A letter to Proffer from Zita D. Dabars of the Department of Slavic Languages and Literatures invites Brodsky to give a lecture, dated 26 February 1973 (JBP, S.1, GC, 'Uni'-'Uto' general, 1972–95, Box 15, Folder 404).

Illinois,[13] Oakland University,[14] the Ohio State University,[15] Davidson College by invitation of Harry Thomas and the University of San Diego.[16]

Usually, Brodsky was invited to recite his poetry in Russian followed by the translation read by somebody else. In some cases, the universities also extended their invitations for Brodsky to give a lecture or a public reading. This was a fantastic opportunity for Brodsky to be introduced to most Slavists in US universities. All universities offered Brodsky an honorarium ranging from $85 to $2,500, depending on the number of events organized during his visit, with most of the travel and accommodation expenses covered. It is impressive that in some universities they expected the audiences to amount to hundreds of people.

Brodsky used his English intensively as he was teaching and giving many talks in the first years of his life in the United States. His growing confidence in his second language is also reflected in his decision to start writing in English. Brodsky gives slightly contradictory accounts of when he actually started writing in English, whether it was in the summer of 1977 when he 'purchased in a small typewriter shop on Sixth Avenue a portable "Letters 22" and set out to write (essays, translations, occasionally a poem) in English' ('To Please a Shadow', Brodsky 1986: 357) or in 1976 when his 'Less Than One' essay was published. No matter what year it was, it is important for Brodsky to establish a rite of passage in his use of the English language. Elizabeth Beaujour suggests that differences between individuals who are bilingual and bilingual writers lies in the fact that the writer has to make a deliberate choice to be bilingual. Brodsky's retrospective description of purchasing Lettera 22 and establishing

---

13. A letter from Patrick Persaud to Proffer confirms the details of Brodsky's visit to the college, dated 25 October 1972 (JBP, S.1, GC, 'Roc-'Rud' general, 1972–94, Box 12, Folder 326).

14. A letter from Mrs Dorothy Owen to Proffer confirms their invitation to Brodsky to read his poetry at the Village Women's Club, dated 29 November 1972 (JBP, S.1, GC, 'Oak'-'Oli' general, 1972–94, Box 15, Box 11, Folder 290).

15. A letter from the Department of Slavic Languages and Literatures to Proffer confirms a weekly stay for Brodsky in May 1973, dated 22 February 1973 (JBP, S.1, GC, 'Oak'-'Oli' general, 1972–94, Box 15, Box 11, Folder 290).

16. On 23 April 2020, Harry Thomas confirmed to Rulyova by email that he had invited Brodsky to read poetry at Davidson college: 'It took place in the college's biggest auditorium, and when we walked out on to the stage we realized the place was packed, with some forced to stand along the walls. He recited his poems, as he always did, and I read the English translations, as I did on several occasions'. In the same email, Thomas notes that Brodsky gave a reading at the University of San Diego when Thomas worked there, adding: 'he gave an extraordinary powerful reading, his voice threatening, it always seemed, to bring down the walls.'

that this was the beginning of his bilingual stage is significant for his personal mythology.

As for the reasons to write in English, Brodsky has given a few on various occasions. In the above-mentioned essay 'Less Than One', he writes:

> So I am writing all this not in order to set the record straight (there is no such record, and even if there is, it is an insignificant one and thus not yet distorted), but mostly for the usual reason why a writer writes – to give or to get a boost from the language, this time from a foreign one. The little I remember becomes even more diminished by being recollected in English. (Brodsky 1986: 3–4)

He also wants to re-acquire his relevance and re-establish his literary persona in a new space through finding a new audience without a distorting mirror of translation. In the essay 'To Please a Shadow', Brodsky provides yet another reason for writing in English, that is, to find himself 'in closer proximity' to Auden', whom he considered the 'greatest mind' of his time and writing in his language was a way to understand him better (Brodsky 1986: 357). (For further discussion, see the section on W. H. Auden.)

Since Brodsky acquired a Letters 22 he always possessed two typewriters, one for writing in Russian and the other one in English. In 1982, in the interview with W. G. Westsijn, he described writing in English as 'inevitable' (Polukhina 2000: 197). When asked whether he wanted to become a bilingual poet, he replied: 'No, I have no such ambitions.' During the late 1970s and in the 1980s, he did not see himself as an English-language poet and claimed not to have the ambition to become one; he just wanted to write 'decent, readable poetry in English':

> I will continue to write poetry in Russian, I am sure of that. As for the essay, it is a rarely used genre in Russian literature. The Russian language rebels, resists – it is not suited for this, but English language is. I am glad that I can use this wonderful means.[17] (Polukhina 2000: 197)

Brodsky is not the only one who starts writing in a different genre in the second language. Christine Brooke-Rose writes about her husband, the Polish exile writer Jerzy Peterkiewicz. Like Brodsky, he was recognized as a 'highly original poet' before his exile, in Poland. Living in exile in Britain, he underwent 'the mutation: he not only stopped writing poetry, he turned to novels, and in English' (Brooke-Rose 1998: 18). Another thing that the two poets had in common was that they needed help when they started writing in their second language. Peterkiewicz was helped by his wife, and Brodsky had a broader network of friends and colleagues to rely on. In the following chapters, I reveal the complexities of Brodsky's collaborative translation and self-translation and

---

17. Here and henceforth, translation from Russian is mine unless it is stated otherwise.

identify the three main stages through which Brodsky moved as a self-translator and author in the twenty years of his bilingual career, between the mid-1970s and the mid-1990s. In Chapter 3, I consider five modes of collaborative writing that Brodsky practiced as he was mastering the English language.

Like all great poets, Brodsky drew on his predecessors including many English-language poets, such as W. B. Yeats, T. S. Eliot, Ezra Pound, Wallace Stevens, Auden, Thomas Hardy and Robert Frost. Reading them in the original language was a way to get a better understanding of English. As an autodidact, Brodsky had an enviable skill to learn independently and quickly. His knowledge of English and American poetry was remarkable, and although he could have mispronounced English words in the poems that he was reciting to students in his lectures, his insights into English-language poetry were thought-provoking and truly original. This is evident from the two remarkable volumes of essays *Less Than One* and *On Grief and Reason*.

Reviewing *Less Than One*, Lezard (2011) admires Brodsky's 'gift for the striking phrase', which, he notes, is somehow improved by Brodsky's being a non-native speaker. Lezard also marvels Brodsky's interpretation of Auden's most celebrated poem 'September 1, 1939' and quotes Seamus Heaney's brilliant lines about Brodsky's reading of Auden in the same collection: 'There will be no greater paean to poetry as the breath and finer spirit of all human knowledge than Brodsky's line-by-line commentary on "September 1, 1939", if commentary is a word applicable to writing so exultant, so grateful and so bracingly ex cathedra' (cited from Lezard 2011). In his review of Brodsky's second collection of essays *On Grief and Reason*, Hugh Kenner writes: 'this collection is occasion for gratitude. It is rare for someone so advantageously situated, within poetry but both within and outside of American speech, culture and experience, to confide in us with such pedagogic confidence' (Kenner 1996). Kenner admires how Brodsky has managed to present American poets to the American reader in a new light, adding that 'Brodsky's essay on Frost "is probably the best piece ever written" on his poetry' (1996). The Russian poet has unpacked what it means to be American from a fresh perspective which was possible only because of his position of being simultaneously an insider and outsider, or being in the position of *strangership* to the Americans who grew up in the United States (see the section on *strangership* and the stranger in Chapter 2).

Being a late bilingual also meant that Brodsky had to simultaneously master both spoken and written modes of English, which require different skills and approaches apart from those occasions when one needs to give a formal speech. Some of Brodsky's speeches were written in advance. For example, he was asked to address the students graduating from the University of Michigan in 1988. Commenting on this speech and Brodsky's other public speeches, Kenner describes some parts of them as examples of his 'verbose buffoonery' which 'infest' many of Brodsky's paragraphs: 'To say the least, you were born, which is in itself half the battle, and you live in a democracy – this halfway house between nightmare and utopia – which throws fewer obstacles in the way of an individual than its alternatives' (Kenner 1996). Despite this, Brodsky's essays in English have been unanimously praised. This cannot be said about Brodsky's poetry in English. Isaiah Berlin observes that 'there is no sense that they [Brodsky's poems in English] were written by a great poet'. He adds that in Russian, 'From the very beginning, as soon as it starts, you are in the presence of genius' (Scammell 2012). Despite these limitations in his second language, he still achieved an unprecedented recognition for a late bilingual poet when, in May 1991, he was named the fifth Poet Laureate of the United States. With this hat on, he made it his mission to bring poetry to every American family. Having observed that in many US hotels guests can find a copy of the Bible in a bedside table, he adopted a similar pattern to distribute some books of English-language poetry.

Homage to W. H. Auden

Brodsky familiarized himself with Auden when he was in internal banishment in Norenskaia, in the early 1960s, 'in rather limp and listless translations', which he found in the anthology of contemporary English poetry subtitled *From Browning to Our Days* (Brodsky 1986: 359–60). Through those poor translations, Brodsky recognized a great poet. Auden's verse struck him by its 'self-restraint' with a 'threatening touch of absurdity', by his 'honesty', 'clinical detachment', 'controlled lyricism' as opposed to 'emphatic and self-asserting diet of Russian verse' (Brodsky 1986: 369, 360).

One of the first Auden's poems that Brodsky read was 'In Memory of W. B. Yeats'. He was particularly struck by the lines about time and language:

> Time that is intolerant
> Of the brave and innocent,
> And indifferent in a week
> To a beautiful physique,
>
> Worships language and forgives
> Everyone by whom it lives.
>
> (W. H. Auden 1989: 242)

Brodsky admits that these lines had a remarkable effect on him:

> the train of thought that statement set in motion in me is still trundling to this day. For 'worship' is an attitude of the lesser toward the greater. If time worships language, it means that language is greater, or older, than time, which is, in its turn, older and greater than space. That was how I was taught, and indeed felt that way. (Brodsky 1986: 363)

Polukhina sums up Auden's impact on Brodsky: supported by Auden, Brodsky's reverence to language is reflected in his interpretation of language as the 'poet's master' and the poet as a 'language's slave' (Polukhina 1989: 86). In Brodsky's poetic hierarchy, language is the only phenomenon that can be greater and more important than time in the sense that language can reorganize the linear passage of historicist time. Brodsky was not usually keen on accepting the fact of another poet's influence on him but Auden became an exception: 'This is, I suppose, what they call an influence' (Brodsky 1986: 360). It could be argued that this Brodsky's interpretation of Auden's lines gave rise to the Russian poet's distinctive poetics and mimetic approach to poetic translation, as both are rooted in acknowledging the superiority of poetic form due to its metric quality and its capacity to create rhyming patterns. John Maxwell Coetzee explains Brodsky's position was not far

> from that of the educators of ancient Athens, who prescribed for (male) students a tripartite curriculum of music (intended to make the soul rhythmical and harmonious), poetry, and gymnastics. [. . .] The powers Brodsky claims for poetry would seem to belong even more strongly to music. For instance, time is the medium of music more clearly than it is the medium of poetry. [. . .] Music restructures time in which it is performed, lending it purposive form more clearly than poetry does. (Coetzee 1996: 29)

Coetzee notes that the crucial difference between a poem and a piece of music is the former's semantic meaning, and he comes to the conclusion that Brodsky's theory can lead to a new poetics only if semantics is treated along with prosody 'in a unified and an historical way' (Coetzee 1996: 29). Writing and translating poetry, Brodsky is indeed concerned with both, prosody and semantics, with the focus on the rhyming words which, in his view, carry extra meaning. In 'Child of Civilization', Brodsky writes: 'Meters in themselves are kinds of spiritual magnitudes for which nothing can be substituted. They cannot be replaced even by each other', let alone by free verse (Brodsky 1986: 141). However, to what extent mimetic translation can be universally successful between different languages is discussed in Chapter 2.

Auden's influence on Brodsky was profound. Even Auden's face incited a sense of awe in the Russian poet. Aleksandr Genis wrote that Brodsky loved to repeat Akhmatova's words that 'everybody is responsible for their own facial features' (Genis 1998: 10). Auden's face for Brodsky was the quintessence of the English poet's style – 'of a physician who is interested in your story though he knows you are ill. A face well prepared for everything, a sum total of a face' (Brodsky 1986: 371).

The extraordinary sense of awe which W. H. Auden inspired in Brodsky also was one of the reasons to master poetry in the English language. The 'assimilation' with the language of his beloved poet was the only way to bridge the gap and better understand Auden, as he described in his essay 'To Please a Shadow':

> My sole purpose then, as it is now, was to find myself in closer proximity to the man whom I considered the greatest mind of the twentieth century: Wystan Hugh Auden.

I was, of course, perfectly aware of the futility of my undertaking, not so much because I was born in Russia and into its language (which I am never to abandon – and I hope vice versa) as because of this poet's intelligence, which in my view has no equal. (Brodsky 1986: 357)

For Brodsky, Auden represented the Anglo-American poetic tradition of philosophical, 'existential' verse that developed out of the English metaphysical poetry.

Brodsky recalls with an uncharacteristic precision that he first met Auden on 6 June 1972, 'some forty-eight hours' after he left Russia (Brodsky 1986: 374). Upon Brodsky's arrival in Austria, Auden helped him in various ways. Auden knew about Brodsky, having read his verse in the translation of Kline, who was preparing a volume titled *Selected Poems* the Penguin edition. When Kline asked Brodsky whom he wanted to write an introduction to the book, Brodsky suggested Auden 'because England and Auden were then synonymous' in his mind (Brodsky 1986: 376). Auden personified Anglo-American verse, literature and the whole English language for the Russian poet.

In this light, Brodsky's desire to master English and to 'find himself in closer proximity' to Auden through translation and the 'assimilation' with the English language can be seen as a type of 'metempsychosis', which Tomlinson identifies in Ezra Pound's translations (Tomlinson 1983: 72–97). Tomlinson cites T. S. Eliot commenting on Pound: the good translator 'is giving the original through himself, and finding himself through the original' (Tomlinson 1983: 76). Translating Auden from English to Russian and learning English through this process helped Brodsky shape his own poetic voice in English.

So it is not surprising that Roy Fisher finds so many dazzling similarities between W. H. Auden and the English Brodsky as the Russian poet imitates some peculiarities of the English poet's style. He finds Brodsky's writing in Russian and in English, in original or in translation, somewhat unusual and uncharacteristic of contemporary English poetry. In his view, Auden developed a particular style or even a range of genres between the 1930s and the 1950s, and Brodsky was influenced by them and used them as a way into English poetry (Polukhina 2008: 283).

In her discussion of Brodsky's elegy titled after W. H. Auden's birthplace, Polukhina also pinpoints at some similarities between Brodsky's and W. H. Auden's stylistic features, in particular, 'the same technique for constructing the poetic line', whose 'unity – rhythmic, melodic, grammatical – is broken either by long words, or repetitions, or the syntax'. In addition, she argues that Brodsky's 'heterogeneous lexicon' follows the model of Auden and English metaphysicals (Polukhina 1989: 92). Polukhina shows

> that almost all the features of Auden's style that Brodsky has isolated are characteristic of his own work. He has dubbed Auden 'a master of understatement', a 'self-disgusted moralist', and 'the most humble poet

of the English language'. He has praised Auden's capacity for 'objective, dispassionate discourse', 'his dryness of tone', and 'detached posture', that is for those qualities are, to the highest degree, characteristic of his own style. (Polukhina 1989: 99)

Reflection on exile

Brodsky theorized exile as a non-return by paraphrasing Heraclitus: 'You can't step twice on the same asphalt.' He rejected the idea of going back although, apparently, he played with the idea of returning incognito with Mikhail Baryshnikov (Pitkethly 1999). Gordin recalls that when he was seeing Brodsky off at the airport in Leningrad, the customs officer told Brodsky that in his circumstances, instead of saying 'good bye', he should say to his friends 'farewell', as recorded in the film *A Maddening Space*. These words became a prophecy. When interviewed in the United States later, he said: 'I'll tell you honestly, I'm a little bit afraid of that [going back]. [...] I don't know if I'm in a state to come as a tourist. [...] I'm not a metronome. Swinging back and forth. I probably won't do it. It's just that a human being moves only in one direction' (Graffy 1992: 142–3).

Having settled in the United States, Brodsky made a deliberate decision 'to pretend that nothing had happened', as he put it in conversation with Derek Walcott in the above-quoted film *A Maddening Space*. The effort to pretend and forget reveals the anxiety and emotional scarring that his banishment imprinted upon him. The success of his pretence is due to his apolitical theorizing of a country as just a 'continuation of space', a type of landscape. The landscape in Massachusetts where he rented a house reminded him of the St Petersburg area, and, arguably, made it possible for him to feel at home.

According to Brodsky, an important feature of exile that makes it a worthwhile experience for the writer is that it provides the necessary separation from the mainstream by positioning the poet on the margins. When Walcott asked Brodsky whether he ever felt displaced, he said 'no' because to be on the outside is not to be displaced for the writer; indeed, it puts him in the advantageous position of the observer. So, Brodsky embraced the 'positive' experience of exile, but not by turning tragedy into 'romance', in Thomas Pavel's words, who distinguishes between the desired, voluntary exile – 'romance' – and the forced, involuntary banishment – 'tragedy' (Pavel 1998: 25–6). Brodsky's stoic response comes out of his embracing 'tragedy' for the benefits of being on the margins but avoiding the martyr's syndrome.

The poet remained distanced from the mainstream and 'intellectual fashions' of his new milieu in the United States. Milosz finds the roots of his intellectual independence in his self-education. Self-trained to be impenetrable to the Soviet propaganda, Brodsky also managed to stay critical of the Western thought. Politics, in general, did not interest Brodsky. As Michael Scammell notes in his review of Loseff's *Joseph Brodsky: A Literary Life*, 'he found politics of any description pointless and boring' whether it was related to émigrés or not (Scammell 2012). In a letter to Andrei Sergeev, the poet writes: 'Émigrés hate me. They think that I embarrass them. They like to talk about freedom: the psychology of the slave who ran away from his owner – the slave dreams of boots' (Sergeev 1997: 151). Brodsky avoided the gatherings of exiled writers. For instance, he did not attend the conference of writers in exile held in December 1987 in Vienna, but he submitted the essay titled 'The Condition We Call Exile', which caused a lengthy and heated discussion.

In his other essay 'The Child of Civilization', he interprets exile as the poet's destiny, a 'linguistic' disobedience which establishes kinship with other exiled writers, in particular with Osip Mandelshtam, whom he presents in the essay to the English reader.

> When a man creates a world of his own, he becomes a foreign body against which all laws are aimed: gravity, compression, rejection, annihilation. [...]
> A poet gets into trouble because of his linguistic, and, by implication, his psychological superiority, rather than because of his politics. A song is a form of linguistic disobedience, and its sound casts a doubt on a lot more than a concrete political system: it questions the entire existential order. And the number of its adversaries grows proportionally.
> [...] It was the immense intensity of lyricism in Mandelstam's poetry which set him apart from his contemporaries and made him an orphan of his epoch, 'homeless on all-union scale'. For lyricism is the ethics of language and the superiority of this lyricism to anything that could be achieved within human interplay, of whatever denomination, is what makes for a work of art and lets it survive. That is why the iron broom, whose purpose was the spiritual castration of the entire populace, couldn't have missed him.
> (Brodsky 1986: 134, 136, 137)

Everything that Brodsky says above about Mandelshtam could be said about Brodsky himself. By creating his autonomous, independent and free world, the poet inevitably opposes himself to the surrounding environment with its norms and laws. It was characteristic of Brodsky to be fascinated with those features of other poets that he developed in himself; thus writing about others he often wrote about himself. Bethea remarks: 'Everything he [Brodsky] says about the character of Hardy's "autoelegy" could be said about his own' (Bethea 1998: 251). The song's 'linguistic disobedience' inherently causes the alienation and separation of the poet no matter what historical and political situation is around. Ishov discusses Brodsky's representation of exile and his affiliation with Dante and Mandelshtam in 'December in Florence' (Ishov 2017).

Brodsky's view of the writer as exiled into his own, self-created literary and linguistic space is far from being uncommon: 'Any writer, as a poet, is exiled in language itself, in the language of communication; he creates the space in which he can write his own language. By definition, the situation of any artist is an interior exile' (Bethea 1994: 164–5). As for Brodsky, Bethea (1994: 44) remarks on 'Brodsky's own relentlessly centrifugal, "self-estranging" exilic consciousness'. Efraim Sicher (1995: xxi) describes Brodsky as 'Mandel'shtam's ideal of the man of world culture who eschews any self-conscious ethnic identity even as he continues a Russian literary tradition'. Leon Burnett traces affinities between Brodsky and Mandelshtam, which originate in their 'nostalgic concern' for world culture, which 'makes the "acoustics" of their poetry equally suitable to serve as a "great cupola" for Classical Literature [and] for Russian' (Burnett 1990: 13).

In this view of exile Brodsky follows many poets including his poetic mentor Marina Tsvetaeva who, as Dietz observes, promotes the 'popular post-Romantic concept of the creative artist [. . .] [that] an artist never truly belongs to or fits into any society' (Dietz 1992: 46). In her essay 'The Poet and Time', Tsvetaeva formulates her position: 'Every poet is essentially an *émigré*, even in Russia. *Émigré* from the Kingdom of Heaven and from the earthly paradise of nature. [. . .] An *émigré* from immortality in time, a non-returner to his own heaven' (Tsvetaeva 1992: 93).

Brodsky develops this idea of the poet as an exile from society by prioritizing art above state and society: 'The philosophy of the state, its ethics – not to mention its aesthetics – are always "yesterday"' (Brodsky 1995: 48). Belonging to 'tomorrow', the poet is misunderstood and mistreated by 'yesterday', in other words, is exiled in time. Brodsky defines his citizenship and 'patriotism' through his linguistic rather than civic affiliations: 'For a writer only one form of patriotism exists: his attitude towards language. The measure of a writer's patriotism is how he writes in the language of the people among whom he lives. Bad literature, for example, is a form of treason' (Brodsky 1972). Brodsky was determined to become a citizen of his new language.

Thus, as a condition, exile leads to even greater linguistic isolation, and enhances the intensity of the poet's relationship with language:

> to be an exiled writer is like being a dog or a man hurtled into outer space a capsule (more like a dog, of course, than a man, because they will never retrieve you). And your capsule is your language. To finish the metaphor off, it must be added that before long the capsule's passenger discovers that it gravitates not earthward but outward.
>
> For one in our profession the condition we call exile is, first of all, a linguistic event: he is thrust from, he retreats into his mother tongue. From being his, so to speak, sword, it turns into his shield, into his capsule. What started as a private, intimate affair with the language in exile becomes fate – even before it becomes an obsession or a duty. (Brodsky 1995: 32)

In 'The Condition We Call Exile', Brodsky sums up political and literary consequences for an exile writer from a totalitarian country to an economically advanced and democratic world in the twentieth century, which he defines as 'tragicomedy'. The writer has to make a 'transition from a political and economic backwater to an industrially advanced society with the latest word on individual liberty on its lips' (Brodsky 1995: 24). But, ironically, moving to a more advanced society deprives the writer of his 'meaningful role', his significance. In turning to English as his means of expression, Brodsky challenges himself to re-acquire his relevance, and re-establish his literary persona in a new space through finding a new audience for his books.

> Life in exile, abroad, in a foreign element, is essentially a premonition of your own book-form fate, of being lost on the shelf among those with whom all you have in common is the first letter of your surname. (Brodsky 1995: 31)

The comparison of an exile writer's destiny with the fate of his books is particularly telling in the context of Brodsky's 'sentiment' for his lost reader in Russia. In 'Maddening Space', looking at the photos of his Russian friends, he points out that he cares less about his books being read by following generations than by his contemporaries with whom he grew up as a writer, whose audience he was being denied, and whom he lacks in exile. Brodsky shares this sentiment for the lost reader with the Russian writers of the first emigration, of whom Dietz writes:

> In an effort to retain their Russian identity, these poets looked to the past, to life in Russia as they knew it or nostalgically remembered it – a time when life was better or at least when they felt secure of their place in the culture, where, as Khodasevich reminisces in a poem written in exile, 'Everyone listened to my verses [*Vse slushali stikhi moi*].' (Khodasevich, 'Petersburg'/'Peterburg'). (Dietz 1992: 45)

Sufaru discusses the representation of the poet's 'I' in Brodsky's English-language essays and his displacement as a result of exile: 'the exiled writer becomes an exilic self, which has grown out of his roots, i.e. territory, and into a rhizome: both subject and object, and neither one, a multiplicity of interconnected heterogeneous selves, a cartography of territories and languages, an absolute in-between who is in constant negotiation with his context, constantly adapting, constantly performing, constantly becoming' (Sufaru 2016: 193).

Brodsky's view of language and enchantment with a new muse

Brodsky's view of language is poetic, hierarchical and playful. He treats language as the poet's 'master' and the poet as a 'language's slave'; language dictates the poem's form and content, brings about imagery and memory. In addition, each national language and its literature inspire a different style of writing, a particular approach and attitude to reality. In addition, he poeticizes and personifies individual languages based on their morphological structure by ascribing them specific 'characters'. As Bethea points out,

> English and Russian, argues Brodsky, have different morphological, semantic, and syntactic forms, and these differences have a direct impact on the sort of poetry that each tradition can create. Each language has a different 'personality', and this personality underlies anything that is said through the language. Brodsky, it turns out, gravitated toward English for reasons that were simultaneously ethical and aesthetic. Russian was a 'magnificently inflected language capable of expressing the subtlest nuances of the human psyche', but its very subtlety, its tendency toward what the poet, using the English phrase, calls 'loose ends', left it open to infinite moral compromise. [...] English [...] is more 'analytical' and less 'intuitive'. (Bethea 1994: 121)

As a bilingual author, Brodsky sees himself as someone who has access not only to two different languages but to two different worlds and two literary traditions. He describes the bilingual author as a 'common denominator' of the two languages. In a letter to Andrei Sergeev dated 29 March 1976, Brodsky writes:

> I am inclined to think more and more that the US and Russian literatures (like the languages themselves) are not so much the manifestations of two opposing cultures but rather two opposite ends of the same civilization, the civilization of the whites. I have always been guilty of ethnocentrism [...] now I have the advantage. There is a difference between the analytical and synthetic attitude to reality. The former allows to have control over reality but sacrificing [losing?] half of it in the process. The latter encourages to develop perception (to the highs of Leo Tolstoy) but at the expense of being able to take action. The difference is the same as between a sofa and a car, but the common denominator is the same, me, for example. (Sergeev 1997: 151)

This playful and amusing comparison of Russian with a sofa and English with an automobile in the letter gives us a new dimension as to how we can understand the poem 'Centaurs II' ('Kentavry I').[18] The described centaurs in the poem refer to the comparisons made in the letter. The more 'intuitive' Russian language, the poet's mother tongue, with its tendency to inflections, is represented as a female centaur: 'Part ravishing beauty, part sofa, in the vernacular – Sophie,' and English that is more analytical appears to Brodsky masculine: 'Two-thirds a caring male, one-thirds a race car – Cary.' With ironic undertones, the poem describes an affair between the two centaurs who go to the theatre to enjoy 'a drama about the life of puppets / which is what we were, frankly in our era' (Brodsky 2000: 366).

18. The first poem in the Russian sequence 'Kentavry I' corresponds to the second poem in the English sequence 'Centaurs II'.

Apart from being playfully represented as different characters that inspire specific styles and approaches, languages can also be seen as spaces: linguistic spaces versus geographical and political ones. Brodsky compares mastering a new language with receiving a new linguistic citizenship: 'there is every chance for you to become citizens of the Great English Language' (Brodsky 1986: 310). The English language becomes the poet's new space and muse; it inspires, enchants and calls the poet:

> The purpose of evolution, believe it or not, is beauty, which survives it all and generates truth simply by being a fusion of the mental and the sensual. As it is always in the eye of the beholder, it can't be wholly embodied save in words: that's what ushers in a poem, which is as incurably semantic it is incurably euphonic.
>
> No other language accumulates so much of this as does English. To be born into it or to arrive in it is the best boon that can befall a man. (Brodsky 1995: 207)

This view of the English language is an extension of Brodsky's familiarity with and adoration of the Anglo-American literature. Apart from Auden, he revered the works of English metaphysical poets, in particular John Donne. The English language for Brodsky represents the whole tradition of the Anglo-American literature and cannot be separated from it; and that is the reason why the Russian poet expresses such sheer and ultimate homage to it. In his review of *A Part of Speech*, Michael Schmidt observes that Brodsky 'owes to Donne and the Metaphysicals (whom he has translated into Russian) certain debts of metaphor, organisation and tone' (Schmidt 1980).

Despite all his love for the adopted language, Brodsky still needed his native tongue to articulate what it meant to remain himself in a foreign country. In an interview with Richard Eder, Brodsky elaborates the meaning of the native language in a foreign element: 'It helps you to win the notion of yourself unimpeded [. . .] it's not pleasant but it is a more clinical notion of yourself. The relationship with your own language becomes more private and intricate; it hovers on the verge of esoteric' (Eder 1980: 2).

Brodsky also sees language as a means of accumulating a people's memory. A people's experience is imprinted in it; thus, a national language, according to Brodsky, is the record of a nation's history. Brodsky states that as experience is recorded and maintained by a language, then there can be no experience outside of language. That is why, he claims, the experience of a people is recorded in one language and sometimes cannot be translated into another. As a consequence, Brodsky deprives certain languages of the capacity to express certain emotions and experiences. For example, he thinks that the English language is not capable of expressing evil in the same way as the Russian language.

> The sad truth is that words fail reality as well. At least it's been my impression that any experience coming from the Russian realm, even when depicted with photographic precision, simply bounces off the English language, leaving no visible imprint on its surface. Of course the memory of one civilization cannot, perhaps should not, become a memory of another. But when language fails to reproduce the negative realities of another culture, the worst kind of tautologies result. (Brodsky 1986: 30–1)

Brodsky is convinced that the horrible events which occurred in Soviet Russia do not have equivalents in English because the different – more democratic – history of the Anglo-Saxon communities makes it impossible for them to be expressed in English. Hence he thinks that Platonov's prose is 'quite untranslatable' (Brodsky 1986: 290).

> These words themselves bear witness that I am far from accusing the English language of insufficiency; nor do I lament the dormant state of its native speakers' psyche. I merely regret the fact that such an advanced notion of Evil as happens to be in the possession of Russians has been denied entry into consciousness on the grounds of having a convoluted syntax. One wonders how many of us can recall a plain-speaking Evil that crosses the threshold, saying: 'Hi, I'm Evil. How are you?' (Brodsky 1986: 31)

Here Brodsky expresses a poetic but circumscribed view of language. He deprives it of its universality. If taken to the extreme, such an understanding of language can lead to the conclusion that translation or even comprehension within one language is impossible because every person's experience is singular and unique. But such a conclusion is contradicted by Brodsky himself; for he wrote in English about his Soviet past, his school, his parents, his hometown Leningrad, addressing English audience in English. He tries to circumvent the contradiction which results from his theory by claiming that he is trying to prevent 'tautology': if his experiment of translation succeeds, then the Soviet concept of evil will penetrate into the memory of the Anglo-Saxon community without being experienced. When writing about his parents in English, in the United States, Brodsky sees the process of writing as an attempt to resurrect their images in the space of his adopted language, 'This is their only chance to see me and America. This is the only way for me to see them and our room' (Brodsky 1986: 457). Brodsky wants to make his and his parents' experience available for the English reader.

Recent research in bilingualism, and especially in late bilinguals (Keysar, Hayakawa, and An 2012), suggests that 'thinking in a foreign language provides a greater emotional distance than a native tongue' (also see Pavlenko 2012). Brodsky's description of writing in English as if he were constructing a poem rather than creating it makes sense in the context of these linguistic findings. Aptly, he describes English as a more analytical language than Russian. Although, in his view, it was caused by some 'objective' linguistic qualities of the English language, in the light of recent research in bilingualism, his statement should be understood in the context of the English language being his second tongue, which he learnt late in life and, as a result, the English provides him with the opportunity for 'disembodied cognition' because the second language reduces decision biases (Pavlenko 2012). Therefore, to him English appears more analytical and further removed from emotion. This also explains why Brodsky claimed that some evil experiences that were 'lived in' the Russian language could not be translated into English. His claim is meaningless in objective terms because English-speaking people have had many 'evil' experiences that they lived through and that have been recorded in their language (among many other examples, just think of the bloodshed in Shakespeare's plays, or witch trials written about by Henry Miller). Subjectively speaking, on the other hand, Brodsky's claim makes perfect sense: for him, as a late bilingual, English does not have the same emotional charge as his native Russian and therefore evil described in English does not have the same visceral feel to it for him. This does not mean that he could not experience emotion in English – the new experiences and emotions that he lived through in English, after his exile, were for him associated with the English language.

From a mongrel to the fifth poet laureate of the United States

According to Brodsky, 'mongrel' is someone who cannot 'come up with the right word instantly' in a right language. In his essay 'Collector's Item', he describes a moment of linguistic tangle and a lapse of memory in a shop while trying to buy a stamp: 'I stood there groping for an English word to shield my wits from the familiarity that Cyrillic letters exuded. As is often the case with mongrels, I couldn't come up with the right word instantly, and so I turned and left the store. I only remembered the word well outside' (Brodsky 1995: 193). Later he continues: 'Who are you, the author asks himself in two languages, and gets startled no less than you would upon hearing his own voice muttering something that amounts to "Well, I don't know." A mongrel, then, ladies and gentlemen, this is a mongrel speaking. Or else a centaur' (Brodsky 1995: 150). My interpretation of Brodsky's *mongrelization* is primarily linguistic and is underpinned by the theory of *strangership* (see Chapter 2). However, it is also connected to his state of exile, which, as was pointed out by Sufaru, 'translates into displacement and estrangement from both cultures and languages' (Sufaru 2016).

Linguists who study bilingualism have analysed exactly what Brodsky describes as being a mongrel: forgetting the words that you need at the right moment, getting confused with your lexis. The bilingual person may struggle to remember either the words of the second language or of the native tongue but for different reasons. The latter occurs as a result of attrition and the former is the problem of retaining new vocabulary. For a late bilingual poet this 'mongrel' stage is associated with self-translation; it is frustrating but is yet potentially productive, as described by Elizabeth Beaujour: 'self-translation is frequently the rite of passage, the traditional, heroic psychic journey into the depths of the self (a version of Sigmund Freud's self-analysis or Joseph Campbell's archetypal voyage) that is a necessary prelude to true self-knowledge and its accompanying powers'; Beaujour also adds that 'Self-translation is the true test of whether a bilingual writer can ever totally coincide with himself' (Beaujour 1989: 51).

Arguably, this coincidence with oneself in the second language is possible only for the writers who not only are equally fluent in both languages but also write in 'symmetrical' languages, that is, not the languages that might have been in a subordinate relationship with each other (e.g. the language or colonizers and the language of the colonized). Although English and Russian are usually considered by translation studies scholars as the languages of comparable importance, Brodsky ascribed different qualities to each language based on the experience lived by their peoples (as discussed earlier), which leads to potential difficulties for the poet who strives to coincide with himself in his second tongue. Another reason for difficulties to coincide with oneself is the self-translator's ability to achieve the same fluency in both languages. For a late bilingual writer, like Brodsky, this was the main obstacle.

It is possible to see how the poet attempts but fails to coincide with himself when we compare the Russian poem 'Ia vkhodil vmesto dikogo zveria', written on the poet's fortieth birthday, and its English self-translation 'May 24, 1980'.

Я входил вместо дикого зверя в клетку,	I have braved, for want of wild beasts, steel cages,
выжигал свой срок и кликуху гвоздем в бараке,	carved my term and nickname on bunks and rafters,
жил у моря, играл в рулетку,	lived by the sea, flashed aces in an oasis,
обедал черт знает с кем во фраке.	dined with the-devil-knows-whom, in tails, on truffles.
[. . .]	[. . .]
жрал хлеб изгнанья, не оставляя корок.	. . . Munched the bread of exile; it's stale and warty.
Позволял своим связкам все звуки, помимо воя;	Granted my lungs all sounds except the howl;
перешел на шепот. Теперь мне сорок.	switched to a whisper. Now I am forty.
Что сказать мне о жизни? Что оказалась длинной.	What should I say about life? That it's long and abhors transparence.
Только с горем я чувствую солидарность.	Broken eggs make me grieve; the omelet, though, makes me vomit.
Но пока мне рот не забили глиной,	Yet until brown clay has been rammed down my larynx,
из него раздаваться будет лишь благодарность.	only gratitude will be gushing from it.
1980	1980
	(translated by the author, quoted from *Collected Poems*)

Source: Brodsky 2000: 211.

The English self-translation was not very well received by many English-speaking critics who described Brodsky's English as 'unidiomatic and just awkward' (Simic 2000). But the asymmetry between the much admired Russian original and its self-translation is inevitable. The English language is young to Brodsky, compared to the Russian, and that is particularly important in a poem on a birthday – English is old enough, but Brodsky is not old enough in English to do just what he needs to rewrite the Russian. So we have the younger poet looking back on the older poet in a new language. The Brodsky-in-Russian is an experienced writer, and the Brodsky-in-English is still a bit adolescent, talented and bold, but lacking the experience of the former.

Most critics and scholars of Brodsky have taken sides, either defending Brodsky's idiosyncratic English (Henry Gifford, D. M. Thomas, Derek Walcott, Seamus Heaney, Lachlan Mackinnon, Susan Sontag, Kees Verheul, Ishov, Berlina) or criticizing it (Simic, Weissbort, Clarence Brown, Michael Schmidt, John Bayley, Christopher Reid, Donald Davie, Craig Raine) (see further discussion of opposing views in Chapter 2). The purpose of this book is not to join any of the two camps and support their argument with more comparative readings of Russian originals and English self-translations as has been done by Berlina, Ishov, Oslon and some others. My aim is to study *how* Brodsky became a bilingual writer by examining archival papers, the poet's correspondence and other relevant documents that can shed light on the process of Brodsky's mastering the English language. As an example, let us see how Brodsky approached 'May, 24 1980' by looking at his notes on the manuscript in English, which are held in the Brodsky Archive at Beinecke library. The folder, which contains the manuscripts, translations and notes related to this poem, has three handwritten sheets with a glossary drafted by Brodsky as he was preparing to self-translate the poem (Picture 1.1).

Nearly every word of the Russian original is translated individually through the laborious process of finding equivalents. If nothing else, this demonstrates how different is the process of writing a poem in the second language for a poet who is searching for the right words in his adopted tongue. Unlike Russian words, these do not come 'naturally' but are found in the dictionary. On top of this, Brodsky persisted on using equivalent rhyming and rhythm patterns in English as he did in Russian. So, having found all the right words, Brodsky then had to solve the riddle of putting the poem into shape. Looking at the poet's notes and manuscripts helps us understand what Brodsky meant when he said that writing poetry in English was 'like playing chess or building with blocks' (Glad 1993: 110).

It is therefore necessary to define the difference between writing in the native language and self-translating into a second one. A poem written in the original language is a product of the primary creative impulse. The drafts of Brodsky's Russian originals are usually typed by the poet, after he works them out schematically in a notebook in some cases, and have very few corrections on them. There are no visible signs of other people's intervention in his original

1. Joseph Brodsky

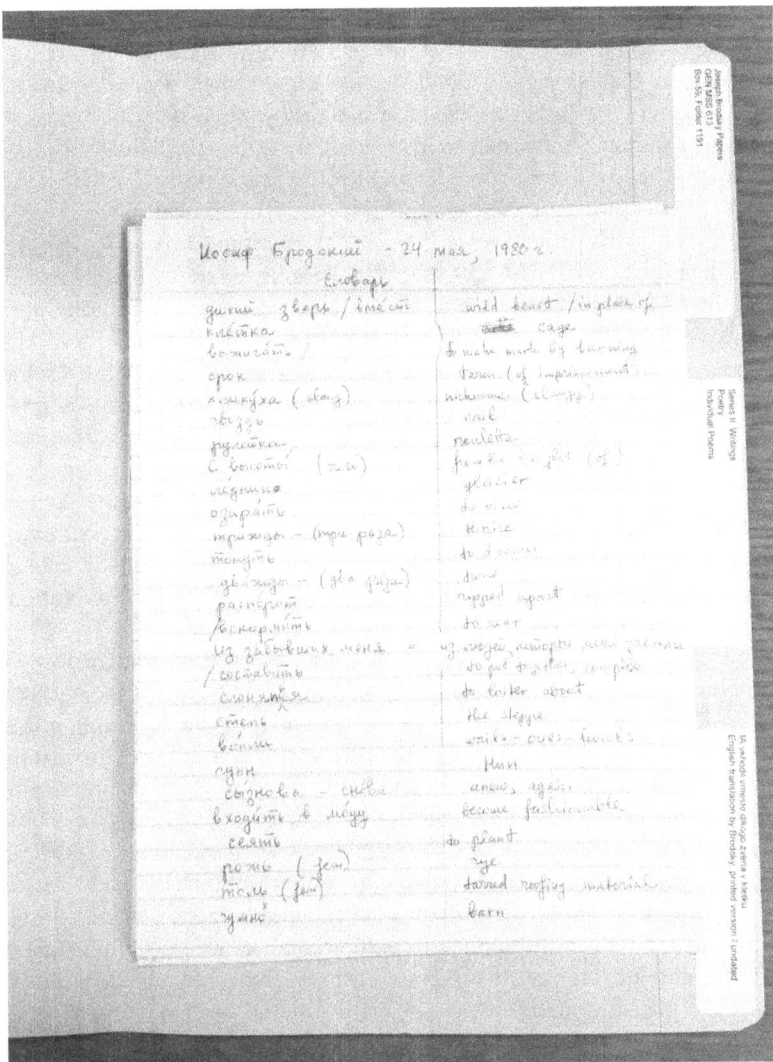

Picture 1.1 'Ia vkhodil vmesto dikogo zveria', English translation by Brodsky: Glossary.

Russian texts, so there is evidence to argue that Brodsky wrote them solo. Brodsky's English self-translations, on the other hand, have signs of laborious work by the poet in collaboration with others. Translations as well as self-translations are both inspired and limited by the original Russian poem, or the ST. Following Brodsky's mimetic approach, they tend to mimic the original's meaning and its form. Attempting to reconstruct the poetic structure of the ST, they require a lot of hard work and dedication from the self-translator and his co-translators. Brodsky's collaboration is manifested in different ways depending on when the poem was translated. Brodsky's translations and self-translations in English can be divided into several types, according to the dominant patterns of authorship: (1) translations by others without Brodsky's involvement (these include the unauthorized translations by Bethell (Brodsky 1967) as well as some individual translations which Brodsky has approved with no interference and the unauthorized translations which were made without his knowing or approving them); (2) translations by others with the author's help/or interference (e.g. most translations made for the volume *A Part of Speech*); (3) self-translations with translators' help, where translators were acknowledged (e.g. some self-translations made for *To Urania*); (4) self-translations with collaborators' help, in which collaborators (or, all least, some of them) were not acknowledged (e.g. the translation of 'Eclogue IV: Winter', which was self-translated based on Masha Vorobiov's interlinear translation); (5) self-translations without evident help from others except for minor corrections by Kjellberg, Brodsky's secretary, or others (in the 1990s); (6) texts written in English with others' help (the late 1980s and the 1990s); (7) texts written in English mostly without others' help except for minor corrections by Kjellberg or others (in the 1990s). Chapter 3 discusses different types of collaboration, providing archival evidence.

Throughout all chapters, I argue that the process of self-translation is complex and has two sides to it. On the one hand, it reflects the author's vulnerability in the use of a new language, especially at the beginning of his bilingual stage. On the other hand, the self-translator compensates for that by having the opportunity to exercise his authorial power, his rights of authorship, ownership, censorship and copyright over the translated text. In the work by a late bilingual author, like Brodsky, it is possible to observe with more clarity how these two sides of self-translation are manifested: how the established Russian poet is humbled when he starts writing in 'the Great English language' that he admires, and yet how he applies his authorial power when commissioning translators and judging their work from his perspective of both the eminent Russian poet and a 'mongrel'.

Chapter 2

FROM SOLO WRITER IN RUSSIAN TO COLLABORATIVE SELF-TRANSLATOR IN ENGLISH
THEORETICAL FRAMEWORK AND INSIGHTS INTO THE PRACTICE OF SELF-TRANSLATION

> ... A victim of shipwreck,
> in twenty years I've sufficiently domesticated
> this land (though perhaps it's a continent) ...
> ('Robinsonade', trans. Jonathan Aaron with the author, *Collected Poems* (Brodsky 2000: 493))

In this chapter, I contextualize Brodsky's journey to bilingualism by examining recent developments in the emerging fields of self-translation and collaborative translation, which are linked to the 'social turn' in translation studies. I draw on historicist debates about bilingualism and bilingual writing to understand the poet's approach to and practice of self-translation. The sociologist Georg Simmel's concept of *strangership* (Simmel 2016)[1] helps me unravel Brodsky's references to being a 'mongrel' when the poet describes how he felt upon arriving in the United States. I reveal that when Brodsky decided to write in English, he had to re-adjust writing practices and move from solo writing to collaborative self-translation, from single to multiple authorship. Focusing on Brodsky's work allows me to review Jack Stillinger's definition of 'multiple authorship' (Stillinger 1991) in light of Brodsky's relationships with his translators and collaborators.

Then I map out three main stages through which Brodsky moved as an author and self-translator. The first stage was when Brodsky had no control over the translations of his poems in English, while he was still living in Russia

---

1. In this book, I use Ramona Mosse's translation of the famous essay by Georg Simmel (1908). Recently, there has been some renewed interest in Simmel's concept of *strangership* in relation to the European crisis with an inflow of refugees and related outbreaks of xenophobia.

up to 1972. The second stage started when he settled in the United States and found himself in a position to manage a team of commissioned translators while preparing the collection *A Part of Speech* (Brodsky 1980). He translated collaboratively, edited the work of his translators and then he began to self-translate with the help of his collaborators. This was the longest and most prominent stage of his bilingual career. Finally, the third stage is when Brodsky began to write in English with only minor assistance provided by his editors.

Redefining self-translation: A move from 'cultural' to 'social turn'

Self-translation has recently emerged as a field of translation studies. According to Rainier Grutman (2013b), there was an impressive increase in scholarly literature on this topic between 1998 and 2013. Even the name of the discipline was not yet fixed in 1998 when Grutman wrote his entry 'Autotranslation' in the original *Encyclopaedia of Translation Studies* (Grutman 1998). By 2013, the term 'self-translation' became the norm. Since then, there have been a number of edited books and special issues of academic journals focusing on self-translation in English and other European languages (Cordingley 2013; Lagarde 2015; Puccini 2015; Falceri, Gentes and Manterola 2017; Castro, Mainer and Page 2017; Ceccherelli, Imposti and Perotto 2013; Ferraro and Grutman 2016; Lagarde and Tanqueiro 2013).[2]

For years translation studies scholars did not consider self-translation worth separating from translation overall, as stated by Susan Bassnett:

> How useful is the term 'self-translation' in any case? For if all translation is a form of re-writing, then whether that rewriting is done by the person who produced a first version of a text or by someone else is surely not important. What matters are the transformations that the text undergoes, the ways in which it is re-shaped for a new readership. [. . .] The writer who undertakes this kind of task is hardly 'privileged' over the other kinds of translator, but then, in my view, since all translation is rewriting, it is a waste of time trying to distinguish between self-translation and other forms of translation. (Bassnett 2013: 6)

Elsewhere Bassnett explains that the idea of looking at translations as 'rewritings' was proposed by André Lefevere 'to move away from the constraints imposed by traditional ideas of translation as a second-rate literary activity' (Bassnett 2014: 163–4). This has helped affirm the translator's creativity. Bassnett's view of self-translation is underpinned by the same idea of seeing translations as rewritings. Reflecting on Nancy Huston's bilingual work, Bassnett admits that

---

2. For full bibliography on self-translation, see Gentes (2017)

self-translation offers 'an opportunity for some writers to rethink and then rewrite, shifting between languages, so that both texts are original, albeit in different ways' (Bassnett 2014: 163). Bassnett takes this example to emphasize the idea that self-translations have the same status as the STs; they are just as 'original' and as 'authentic' as each other. From her point of view, however, there is no fundamental difference between rewriting by the translator or by the author of the ST. In either case, her primary focus is on the text, not on the agent of translation.

It takes some refocusing to appreciate that any translation can be seen 'as both an enactment and a product', and 'is necessarily embedded within social contexts' (Wolf 2007: 1). A fairly recent rise in the interest in social approaches to translation has become known as a 'social turn' in translation studies. Among the scholars who brought to our attention the value of sociological theories and methodologies in relation to translation are Anthony Pym (2006), Michaela Wolf and Alexandra Funari (2007). Drawing on the view of translation as a 'socially regulated activity' (Hermans 1997: 10), Wolf emphasizes the role played by individuals and social institutions in the process of 'the selection, production and distribution of translation' and 'the strategies adopted in the translation itself' (Wolf 2007: 1). Contributors to *Constructing a Sociology of Translation* (Wolf and Funari 2007) pay special interest to the role conventionally played by translators in society (Prunč 2007), to the practice of translation as a norm-governed activity continuously negotiated by individuals and institutions, to the role of power in the process of translation taking place in 'a communicative, socio-cultural context' (Hermans 2007), to the construction of translators' identities through the prism of gender, ethnicity, social class, geographical or cultural contexts in which they work, and to the traditionally low status of translators in light of Pierre Bourdieu's notion of *habitus* (Simeoni 2007). With the 'social turn' scholars' focus on the translator as an agent, translation networks and the process of translation, self-translation has a greater chance to develop into a branch within translation studies than it did in the work by 'cultural turn' scholars.

Independently of 'social turn' academics, Anthony Pym developed his own methodological framework for the historical study of translation to move from the text to the stories of individual translators as the main object of research (Pym 1998). His approach – 'humanizing translation history' – alerts scholars to the social roles played by translators mediating between cultures (Pym 2017). In the move from the text to the agent, he states that text modifications can be seen 'as negotiations' within social networks where ideology, gender and ethnic identity can play significant roles (Pym 2017: 23). His two methodological principles include studying translators *before* texts and looking for professional 'intercultural', that is, the space where cultures 'overlap' and 'intersected' (Pym 2017: 31, 37). He observes that translators do not move from one culture to another; they work in that intercultural space.

Lawrence Venuti (1995) and feminist translators have also contributed to socially aware approaches to translation. Venuti brings the translator to the fore as the author of the target text who may choose *foreignizing* as a resistant method of translation, as opposed to the conventional methods of fluent translation, which renders the translator invisible and insignificant in comparison with the author of the ST. The role of the translator as an agent has also been underlined by feminist translators. Luise Von Flotow-Evans (1997) discusses the importance of the agent's female gender in the bold translation choices made by Canadian feminist translators, including Barbara Godard who underscores the mission of the feminist translator: 'the repossession of the world by women and the naming of the life of the body as experienced by women' (Godard 1984: 14).

As translation studies have made a 'social turn', scholars have started to review the place of self-translation and its potential contribution to translation studies overall, and a sociology of self-translation is defined as a 'new and complex discipline' (Lagarde 2015). Grutman calls for a move from self-translation as the study of a 'gallery of portraits' to the next stage where this approach is underpinned by a sociological perspective and informed by sociolinguistic theories; he proposes scholars rethink self-translation in order to develop 'scientific, sociological, methods to study self-translation instead of examining individual cases of self-translators "*in splendid isolation*"' (Grutman 2015; 2013b: 69–70; emphasis in original). He demonstrates how informative an examination of a group of bilingual writers could be by focusing on the bilingual authors among the Nobel Prize winners for literature in the twentieth century. They are Frédéric Mistral (awarded the Nobel Prize in 1904), Rabindranath Tagore (1913), Karl Adolph Gjellerup (1917), Luigi Pirandello (1934), Samuel Beckett (1969), Isaac Bashevis Singer (1978), Czeslaw Milosz (1980) and Joseph Brodsky (1987). Grutman's typology of the Nobel Prize–winning writers is based on two factors: (1) whether writers developed bilingualism in their original speech community or whether they have to cross national borders to learn another language (internal/endogenous or external/exogenous), and (2) the place of both languages used by the authors in the symbolic hierarchy of languages (dominated or dominating). Endogenous authors, according to this typology, fall into the category of 'early bilinguals' because they have to 'juggle languages of their native communities' from childhood (Grutman 2013b: 75).

In his other article, Grutman proposes a slightly different typology for sorting different types of self-translators:

(1) 'post-colonial' writers who alternate between their native tongue(s) and the European language of the former colonial powers; (2) recent immigrant writers who expand on work begun in their home country while staking out new ground for themselves in the language of their adoptive country; (3) writers belonging to traditional linguistic minorities because of the multilingual make-up of the State of which they are citizens. (Grutman 2013a: 188)

Whichever of Grutman's typology we use, Nabokov and Brodsky, two Russian writers, end up in the same category of either exogenous bilingual writers or recent immigrant writers whose two languages, Russian (native) and English (second), are in symmetrical relationship to each other. In comparison to post-colonial writers or bilingual authors from linguistic minorities, it makes sense because both Nabokov (or rather his family) and Brodsky were forced to leave Russia for political reasons. The Nabokov family fled St Petersburg soon after the October Revolution in 1917. Brodsky was exiled from Russia as a result of his nonconformist behaviour, as discussed in the Introduction. However, the similarities between the two writers' biographies cease there. Differences between the two, on the other hand, are abundant, especially in terms of their social background and second language acquisition (see Bethea 1995).

As is well known, Nabokov was born into a privileged, aristocratic and wealthy family of the Russian nobility in 1899, before the Russian Revolution. Since childhood, he was regularly exposed to the French and English languages along with Russian, as all three languages were spoken on a regular basis by the members of his family. He could read and write in English before he could in Russian (Nabokov 1969). Soon after the exile in 1917, the Nabokov family found themselves in England where Nabokov enrolled in Trinity College, the University of Cambridge. As a student, he published his translation of Lewis Carroll's *Alice in Wonderland* into Russian (Carroll 1923). Brodsky's second language acquisition was a different story, as we already know from Chapter 1. In addition, Brodsky was primarily a poet while Nabokov wrote predominantly prose. Brodsky admits that comparing himself with Nabokov is not productive because, while for Nabokov, English was a nearly native language as he spoke it since childhood, for Brodsky it was a 'personal stance' ('lichnaia pozitsiia') (Brodskii 2010: 730).

Reflecting on these differences between the two writers, I suggest that Grutman's typologies need further fine-tuning by adding the considerations of the bilingual writer's identity, the social and cultural circumstances in which they write, and, most importantly, the details of their second or third language acquisition; in other words, as proposed by Pym, we should study the authors before their texts (as discussed earlier). In addition, it is crucial to examine the process of self-translation, how self-translations emerge, whether authors work collaboratively with translators and editors, what sort of relationships (if any) they have with the author, and what their contribution is to the authors' work. Such details related to the process of translation and self-translation become evident only in the process of archival study, by scrutinizing the author's drafts, correspondence and notes in the margins of poems. Jeremy Munday has affirmed the importance of a sociologically driven archival approach in his article 'Using Primary Sources to Produce a Microhistory of Translation and Translators: Theoretical and Methodological Concerns' (Munday 2014). My approach is underpinned by Munday's notions of 'microhistories': in Chapter 4, I examine the 'microhistories' of Brodsky's collaborators.

Historicist debates related to monolingual and bilingual writing

Jan Hokenson and Marcella Munson (2007) trace the history of bilingual texts back to the Middle Ages, identifying a significant shift from bilingual texts as a commonplace in multilingual medieval Europe to their decline in mainly monolingual European states with the rise of romanticism and the nationalist approach to literature. In other words, the book examines the shift between the 'horizontal' world of medieval Europe and the Renaissance, and the 'vertical' world of modernity, tracing the origin of our understanding of one's native language as 'the egoic essence of subjectivity' (Hokenson and Munson 2007: 142). According to them, the notion of the monolingual author is rooted in the German romantic philosophy of language, quoting Friedrich Schleiermacher who in 1813 'pronounced the bilingual writer a flat impossibility' because the author can create original work 'only in the maternal tongue' (Schleiermacher 1813).

In her study of bilingualism, Aneta Pavlenko comes to similar conclusions. It was during the eighteenth-century romantic movement that European thinkers, such as Jean-Jacque Rousseau in France and Johann Georg Hamann and Johann Gottfried von Herder in Germany, started to link national languages to the world views of their speakers, viewing language as the organ of thought and arguing that each nation or people (*Volk*) has a unique national spirit (*Volksgeist*) and a distinct way of thinking, reflected in their language' (Pavlenko 2014: 2). This was a reaction to rationalist and universalist assumptions of the Enlightenment. Pavlenko shows that this thinking is reinforced by Wilhelm von Humboldt in the nineteenth century who, in addition to viewing 'languages as self-contained systems that encoded unique worldviews' (Pavlenko 2014: 2), also claims that by learning another language a person can step into a different worldview (Pavlenko 2014: 3). Pavlenko discusses how this view of languages became popular across Europe including Russia in the nineteenth century. She observes that this school of thought leads to linguistic relativity, which was further developed by Franz Boas and his student Edward Sapir who wrote what 'came to be seen as a manifesto of linguistic relativity (Pavlenko 2014: 8).

This linguistic relativity helps us understand Brodsky's view of languages which was discussed in Chapter 1 when he states that evil as was depicted in the Russian language cannot be translated into English referring to the difference in the experience that people had had in the two languages. So, on the one hand, Brodsky sees the two languages as two different world views, or 'stances', but, on the other hand, he also tends to talk about poetic language as something universal which transcends national languages and their particular world views, especially, when he refers to his beloved Auden's quote about language's ruling time. When Brodsky starts self-translating, he has to negotiate between the relativist and universalist views of language, and, in his case, the latter view prevails, which makes it possible for him to turn from a mongrel into a bilingual writer.

The conflict between the two schools of thought – relativist and universalist – is also the reason for 'the long neglect of the bilingual text in twentieth-century critical thought', according to Hokeson and Munson (2007: 146). Scholars associate the return of the interest in bilingualism in the twentieth century with 'globalization, transnational migration, and increased ethno-linguistic diversity in the Western world' (Pavlenko 2014: 19–20).

Further reasons for studying self-translation

The main reasons for studying self-translation that have been identified so far include the aspects of translation inspired by sociological and historicist debates. These encourage the study of self-translators as agents, their identities, their motives for self-translating, their philosophical standpoints and their place in history, as well as their personal and professional networks, and links to translation institutions in which they are involved. Self-translators need to be looked at as a separate group from translators because they are 'largely motivated by certain private, artistic and literary ambitions of a uniquely dual nature' (Hokenson 2013: 40). Their motives could be social or cultural, where 'social' would refer to 'institutional', 'macro-level' forces imposed on an individual and 'cultural' would refer to 'personal', 'micro-level' forces (Hokenson 2013: 44). In addition, the study of self-translation allows us 'to get a better understanding of questions of authorship, identity, and translation' (Boyden and De Bleeker 2013: 177). Self-translation helps challenge Western monolingualism as the norm; it demonstrates the dependency of languages on each other. It helps us review our understanding of so-called infidelities, which are legitimized by bilingual authors in their self-translations; it identifies conflicts and 'points of resistance' within subjective encounters (Shread 2009; Hokenson and Munson 2007; López López–Gay 2006).

Another intriguing concept that the study of self-translation helps us unpack is authenticity and the elusive notion of the 'authentic voice'. How 'authentic' are bilingual authors' voices when they are rewritten in a second language? Is the text translated by the author more 'authentic' than the translation made by a different translator who cannot claim to have the same insight into the original? What about the translations made collaboratively by a translator and the author? Would the author's intervention in the translation produced by a translator make the text more 'authentic'? Or should we do away with the whole concept of the 'authentic' in translation and self-translation, drawing on Lefevere's and Bassnett's understanding of translations as rewritings and new texts? Perhaps, authenticity, as Steven Poole argues, is a 'neoliberal chimera'? (Poole 2013). Or could the concept of the 'authentic voice' be useful to apply to self-translation, at least, to understand why Brodsky and his publishers increasingly wanted to curate his voice in English, to make it more consistently 'his' rather than having him represented by many voices of his translators?

Brodsky's bilingual texts provide some interesting material for reflecting on what may be understood as an 'authentic' voice, how an 'authentic' voice is constructed, the reasons for an 'authentic' voice to be desired, whether it could be translated by others, and whether it should be curated for consistency in the second language. Comparing Brodsky's self-translations with the translations of his poems by English-language poets, Zakhar Ishov comes to the conclusion: 'Despite the brilliance of some of these translations, in them the authentic voice of the poet came across arguably less than in his own self-translations' (Ishov 2008: 138). By authentic voice, Ishov seems to mean the consistency and recognizability of the poet's voice as opposed to what Derek Walcott, in his review of *To Urania*, described as a 'not necessarily desirable variety of an anthology of Brodsky seen through the eyes of contemporary American poets' (Walcott 1988). As will be discussed later in the chapter, Brodsky's decision to increase control over his English-language texts was to achieve greater consistency in his English-language texts as well as to exercise the author's preferred method of mimetic translation. However, Brodsky's self-translations have not brought him a universal approval, and there is a view that having more translations of Brodsky's poems from Russian to English would be beneficial for the poet's legacy. Alexandra Berlina argues that Brodsky in English would gain from having his poems translated by others, implying that Brodsky's 'authentic' voice would not suffer from being re-interpreted by multiple English translations. Does Brodsky gain from having his 'authentic' voice curated for consistency in English or would he have benefited from having more diverse translators rendering his work? (I will come back to this in the conclusion after the comparative analysis of translation drafts in Chapter 3 and the translators' microhistories in Chapter 4.)

For now it is helpful to turn to Samuel Beckett, a symmetrical bilingual author, whose command of two working languages was equally fluent. As has been remarked, Beckett began to self-translate and to curate his voice 'out of the need to preserve his original intention; his authentic voice', which, according to Siccama, 'led to the repetition, and the subsequent dispersal of his primal word' (Siccama 1999: 175). As a result, Wilma Siccama argues, Beckett created versions of his texts instead of the translations of his own originals because his versions were of equal status; none of them could be seen as an original or a translation, none of them originated from the other. This argument is very much underpinned by the idea of translation as rewriting, as theorized by Lefevere and Bassnett, or the cultural turn scholars. Beckett's work has been the focus of many scholars' attention for a reason: he is often described as a 'canonical' self-translator (Boyden and De Bleeker 2013) because he had an exceptionally high command of both languages and used them symmetrically, in a balanced way. His work has been extensively studied (Oustinoff 2001; Sardin-Damestoy 2002; Van Hulle 2007; Ackerley 2008; Montini 2007; Mooney 2011; Grutman 2013a; McGuire 1990). Some scholars argue that Beckett's approach to bilingual writing is more than self-translation; for example, 'the many slippages Beckett introduces between the two versions of his texts to form a crucial part of the new text they create when both are considered together'; Ian Wilson describes this new text as 'ironic' (Wilson 1999: 94). James McGuire (1990) proposes to read Beckett's self-translations as 'parallel texts', which also imply the two versions need to be read next to each other by bilingual readers. All Beckett's scholars admire the author's fluency and accept his ultimate authority in the way in which he created his texts. When asymmetry is discussed, as in the article by Sinead Mooney (2002), it is done so on the understanding that Beckett's knowledge of both languages is equally excellent. Mooney notices a deteriorating use by Beckett of the translating language and explains this phenomenon as a poetic tool, stating that 'self-translation here takes an ambivalent pleasure in killing off the work of the "other" self' (Mooney 2002: 174). All the 'infidelities' in Beckett's self-translations are seen as intentional and as part of his grand plan, or his intellectual bilingual game.

There are two kinds of reasons behind Beckett's symmetrical bilingualism. The first one has to do with the fact that Beckett translated between 'two equally established European languages', as Grutman points out (2013a). Some languages can be described as politically oppressed while others are dominant; hence they do not have the same exchange value on the world market. The dominant languages include English, French, German, Spanish, Italian and Russian, and they serve as source languages for the rest of the world. The other reason for Beckett's symmetrical bilingualism is related to the self-translator's agency, and more specifically, to his ability to reach fluency in both languages and cultures. Not all bilingual authors and a relatively small number of bilingual speakers can ever get to the level of linguistic, literary and cultural competence that Beckett has achieved. Some bilingual writers question their own competence. For example, the established bilingual author Nancy Huston who, like Beckett, writes in English and French, describes herself as a 'false bilingual' (Falceri 2014) because she did not acquire her second language, French, in childhood but started mastering it when she moved to Paris to study at the age of twenty. Her uncertainty and self-doubt may be related to the general use of the term 'bilingual' by most lay people who usually use it to refer to the person who grew up bilingual from childhood.

In linguistics, on the other hand, researchers 'define *bilinguals* as speakers who use two or more languages in their everyday lives' and their fluency in each language could vary (Pavlenko 2014: 20–1; emphasis in original). Drawing on this, I define bilingual writers as people who write regularly and have published in two languages. Brodsky became a bilingual writer from the moment he bought his English typewriter, as suggested in the Introduction. Applying Hokenson and Munson's terminology (2007: 13–14), it is possible to say that Brodsky has progressed from being a 'colingual writer' with one dominant language (in the 1970s) to become a 'competent bilingual writer' who was 'able to write in both alternately and reproduce standard or normative discourse' in the late 1980s and early 1990s. Arguably, he never entirely reached the level of 'idiomatic bilingual writers' who are described as fluent 'in both languages with near-native handling or grammar, idioms, discursive registers, and stylistic and literary traditions'. Both, the critics who criticized Brodsky's English, such as Craig Raine (1996) and Christopher Reid (1988), and those who admired Brodsky's verse in English, including Derek Walcott (1988) and Seamus Heaney (1996), recognized the difference between the standard use of English and Brodsky's 'translationese', but they interpreted this difference according to opposing stances: as a negative impact on the English language or as 'poetic strength', as was put by Lachlan Mackinnon (2001). Focusing on Brodsky as a late bilingual writer and poet who never became as 'symmetrical' in his use of the two languages as Beckett, this book does not only go 'beyond' Becket in the study of self-translation (as encouraged by Grutman (2013a)) but also sheds light on how one's bilingualism is shaped in time, through self-determination and collaborative work.

The author's privilege versus the author's vulnerability

Scholars have described self-translators as those who have more freedom and authority to introduce changes to their self-translations than translators could have dreamed of. This school of thought is represented, for example, by Nibras A. M. Al-Omar who applies *skopos* theory to argue that

> the self-translator is also expected to designate and maintain the *skopos* of the target language text. Unlike the translator *per se*, the self-translator has the privilege of access to the intention of the source language text prior to its production. All these prerequisites contribute to the self-translator's decisions of introducing shifts and changes in the target language text through cultural mediation. (Al-Omar 2012: 211)

As a result, the self-translator can introduce some bold shifts to ensure effective cultural mediation including differences in sociocultural sphere, moral principles and some others. Jan Vansina (2004: 484) also finds that what differentiates the author's self-translation from other translations of the text is knowing the author's intention. Writing about the Chinese author Eileen Chang, Jessica Tsui Yan Li (2006) makes a similar observation: the Chinese writer enjoys her authorial privilege and aesthetic freedom in her self-translation of the short story 'Stale Mates' by introducing some changes in English in her description of physical beauty, which is re-contextualized to reflect differences in the Western and Chinese aesthetics of the body (2006: 99–106).

However, the privileged position of the self-translator has been questioned, in particular, by scholars who have analysed the role of the self-translator in historical perspective. Michael Boyden and Lieve Jooken consider J. Hector St John de Crevecoeur's 'History of Andrew, the Hebridean' in French and Dutch translation. They conclude that the author was 'much more tied to the public image that circulated about him in French society, which, to be sure, he had helped create, but which he could hardly control' (Boyden and Jooken 2013). The author's self-translations were transformed under the pressure applied by publishers who compelled the author 'to revise his views on such contentious issues as the depiction of Native Americans' (Boyden and Jooken 2013). These differences become apparent when the French self-translation is compared to the Dutch translation by an unknown translator, whose version shows that the translator was free of such pressure. Therefore, Boyden and Jooken conclude that 'claims about the "privileged" status of the self-translator are in need of serious modification'. Reflecting on the position of German bilingual self-translators, Verena Jung agrees that they are also under pressure to 'adapt their texts for their new readership in the other language' (Jung 2004: 532).

The privileged position of self-translators is further complicated if they translate into their second language because it is challenged by the long known prestige and privilege of the native speaker. Native speakers' command of language and level of fluency, independent of their regional accent and education, is privileged over the command of the second language acquired by the 'foreigner', as well known in pedagogy (Kramsch 1997: 359). This is particularly poignant for late bilinguals whose command of the second language is visibly foreign and whose linguistic 'strangeness' is evident from their accent. The self-translators who lack a 'native-speaker level' competence in the second language need to compensate for this lack. Brodsky was in precisely this position of an established writer whose second language (English) was still relatively insecure when he arrived in the United States, so he developed strategies for dealing with the lack of native speaker's privilege by creating support networks which consisted of his native English-language translators, editors and friends.

Self-translation by migrant writers is 'a translingual practice', 'which permits new kinds of conversations' and provides 'new speaking positions', to rephrase Sherry Simon (Simon 2000: 28). An example of a new speaking position could take the form of a (self-)editor. In her examination of bilingual work by German authors (Klaus Mann, Stefan Heym, Rudolf Arnheim and Hannah Arendt), Jung looks at them as cultural mediators writing in English in exile and then translating their work into their native German (Jung 2004). She discovers that they act as editors of their own text, making adjustments for a different readership. In some cases, they make rather drastic changes to the meaning in order to appeal to the German audience who are, for example, more interested in the facts or 'the truth' and less captivated by the genre of 'the quaint romance', at least in the view of the self-translator Klaus Mann (Jung 2004: 534). Jung explains this necessary editing through the authors' 'biculturality' and their knowledge of the 'pre-text', that is, national literary context. In other words, the pressure of the national literary discourse and the presumed tastes of the reading public force the authors to make these adjustments.

Diya M. Abdo (2009) discovers something similar in the work by the Arab female author Leila Abouzeid, when Abdo compares the two versions of Abouzeid's autobiography written first in Arabic and then self-translated into English for an American edition *Return to Childhood: The Memoir of a Modern Moroccan Woman*. Abdo observes in which ways the text is transformed through 'translation, editing, and reviewing' (Abdo 2009: 2). However, the difference between the German writers (most of whom are male) translating into their mother tongue and the female Arab author self-translating into English is not just in her own style but in 'the roles of editors, translators, and publishers', which 'cannot be underrated since Arab women writers are often packaged for their audiences in ways in which they might not approve' (Abdo 2009: 2). Abdo quotes Elizabeth Fernea who contends that 'the politics of translating the work of an Arab woman are always governed by the editor's or translator's choice of what will be exciting for or appropriate to the supposed target audience' (Abdo 2009: 2). Abdo's research confirms the existence of stereotypes and preconceptions by giving numerous examples of changes and shifts in the self-translations that were made by the author in response to 'the demands made upon her (by editors and publishers) to cater her work to a western audience' (Abdo 2009: 3). Interestingly, as in the case of the German writers, Abdo finds that some pressures have to do with the choice of genre: 'There is no denying the popularity of the confessional among American readership, as indicated by the popularity of autobiographies in the American publishing market' (Abdo 2009: 10). American readers want to see the markers of 'real' memories and authenticity: 'While the Western audience craves authenticity, exoticism, revelation, confession and self-indulgence, the native Arab, Moroccan, and Muslim audience, to whom autobiography is a "genre little validated", expects privacy and self-effacement, especially for women' (Abdo 2009: 12). Abouzeid struggles to reconcile her competing allegiances, especially as she is positioned in the west as 'Islamic feminist', which Abdo describes as 'not a coherent identity, but rather a contingent, contextually determined strategic self-positioning' (Abdo 2009: 22).

As seen from the above-mentioned examples, self-translators introduce changes of all kinds as they rewrite their texts in the second language. Some of these changes are made as a result of the pressure from editors and new readership tastes, while others may be introduced for other reasons, known only to the author who has access to his own original intention of the text. These tensions could be political, aesthetic or personal. As a political exile from the USSR and a migrant living in the United States, Brodsky experienced similar tensions to the ones described earlier, but his reaction to some pressures applied by editors, translators and readers was often to resist and insist on his own choices. First, like some other immigrants from the USSR, he had to fight against his positioning as a political exile and the stereotypes associated with this status (see Chapter 1). Second, he chose not to adapt to the demands of the popular poetic trends in Western poetry at the time. Unlike Arab female writers or German writers, he chose to resist adapting to the tastes of the majority of poetry readers and insisted on stricter poetic forms associated with Russian poetry. As a result, he was blamed for Russifying the English language and writing in *translationese*. Brodsky's poetic voice in English was shaped in the process of negotiation between him as the author and his multiple collaborators including translators, editors, readers and critics. His example also shows that the distribution of power constantly changes in this process; the author curates his own poetic voice with more confidence and resilience as he feels more bilingual and bicultural.

Types of collaboration in self-translation

Collaborating with the author is not uncommon for translators. Isabelle Vanderschelden (1998) considers various types of relationships between authors and their translators as well as degrees of author intervention to help us understand a variety of their attitudes and practices. There are authors, including André Brink and Marguerite Duras, who prefer not to intervene in translation and believe that each new translation is a new text. They have a 'non-possessive view on authorship' (Vanderschelden 1998: 23). It is, however, not rare when authors cooperate with translators, for example, by correspondence. They might assist translators in various ways: 'clarification on specific problems of comprehension or reference, consultation on translation strategies, and the transfer of formal properties of the source text' (Vanderschelden 1998: 23). It is also not uncommon that authors give preference to the importance of rhythmic and sound patterns over 'linguistic faithfulness', and many authors (including Milan Kundera, Umberto Eco, Jorge Luis Borges and Julio Cortázar) develop collaboration with translators on a systematic basis. Vanderschelden emphasizes a number of advantages of such collaboration for all: authors, translators and target text readers because authors share their profound knowledge of the ST, its style and intention while translators provide their understanding of the target language and audiences. As a result, they avoid unnecessary errors and save translation and production time. There is yet another group of translators who extend their authorial power over translations. They do not only keep a close eye on the process of translation; they can interfere in the production of the target text and even veto a translation, like Milan Kundera vetoed a translation of his novel *The Joke* in English on the grounds of unfaithfulness. Intervening in translation process questions the translator's autonomy and legitimacy by underlining the derivative nature of translation, concludes Vanderschelde. Tracing the author's proprietorial attitude to the TT to the romantic age, Vanderschelde observes that despite postmodern reading practices in literary studies, some authors 'tend to behave like Romantic poets when it comes to translation of their work, while others lead their translators toward rewriting and the creation of parallel texts' (Vanderschelden 1998: 29). She identifies significant problems for translators who have to constantly justify their work, as they hold a different status from authors who have the power to legitimize the TT if they have collaborated on it.

Some of the authors mentioned earlier may not have the intention to translate or collaborate on the translation of their ST, at least, at the start of the process, while other author do. I shall now consider the types of relationships between self-translators, or the authors who intend to render their texts in another language, with their collaborators who can be not only translators but their friends, editors or publishers. The first type of this collaboration could be one with editors and native-speaking friends. In his interview with Maria Recuenco Peñalver, André Brink explains to what extent he asks for help when he self-translates or rewrites his books:

> I could ask specific friends to tell me how they would write a particular expression or something like that. [...] Obviously, I am aware of the fact that I am an Africaans writer, there are many things that come more naturally to an English speaker than to an Africaans speaker. But it's only when I feel stuck with, let's call it, a translation. (Peñalver 2015)

The self-translator Vansina refers to this practice of editing by a native speaker as a regular practice (Vansina 2004: 484). In her analysis of immigrant writers' self-translations, Anastasija Gjurčinova considers the work by a Russian immigrant author Nikolai Lilin who self-translates from Russian to Italian. She notes that the translation of his texts was a two-stage process: he does it himself first, and then the editors of his publishing house '*translate*' his texts into literary language, 'through an intralingual operation we call *editing*, in order to turn them into excellent and successful literary products, as they are and have become' (Gjurčinova 2013: 7; emphasis in original).

Second is the collaboration with publishers who can act as the bilingual author's representative in a new literary space. By acquiring publishing rights for the authors' books, they gain power over their work and can influence on the shaping of their voices in the second language. Third is the author's active collaboration with translators. Even Beckett sought translators' help in some of his projects. In reference to Anthony Cronin (Cronin 1996), Grutman brings to our attention the 'collaborative (versus individual) nature of self-translation' in Beckett's work, describing it as writing 'several versions ... *à quatre mains*', including Beckett's work with Alfred Péron, Pierre Leyris, and the South African poet Partick Bowles (Grutman 2013a). Fourth is the collaboration of the self-translator with translators when translating somebody else's piece of work from a third or a fourth language. For example, as described by Grutman, 'in 1949, he [Beckett] was mandated by UNESCO to translate an anthology of Mexican poetry edited by Octavio Paz (1958) [...] he enlisted the help of an anonymous friend who had a better grasp of that third Romance language' (Grutman 2013a: 3).

Collaboration between the author and the translator has been described in fiction. Judy Wakabayashi explores the fictional representations of the authors' relationships with their translators and finds that 'translation continues to be overwhelmingly presented as subordinate to original writing' (Wakabayashi 2011: 100). She underlines, 'Reification of the singular genius of authors overlooks the reality that publication of their work involves the cooperation of many individuals, often including translators' (Wakabayashi 2011: 96). She provides examples of both 'implicit' and 'overt' relationships between the author and the translator. She then focuses on a particular form of the relationship where the author is threatened by the translator, like in John Crowley's novel (2002), where the Russian author Falin chooses Kit as translator 'precisely because of her lack of creative abilities' (Wakabayashi 2011: 96) – a 'real' poet 'would want to write poems of their own' (Crowley 2002: 173). After some deliberation following the author's death, Kit finally decides to publish her translations of his poems in a book of her own.

Interestingly, Olga Anokhina's study of Nabokov's work with his translators, which draws on the author's manuscripts and correspondence, shows some parallels with the fictional representations described earlier. She finds that Nabokov's strategies differ depending on whether his work is being translated into English or French. In English, Nabokov would find a malleable translator, whether it was his son or another younger person, and ask him (usually a younger male translator) to produce a literal translation of the text. After a literal translation has been completed, Nabokov would sit down with the translator to go over the text word by word and he would often rip it apart, so the translator had to be prepared for these authorial interventions. Anokhina identifies several reasons for Nabokov's use of translators in the English language: (1) he wanted to resist 'the temptation to re-write his work' and (2) he did not want to waste time on this very time-consuming job, especially as he was involved in the long-term translation project of Alexander Pushkin's *Evgeniy Onegin* into English. When Nabokov's texts were translated into French, he was not free to pick his own translators: they were chosen by publishers. He was recommended some established translators from English to French who had strong ideas about their work. As a result, his relationship with his French translators was tense, as they expressed disagreement with the author's suggestions (Anokhina 2017).

Later in this chapter, I show that Brodsky's translations and self-translations in English were often created in collaboration with translators, editors and publishers. The poet's relationships with them were multifaceted and dependent to an extent on the stage of his bilingual career. To begin with, Brodsky was more dependent on his translators but, as his confidence grew, he exerted more power over his English-language texts.

Mimetic approach to poetic translation

There is a lot of literature on the translation of poetry but there is no sign of consensus, especially if we consider different national poetic histories and traditions. Ezra Pound (2006 (1929)) explains the lack of consensus by the fact that no translator can remain faithful to the source poem. His theory is that there are three kinds of poetry: *melopoeia*, which draws on musical qualities of words, *phanopoeia*, focusing on visual imagery, and *logopoeia*, referring to the use of words in multiple layers of meaning. According to Pound, *logopoeia* is the most difficult to translate. But many poems contain aspects of two or all three types of poetry. Most Brodsky's Russian poems would certainly not fit just one type. Take any of his poems, for example, 'The Butterfly', which successfully creates meaning on all three levels. In Brodsky's Russian poems, the meaning emerges from the combination of metric form, rhyming words, rhythmic choices, the use of lexis, imagery, references, allusions, the sonic effect of words and others. As it is impossible to transfer a poem with all its nuances from one language to another without changes, the translator has to prioritize the translation of certain aspects over the others. James S. Holmes (1988) proposes that there could be four approaches to the translation of poetry: two 'form-derivative' and two 'content-derivative'. The first approach is what we know as a mimetic approach to translation, that is, when the form of the original poem is retained in the target poem. The second one is employed by the translators who consider the function of the form in the source language in order to find an equivalent form in the translating language. The third approach is derived from the content of the original poem, which leads to the emergence of a new 'organic form' or a new poem. The fourth one does not derive from the ST and might be called a 'deviant form' or extraneous form.

All translators of poetry have to compromise and make a choice of their translation method. It is interesting that translators who work with the same pair of languages, say Russian to English, do not seem to have any more agreement about the preferred approach to translation despite the fact that they are rendering poems from the same language. In his major study of Russian verse, Michael Wachtel (1998) argues that Russian poetic metres acquire particular thematic associations through the recurrent uses of certain forms. In other words, throughout the history of Russian versification, metres have developed meanings which have emerged as a result of being employed in subsequent texts by different poets. Both Russian poets and Russian readers at large are familiar with these metrical traditions and respond to their use in new poetic texts. However, when it comes to the translation of these metres along with the content of the poems, there is no one universally preferred solution. Brodsky passionately argues for the mimetic school of poetic translation while Nabokov insists on the literal transmission of Pushkin's novel in verse *Evgeniy Onegin*. Comparing Nabokov's and Roman Jakobson's approaches to translation of poetry, Brian James Baer emphasizes that Nabokov insisted 'on the impossibility of translating poetry as poetry, in particular, the poetry of the great Russian poet Aleksandr Sergeevich Pushkin' (Baer 2011: 177). The linguist Jakobson, on the other hand, values 'creativity' and non-literalist approaches to poetic translation. Between these two, there is a great variety of options.

Brodsky's mimetic approach to translation and self-translation came from the Russian tradition of poetic translation. As discussed by Ishov, Brodsky draws on the 'principles of mimetic translation set by Pushkin' in the nineteenth century and formulated by the Acmeist poet Nikolai Gumilev in the early twentieth century (Ishov 2008: 37–8). According to these principles, the translation has to retain the following features of the original poem: the number of lines, metre, rhyme pattern, types of enjambments, rhyme, register, metaphor, special devices and changes of tone. For Brodsky as well as his poetic predecessors, the form is inseparable from the meaning. Therefore, the form of the original has to be transferred to the translating language as closely as possible. Brodsky further fine-tunes the principles of mimetic approach. He insists that a translation had to retain the stanzaic design as well as convey the meaning of the ST. Many of his translators would have agreed with Brodsky on the main principles of mimetic poetic translation, but Brodsky seems to have further demands including having the same words rhymed in the translation as in the original. This is important to him because he believes that rhyming words carry the effect of inevitability, which enhance the impact of the meaning on the reader. Dissatisfied with the existing translations of Osip Mandelshtam's poems, Brodsky writes:

> Translation is a search for an equivalent, not for a substitute. Mandelshtam is a formal poet in the highest sense of the word. For him, a poem began with a sound, with a 'sonorous, molded shape of form', as he himself called it. Logically, a translator should begin his work with a search for at least a metrical equivalent to the original form. (Brodsky 1974)

Brodsky then proceeds to criticize W. S. Merwin's translations of Mandelshtam claiming that they sacrifice the original's unique tone and are renderings into Merwin. Brodsky is equally unapologetic about other translators of Russian poetry into English who have not attempted to retain poetic form, stating that they translate originals not into English but into their own individual languages:

> Russian poetry has set an example of moral purity and firmness, which to no small degree has been reflected in the preservation of so-called classical form without any damage to content. Herein lies her distinction from her Western sisters, though in no way do I presume to judge whom this distinction favours most. However, it is a distinction, and if only for purely ethnographic considerations that quality ought to be preserved in translation and not forced into a common mold. (Brodsky 1974)

Unsurprisingly, Brodsky's bold and normative comments on poetic translation have caused a stir. One of Brodsky's opponents is the scholar and translator Daniel Weissbort who clashed with the poet about his own translations of Brodsky's 'A Part of Speech' (see Chapters 3 and 4). Weissbort has continuously challenged Brodsky's view on poetic translation in his personal correspondence with the poet as well as in his publications. While putting together the edited volume *Translation: Theory and Practice* (2006), Weissbort, as a co-editor, takes the opportunity to clash Brodsky's criticism of Merwin with Merwin's own discussion of his methods. Elsewhere Weissbort turns to Nabokov to demonstrate that recreating formal features of the Russian poem in the English language may lead to the impossibility of finishing a good translation.

> (1) There are far more rhymes, both masculine and feminine, in Russian [. . .] (2) Russian words, no matter how long, have only one stress, whereas polysyllabic English words often have secondary stresses or two stresses; (3) Russian is considerably more polysyllabic than English; (4) in Russian, all syllables are pronounced, without the elisions or slurs that occur in English verse; (5) inversion or trochaic words, common in English iambics, is rare in Russian verse; (6) as against that, Russian iambic tetrameters contain more modulated lines than regular ones. The reverse being true in English poetry. (Weissbort 2004: 39–40)

Brodsky's mimetic view on poetic translation also means that a translation is interpreted as a copy, a product of mimicry, an ongoing work in progress, endlessly striving for improvement not only by the translator but by the author of the original too, if needed. A translation cannot be, as a result, a finite text and the translator is not acknowledged with full authorship rights over the text. For Brodsky, a translation represents the author of the original in the translating language and culture; therefore the author – if she or he happens to be bilingual and present at the time of the translation – had the right to make the final call on the TT, which Brodsky has exercised on various occasions. This desire to curate his voice in English has become a cause for many arguments with some of his translators. His view of translation is reminiscent of Walter Benjamin's somewhat outdated understanding that 'The intention of the poet is spontaneous, primary, graphic; that of the translator is derivative, ultimate, ideational' (Benjamin 1968). By the end of the twentieth century, the view shared by most 'cultural turn' translation scholars was opposite to the one advocated by Benjamin: translation is no longer seen as derivative but as creative process, and the translator's inferior status has also been challenged by Lawrence Venitu (1995), feminist translation scholars and some others.

Brodsky's demands on translation and translators were often uncompromising. He was deeply dissatisfied with the quality of many English translations of Russian poems, especially those written by Russian Acmeists for whom form was an integral part of the poem. Brodsky lamented the quality of poetic translations from Russian to English. He insisted that good translations were an exception and that it was important to have more translations that were faithful to the form of the ST. He believed that Russian poetry would benefit from these translations which should make a majority in the future.

Brodsky's approach to translation was very much linked to his view on writing and composition in the first language. In the Russian poetic tradition, the formal qualities of the poem, its rhyme and metre, remained crucial in poetic composition throughout the twentieth century, especially for a follower of Acmeist tradition. In English, poetic practice developed differently, and by the time when Brodsky moved to the United States, it was a minority rather than a majority of poets who continued to use rhyme and metre patterns. Instead, many poets turned to *verse libre*. Brodsky was relentless in his attacks on *verse libre*:

> In my opinion a regular meter and exact rhymes shaping an uncomfortable thought are far more functional than any form of free verse. Because in the former case the reader gets a sense of chaos being organized, while in the latter a sense of dependence on and being determined by chaos. From what one could call a moral point of view, the former is more important than the latter. Even in the event that it is not organization, but nothing more than a form of resistance to chaos. For in the physical world only resistance is possible. (Brodsky 1973b)

As seen from these remarks, Brodsky ascribes rhyme some powers that go beyond language and help organize not only thought but the physical and social world. Brodsky is adamant that this is a universal quality of poetic language. Therefore an historic literary development within one language, such as decreasing interest in the use of rhyme and metre in English in late twentieth century, cannot justify the poets' and translators' rejection of formal poetry. This point of view is expressed strongly in Brodsky's response to Denise Levertov who criticizes Brodsky for being out of tune with contemporary English-language poetry. Levertov harshly accuses Brodsky of being 'ill-equipped to comprehend poetry written in English' and 'ignorant' in his praise of Wilbur. Levertov explains Brodsky's insistence on the formal use of rhyme and metre patterns by his Russian origin and by the fact that Russian was 'a language of abundance, in vocabulary and in syntactic variations', and she goes on to blame him for 'his ignorance of the "functional" capacities of free verse' (Levertov et al. 1973).

What is clear from this sharp exchange is that Brodsky and Levertov were never going to agree on *verse libre*. Levertov supports a widely spread view that poetic traditions in various languages developed differently and therefore applying similar principles in two different languages would be unhelpful. Brodsky, on the other hand, defends his notion of poetic language as something that is above national poetic traditions and turns to Auden as an example of a twentieth-century English-language poet for whom strict poetic form was paramount. This has also become the basis for Brodsky's idiosyncratic definition of accuracy in the translation of poetry:

> My main argument with translators is that I care for accuracy and they're very often inaccurate – which is perfectly understandable. It's awfully hard to get these people to render the accuracy as you would want them to. So rather than brooding about it, I thought perhaps I would try to do it myself. (Birkerts 1982)

By 'accuracy' in the above paragraph, Brodsky means formal accuracy, that is, the rendering of the form including metre and rhyme patterns, as well as the meaning. Brodsky admitted that his demands were difficult to achieve, but he was neither prepared to compromise on his main mimetic principles of translation nor was he interested in any other approaches to translation, for example, those that identify reception as a key factor in translation, that is, how the audience with their changing historical and cultural views perceive a translation. No translators, even those who shared the poet's views on mimetic translation, such as Kline and Myers, could always meet Brodsky's demands for retaining the metre, rhyming patterns and stanzaic design of the ST.

However, Brodsky's demanding views on translation do not always meet even his own practice of self-translation. A detailed analysis of his self-translation practices, given in the following chapters, shows less rigid, more complicated and changing methods of translation in comparison with the views expressed earlier as, in the course of over twenty years, the poet's translation practices in cooperation with his translators and English-speaking peers go through various transformations.

Debates about Brodsky's English

In 1973, Stephen Spender admired Brodsky's *Selected Poems* translated by Kline for being 'impressive'. In them, Brodsky was 'utterly truthful, deeply religious, fearless and pure', 'loving, as well as hating'. Commenting on Kline's translations, he noted Kline's 'accurate rendering', 'conveying the correctness, density, literalness of lines' of Brodsky but criticized it for not allowing the reader to forget that one is reading 'a second-hand version rather than original poetry' (Spender 1973: 915–16). Two years later, praising Brodsky in his review of the same book, Victor Erlich underlined the author's active part in the translation process: 'These are truly authorized translations, a product of close collaboration and genuine affinity between the poet and the translator' (Erlich 1974: 621). Yet, some translators started expressing their criticism of Brodsky's approach to poetic translation. Raffel Burton inveighed against Brodsky's 'utterly uninformed and indeed incompetent stances' from which Brodsky approached the translation of Russian poetry (Burton 1974). In 1978, Henry Gifford reviewed two books by Brodsky, *The End of a Beautiful Era* (*Konets prekrasnoi epokhi*) and *A Part of Speech* (*Chast' rechi*), claiming that Brodsky's poetry was 'the best poetry in America in recent years' (Gifford 1978: 903). He found Brodsky's English flawless and said that Brodsky should be accepted as a corresponding member of the company of English and American poets: he made 'English his own', took 'the stiffness out of lichés' and restored 'to the language its youthful suppleness'; Brodsky was 'a poet [. . .] reborn into a second parallel life' of a new language' (Gifford 1980: 1158).

However, some further reviews of *A Part of Speech* were less enthusiastic about Brodsky's English, distinguishing between the great Russian poet Brodsky and the not-so-successful translator Brodsky. Clarence Brown criticized his translations for being Audenesque for no 'discernible reason', and for being 'unfocused' and 'incomprehensible'. However, Brown also noticed that Brodsky's poems originally written in English, for example, 'his powerful elegy to Lowell', were more successful because they were not restrained by the self-translator's loyalty to the Russian original (Brown 1980: 16, 18). In his review of the same book 'Lost in Translation', Robert Hass identified general translation difficulties from the Russian language, which is 'inflected, characteristically polysyllabic [. . .], much more flexible in its word order than English'. He noted that the different history of metrical poetry in Russian and English should be held responsible for some decisions made by Brodsky's translators (Hass 1980: 36). In the same year, Michael Schmidt wrote his review of *A Part of Speech*, stating that Brodsky was a 'wit of a high order' who could play 'in and through language'. He also admired Brodsky as 'a fine linguist who had filled his ear with English' but yet described him as 'his worst translator' (Schmidt 1980: 25). D. M. Thomas commended Brodsky's 'controlling hands in the excellent translations' as well as the poems translated by the author solely. Agreeing with Gifford, he declared that every poem in the book read as if English had been 'its first home' (Thomas 1981: 47). John Bayley, on the other hand, criticized Brodsky for not succeeding in the 'daring task of trying to write the same book in both languages'. Bayley stated that 'Brodsky's poetic ear for English was not, could not be, as unerring as his ear for the melodies and nuances of his native tongue', identifying issues with Brodsky's English grammar, style, 'his standardised post-Auden mechanisms', his world view 'generated by an insatiable appetite for competition' and his preoccupation with hierarchy (Bayley 1981: 83–90).

In 1987, Seamus Heaney praised Brodsky, as a Nobel Prize–winning poet, for his 'world-ness', identifying the conflict between the Russian language, which provided the energy of Brodsky's texts, and English, which could appear both 'animated and skewed' in Brodsky's treatment; however, this dichotomy, in his view, made Brodsky's English poetry 'yield with that unbounded assent that only the most triumphant art can conjure and allow' (Heaney 1987). The Nobel brought Brodsky a strain of responses full of praise and appreciation, but even this was contradicted by Christopher Reid's harsh criticism in his piece titled 'Great

American Disaster' (Reid 1988). He identified grammatical and stylistic mistakes in Brodsky's English, questioned his ability to critique English poetry and suggested a lack of ear for the English language: 'though no fault of his own, the poet has seemed to occupy the position of statelessness somewhere between Russian and English, in the neutral zone called *Translationese*' (Reid 1988: 17). In the same year, Donald Davie described Brodsky as a 'conscientious artificer', coming to the conclusion that Brodsky's problem with English lay in the fact that the poet tried to impose Russian metre and metaphor on English (Davie 1988: 1415). Expressing a completely opposite view, Derek Walcott, a Nobel Prize winner himself, wrote in delight about Brodsky's 'phenomenal [. . .] effort' 'to render almost to deliver, the poem from its original language into the poetry of the new country. To give the one work, simultaneously two mother tongues' (Walcott 1988: 35).

In 1996, Craig Anthony Raine accused Brodsky of poor and insufficient English in his review of *So Forth* and *On Grief and Reason*. He dissected Brodsky's English self-translation 'May 24, 1980', describing it as mediocre (Raine 1996: 17). He then wrote another critical piece about Brodsky's English in 2001 (Raine 2001). This attack was challenged by Lachlan Mackinnon who justified some Brodsky-isms and defended Brodsky's literary criticism, which had also been condemned by Raine. Mackinnon asserted that Brodsky had 'succeeded in finding a unique voice', and he 'might yet have a tremendously liberating effect on English verse' (Mackinnon 2001: 9–11), comparing him to outstanding bilingual writers Joseph Conrad, Vladimir Nabokov and Samuel Beckett. Raine then counter-attacked Mackinnon in a Letter to the Editor, confirming his view of Brodsky's English poetry as 'wonky', 'awkward and skewed', 'uneven' and flawed (Raine 2001: 17).

In 1999, Robert Reid underlined Brodsky's 'ability to exploit the deep structure of English' but left a reservation in brackets: '(though occasionally this master of linguistic acclimatisation strikes a wrong note in the adopted language)' (Reid 1999: 193). Charles Simic also found that Brodsky could 'be deaf to nuances of usage in his adopted one [language]' (Simic 2000: 9). This critical account of Brodsky's English was again counterbalanced in a positive assessment by Susan Sontag in her essay, which she had written in 1998 for the book published in 2001: she praised the world poet Brodsky for his poems with 'their extraordinary velocity and density of material notation, of cultural reference, of attitude' (Sontag 2001: 332). And yet again, for every favourable essay about Brodsky's English there is a dissentious review. Reflecting on the posthumous *Collected Poems in English* (2000) for *The Telegraph*, Vernon Scannell (2001) insisted that only 'the versions by gifted American poets [. . .] convey something of the brilliance that captivated Akhmatova and other discerning Russian readers' in the poetry by Brodsky. According to him, American poets none of whom knew Russian were his best translators. However, even this was questioned, as some thought that having translators with strong voices made Brodsky's collections look like an anthology.

The curious thing about these debates about Brodsky's English is that sometimes readers' opinions completely diverge about the same poems. What Raine (1996) found 'inept', 'cliché' and melodramatic in the poem 'May 24, 1980', Mackinnon supported as a fair point about 'gratitude for existence'; what Raine marked as a grammatical mistake (the use of the future continuous in the twentieth line as opposed to the future tense), Mackinnon interpreted as an expression of an 'involuntary response' of the poet's gratitude. Raine also pointed to the sixth line as unnecessarily melodramatic, exaggerated, especially, in comparison with the Russian equivalent that read simply and laconically: 'I was torn apart twice' (in literal translation). Mackinnon himself remarked on how Brodsky's English had split English-speaking readers into two opposite camps: for some he was 'the greatest English (or rather American) poet of the post-war years', and for others, 'barely competent outside his mother tongue' (Mackinnon 2001). In his *Independent* obituary of Brodsky, Mackinnon (1996) wrote:

> Brodsky was engaged in creating a new idiolect, precisely the half-English of a deracinated man. From his mentor Auden he learnt to rummage in the more arcane areas of English vocabulary, and the resulting style is, while sometimes disconcerting, usually self-consistent and achieved. (Mackinnon 1996)

Michael Hoffman who is fully bilingual himself in German and English arrived at a similar conclusion, identifying 'something binaral or bipolar' about Brodsky's writing and adding that the poet was good enough 'to play by two sets of rules' and his poems had 'irresistible verbal authority' even in English. Hoffman also described Brodsky's writing as 'arrant and wilfully provocative *translationese*', and suggested that Brodsky's growing 'tolerance for eccentric English' had 'less to do with translation than authorship' (Hoffman 1997: 6–8). In his short review of *To Urania*, George Steiner endorsed this view of Brodsky's English, suggesting that it was possible to see through Brodsky's 'translationese' and recognize 'the lyric prodigality of invention' and yet there was 'more than an edge of strangeness, a flicker of the forced' (Steiner 1988). So, if there is one thing that scholars, poets, reviewers and readers of Brodsky's English poetry agree on is that Brodsky's English does not sound entirely idiomatic; it disrupts the way in which native English-speaking writers use their language, and this difference provokes a full range of readers' reactions, from admiration to abomination. All the above readers have associated Brodsky with authority, confidence, eccentricity and even arrogance and no one has commented on his vulnerability as a late bilingual writer.

Self-translation by a late bilingual as a form of linguistic 'strangership'

Whether English-language readers accept Brodsky's idiosyncrasies or not, whether they see brilliance and novelty in his voice or awkwardness and mistakes, all of them agree on one thing – Brodsky's self-consciously constructed voice in English is different from any native speaker born into the English language – Brodsky's English is often unidiomatic, accented and forced but yet it can be enriching, refreshing and introspective. It is the English language spoken by a stranger, by a late bilingual who brings his native tongue, literary culture and, most unusually, the poetic tradition of Russian versification into his second language.

Being in a relationship of *strangership* involves crossing boundaries, both physical and symbolic (Simmel 2016). Brodsky crossed physical, geographic, political but more importantly literary and poetic boundaries, and he did not accept the popular poetic and literary norms as given; rather, he challenged them based on his own, a stranger's understanding of English poetry. For example, his essay on Robert Frost was admired by many American readers precisely for his ability to see in the American poet something different, illuminating the aspects of Frost's poetry that were beyond conventional reading of the poet.

To understand this relationship of 'strangership', it is helpful to turn to the sociologist Georg Simmel's notion of it. According to Mervyn Horgan who further develops Simmel's ideas, *strangership* is 'a social relation that both produces and is produced by the society and culture in which it is invariably enmeshed'; it is 'a product of social interaction' (Horgan 2012: 613). Like friendship, which requires that 'friends must mutually recognize one another as friends for friendship to exist', *strangership* requires that 'strangers must recognize one another as strangers for *strangership* to exist' (Horgan 2012: 614). *Strangership* is intersubjective and is produced in the process of communication between people.

For a poet, the greatest challenges of *strangership* are linguistic, literary and poetic. No matter how much Brodsky loved English poetry and how closely affiliated he felt with Auden, he remained a newcomer to the English language, who had to deal with having his work translated. His linguistic and poetic *strangership* was manifest in the differences between his linguistic choices and the choices made by his translators: he would insist on a certain wording for reasons of form (though not only!), but his translators would make linguistic choices which would sound more idiomatic in English. The default position in this context is that the native speaker knows better but not if we are dealing with an eminent writer who has a command of both languages albeit it being limited in the case of English. Brodsky often disagreed with his translators and insisted on keeping his phrasing and his choice of rhyming words. He would knowingly keep this difference, which would make his English texts sound strange to his translators and therefore to his readers. He insisted that he did it for the sake of rhyme and metre, and even for the sake of the English language. In addition, according to Kjellberg,

> he was very conscious of register: he did not like for poems to sound pious or earnest [see Brodsky's letter to Kline later in this chapter]; he did not want the poems to lose their edge. I always felt that he was resisting the tendency

2. From Solo Writer in Russian to Collaborative Self-Translator in English

in American poetry to uniformly colloquial or conversational. Brodsky had a greater variety of rhetorical modes than was common in American poetry at that time. Joseph's immediate predecessors had worked in a self-consciously crafted mode than the predecessors of his American contemporaries. Compare, say, Mandelshtam to Allen Ginsberg. (Kjellberg 2020)

In the end, these differences shaped his 'authenticity' in English; they were consistent and recognizable as Brodsky's voice, what was described as his idiolect. Therefore, *strangership* manifested in those linguistic and poetic differences formed Brodsky's self-consciously cultivated poetic identity in English.

Brodsky's *strangership* was enhanced by the fact that he was an autodidact. His original perspective on everything shaped by self-education became completely unique when he acquired a double vision thanks to the acquisition of the second language. This vantage point was characterized by a dialectic relationship between closeness and remoteness and allowed for fresh perspectives and new angles. This relationship of *strangership* put him in a more vulnerable position, when it came to native speakers' judgement of his grammatical and other errors, but, at the same time, it made him more resilient and powerful because he could project more universal views and values enabled by his position as a stranger.

Brodsky describes his relationship of *strangership* in his poem 'Robinsonade' (see the Epigraph). One of the strengths of looking at Brodsky's 'domestication' through the concept of *strangership* is that it allows us to see this process in its dynamic, or dialectic change, through the prism of his changing position along the closeness–remoteness axis, from being remote to becoming 'domesticated'. This movement was reflected in the shifting of his translation strategies and working practices, which changed despite his loyalty to one method of mimetic poetic translation. As he was becoming more 'domesticated', more fluent and better networked, his collaboration practices took different shapes, as shown in the diagrams in the second part of this chapter.

The concept of *strangership* is also helpful when applied to the principles of translation. Gideon Toury, the pioneer of descriptive translation studies, argues that translation can have one of two aims. It can either lean towards the translating culture – by eliminating the 'incompatibilities' of the ST – or towards the original – by undermining the norms of the target language:

> the pursuit of adequate translation, may well entail certain incompatibilities with target norms and practices, especially those lying beyond the mere linguistic ones. If, on the other hand, the second stance is adopted, norm systems of the target culture are triggered and set into motion. Shifts from the source text would be an almost inevitable price. Thus, whereas adherence to source norms determines a translation's adequacy as compared to the source text, subscription to norms originating in the target culture determines its acceptability. (Toury 1995: 56–7)

Instead of adopting the convention of assimilating the differences and positioning the other in 'domestic intelligibilities' with their established 'values, beliefs, and representations', Larence Venuti proposes an approach to translation that emphasizes differences within the diversity of the English language (Venuti 1995: 78). Inadvertently, this is what Brodsky ends up doing, insisting on formal rhyme and scheme patterns which, in the first place, are inspired by the Russian poetic tradition but also are an attempt to use the English formal poetic canon of the past. So, arguably Brodsky is deploying variations of the English poetic language currently used by a minority to emphasize the difference between how most English-language poetry readers expect to see a poem now and how he would like his poem to appear. Unlike other self-translators he refuses to follow the established canon and propels the one notion of poetic form that he considers right. In fact, he describes it as his mission to set rules for translation from Russian to English and to encourage formal poetic composition in English. In addition, he makes some lexical and stylistic choices that only a stranger would opt for. By doing all this, he meets Venuti's requirement for what a translated text should be, that is, 'the site where a different culture emerges, where a reader gets a glimpse of a cultural other, and resistancy, a translation strategy based on an aesthetic of discontinuity', by reminding the reader of 'the gains and losses in the translation process' (Venuti 1995: 306). While Venuti's foreignizing approach has been criticized, it provides a helpful angle from which to approach Brodsky's self-translation practices. What Venunti describes as 'foreignizing' is often inadvertently present in his writing in English.

Is collaborative self-translation the same as multiple authorship?

Having established that collaborative self-translation is a fairly common phenomenon and can take a variety of forms, it is worth asking the question whether it is any different from collaborative multiple authorship which has been examined and theorized by Jack Stillinger (1991). Stillinger's understanding of multiple authorship is based on a biographical approach to the study of literature. Moving away from the textual, structuralist and post-structuralist approaches, which had dominated the field and focused on the text at the expense of the author, Stillinger proposes to refocus on the author's life in the relevant historical, social and cultural context as well as the production and reception of the text, including

> investigation of how an author wrote and revised a work; recovery of the circumstances of the transmission of a text, publication, and original and subsequent reception; consideration of an author's reading and education; study of comments that an author makes about a work (or about writing in general) in letters, journals, diaries, recorded conversations; relationship

of details in a work to details of the author's life (and to the lives of people among the author's acquaintance); relationship of a work to other writings by the same author and to writings by other authors; study of an author's language and its sources; study of an author's ideas and their sources (and their relationship to ideas of the author's time and earlier); study of the historical, political, social, and cultural contexts that, although beyond an author's control, are channeled through the author into a work. (1991: 8–9)

Stillinger's approach resembles a similarly biographical approach in translation studies developed later by Pym (1998) who states that we should study the author before we study the text. Stillinger's method with its emphasis on the agent, the agent's networks, social circumstances in which the text was created and the production of the text would sit comfortably within a social turn in translation studies, especially as Stillinger demonstrates that collaborative multiple authorship is characteristic of many writers and therefore is a widely spread phenomenon. He argues that many literary texts have been produced in collaboration and identifies different types of multiple authorship:

> the young Keats being refined, polished, and restrained by well-intentioned friends and publishers; the middle-aged Mill being spruced up by his wife for attractive autobiographical presentation; the old Wordsworth rewriting his younger self; Coleridge constructing his philosophy with lengthy extracts taken over verbatim without acknowledgment from the Germans; Eliot seizing on the revisions and excisions of his mentor; novelists routinely sharing their authorship with friends, spouses, ghostwriters, agents, editors, censors, publishers; playwrights and screenwriters disappearing in the ordinary processes of play and film production. (Stillinger 1991: 182)

Any form of involvement in the production of the text is described by Stillinger as 'multiple authorship': from collaborative writing actively sought by the author while working on a draft to editing and copy-editing at the latest stage of the production of the text. Stillinger even goes a step further and stretches his definition of multiple authorship to include some forms of reception. He gives an example of how a lecturer who projects on the screen William Blake's 'illuminations', which were handcrafted by the author and added to his books to illustrate his poems, can distort Blake's original intention, which was 'to epitomise example of single authorship', and therefore the lecturer inadvertently becomes a co-author of Blake's work (Stillinger 1991: 183–4). Stillinger's examination of multiple authorship is helpful because it brings to light its complexity, but yet it fails to be specific enough because its definition attempts to accommodate both text production and reception, whether with or without the author's awareness of changes made to the text or its presentation.

I propose to redefine 'multiple authorship' as *collaborative* multiple authorship [emphasis mine]', which allows me to emphasize the author's *intention* to collaborate and *awareness* of 'multiple authorship', that is, other people's contribution to the text. I do not consider as 'collaborative multiple authorship' a type of co-authorship of which the author is not aware. The author may be unaware of the contribution of others to the text for a few reasons. First, some changes to the author's collaborative translations may be made posthumously. I do not consider these in my analysis because I examine only the translations and self-translations into English conducted with the author's own permission. Second, the author may be unaware of the changes made to the text as a result of plagiarism or some unauthorized intervention in the text. For example, the author may have moved abroad or may have been exiled from the country of his origin. As a result, somebody may intentionally or not make changes to his or her text while publishing them without the author's permission. In Soviet Russia, Brodsky's texts were copied and distributed in *samizdat* (self-publishing). It is perfectly possible that while copying Brodsky's poems someone may have made a mistake or an omission in his poem, which, in my view, should not be considered as 'collaborative multiple authorship' because the author has not given permission for this change to the text. The definition of collaborative multiple authorship used in this book is based on the author's consent to and/or awareness of others' contribution to the text. I would argue that this definition would also work for the texts published online. If the text was published and the author asked for contributions of others, then it would be seen as a product of collaborative multiple authorship. If the author or the authorized person has not agreed on the changes made or has not invited others to contribute, then the changed text should be seen as plagiarized, or changed without the author's permission. It is possible to apply this definition of collaborative multiple authorship during both production and reception – as long as the collaboration has been authorized by the author or by his or her designated person.

It is worth noting that both the monolingual image of the author, as argued by Hokenson and Munson, and the vision of the poet as a single or solo author as opposed to multiple authorship (see the discussion later in this chapter) are rooted in European romanticism, which played a dominant role in shaping the perception of the poet in Russian literature and culture: most notably, Alexander Pushkin, the so-called father of Russian literature, was influenced by both German and English romantic poets. In Russian culture Pushkin the poet is perceived to be a prophet and a sufferer who occupies an elevated space in public consciousness. Brodsky in Russian has been described as a twentieth-century Pushkin due to his extraordinary contribution to Russian poetic tradition. Yet Brodsky's decision to become a bilingual poet in the United States turns him into an international and bilingual author, who is beyond the romantic definition of the poet. By demystifying the process of writing in a second language, this book problematizes our understanding of the poet as both a solo writer and a monolingual poet by analysing how Brodsky approached writing in English through collaboration while continuing to write in Russian as a solo author. Studying work by self-translating bilingual writers makes us review our understanding of the creative process, authority, collaborative writing and originality while comparing self-translators to translators makes us also question the very motives behind their desire to self-translate.

Another problem that I can see with Stillinger's definition of multiple authorship, which could also be seen as its strength in some ways, is that it does not differentiate between different types of collaboration, depending on the number of collaborators, the amount and the type of work they have contributed, the stage of production or reception during which they have made their contribution, the impact that their contribution has had on the text and its reception, the circumstances in which their contribution has taken place. For example, in one case the author could have borrowed from his one writer-friend who came up with some helpful lines and the title of the text. In another, the author could have created the text as a solitary writer, but his text might have been subjected to some minor editorial changes. Or the author or a translator could have drawn heavily on an interlinear translation.

Depending on the author and the author's relationship with collaborators, Lorraine Mary York (York 2002) identifies two types of collaborative writing: overt, that is, when the author openly works with other contributors and fully acknowledges their work, and implicit, when collaborators' work is not fully acknowledged and takes place behind the scene. These are similar to the earlier discussed types of collaboration in self-translation. Stillinger and York discuss multiple authorship only in the monolingual context when authors collaborate on writing a text in one language. But how different is collaboration and multiple authorship in bilingual writing when co-authors are also translators? The following sections of this chapter and Chapter 3 will analyse the complexities of the poet's support networks and processes involved in text production, revealing both overt and covert types of collaboration and the specificity of these relationships caused by the bilingual context in which they develop.

Brodsky's changing translation strategies:
From no control to remote control

This part of the chapter and Chapter 3 focus on how Brodsky started to gain authorial control in English but yet how he was dependent on working collaboratively with his translators and editors throughout his bilingual career. Volgina (2006), Ishov (2008) and Berlina (2014) all take it for granted that Brodsky's voice in English was 'authentic' from his first self-translation 'December in Florence'. My archival study of Brodsky Papers reveals that Brodsky's self-translations, including 'December in Florence' (discussed in Chapter 3), were products of co-translation and re-translation. In his second language, Brodsky had to rely on his collaborators, translators and editors, from whom he borrowed and from whom he learnt as he was working on his self-translations. His 'authentic' voice in English was shaping in response to and in collaboration with his co-translators. Brodsky's Russian manuscripts are usually typed by the poet himself. There is plenty of evidence of this from available documentary footage, photographs, memoirs and other documents. Writing in his native Russian for Brodsky was a solo activity. For him, 'art is always individual: at the moment of creation by the artist and at the moment of consumption (perception) by the viewer.' By individual, he means 'solo', created and consumed by one person alone. In this essay to *The New York Times* (1972), Brodsky discusses the destiny of the writer who, as he reiterates in the final paragraph of the letter, is a 'lonely traveler, and no one is his helper'. Brodsky's manuscripts of his original poems in Russian are manifestations of his understating of writing as a solo activity, a sacred moment of creation when language speaks through the poet where language, especially poetic language, is understood by Brodsky as a phenomenon that is bigger, more important and powerful than the poet and even the passing of time. (See Chapter 1 for further discussion of his view of language.)

This romantic[3] understanding of the process of writing and of the poet as a singular figure opposed to society, as presented in the above-mentioned letter to *The New York Times*, throws light on Brodsky's attitude to translation and translators. Translation is seen as an imitation, an interpretation, a copy, a version of the inviolate original. There is only one original, which is *singular* and *definitive*, but there are many mushrooming translations with commentaries, corrections and remarks; they can be edited, adjusted, changed and completely rewritten. According to Brodsky, translation aims to imitate the ST instead of being an original expression in its own right. It is a copy that can be improved, edited, returned to as many times as necessary.

My conversation with Kjellberg, who closely worked with Brodsky for many years, confirms that Brodsky's translations were created in collaboration: 'We were all working on these poems *because* we admired and appreciated Joseph and wanted translations to be equal to his expectations and standards' (Kjellberg 2020; emphasis in original). By 'we', she refers to herself as his secretary at the time and the network of translators working with Brodsky. There is also plenty of evidence of Brodsky's collaborative translation and self-translation in the poet's correspondence, translation drafts, notes in the margins, interviews with the poet and his translators.

The very first translations of Brodsky's poems from Russian to English were done by George L. Kline and published in *The Russian Review* in 1965 and 1966. Then, Nicholas Bethell published a book of his translations of Brodsky's early poems *Elegy to John Donne, and Other Poems* (Brodsky 1967). Bethell was a British translator who learnt Russian during his national service. The book

---

3. For further discussion of how the concepts of 'solo writing' and 'monolingual writer' have been shaped during romanticism, see Hokenson and Munson (2007).

came out without Brodsky's consent when he was still living in Russia and had no editorial control over this publication. Later, Kline, the translator of Brodsky's second collection in English, described this first book of Brodsky's translated poems as 'hasty, inaccurate and awkward' (Kline 1996: 15–16). Although Bethell's book did not make much of a mark, his translations provoked interest in Brodsky's poetry among some English-language audiences, especially after the BBC programme about the poet's trial in the USSR. Richard McKane, a translator of Akhmatova's poems, first encountered Brodsky's poems as a pupil at Marlborough College in Bethell's translation, as McKane mentions the impact Brodsky's poems had on him in his letter to Brodsky dated 15 December 1973:

> I read in *Encounter* excerpts from your trial. This stimulated me into getting the transcript from the BBC, and within weeks I staged a trial of Joseph Brodsky playing you and reading the poems in the Bethell translations, in fact following the BBC script. [. . .] So it was in a sense you who gave me my first blooding in poetry on the stage of life, and very exciting and emotional it was too. (JBP, S.I, GC, Richard McKane, 1973–91, undated, Box 10, Folder 256)

The second book of Brodsky's poems in English *Joseph Brodsky: Selected Poems*, which was translated by Kline with a foreword by Auden, came out in January 1973, less than a year after Brodsky's banishment from Russia. The work on translations and the foreword took place when Brodsky was still in Russia between 1968 and 1972. Kline, professor of philosophy at Bryn Mawr, a meticulous scholar and translator, describes how he sought Brodsky's advice and consent regarding his translations with the help of hand-carried messages delivered by visitors who went from the West to Russia:

> These exchanges took three related forms: I sometimes sent a list of questions which Brodsky would answer orally or in a separate note. In other cases he jotted down his answers (often in red ink) on the typed sheet with my questions and gave this to the visitor to bring back to London or Paris or New York. (Kline 1977: 26)

While most of the work had been done by correspondence, Brodsky fortunately arrived in the United States just in time for the final proofs of *Selected Poems*. On 6 July 1972, Kline welcomed Brodsky in Ann Arbor and invited him to read the revised translations and give his final approval. From Kline's carefully recorded correspondence and notes, it is evident that the translations for this collection were done by Kline in consultation with Brodsky, so the book was a collaborative project, initiated and led by the translator. Kline recollects that, at the time, Brodsky and Kline wrote to each other in their respective language with 'sprinklings' of the other's language and comments on how much Brodsky's English had improved between their first meeting in Russia in 1967 and 1972 when they were going through a typescript of Kline's translations for *Selected Poems*. According to Kline, Brodsky 'missed very few of my errors and misreadings of his tone (e.g. my failure to detect the irony of given lines)' (Kline 1977: 25). In retrospect, Brodsky's interpretation of this is different: in his letter to Weissbort, he recalls that in 1972 he was not yet able to engage with translations in the way that he did later because his command of the English language was not yet sufficient. All in all, Brodsky's role in *Selected Poems* was that of a remote author-consultant apart from one week in July 1972, which he spent with the translator 'in the Berkshires' reading through Kline's typescript. In addition to being consulted on the translations, Brodsky had the opportunity to read Auden's foreword to this book, which was delivered to him in Russia in May 1970, as Ishov discovered (Ishov 2008: 227).

Kline was generally in agreement with Brodsky's approach to translation: he wanted to retain the form as much as possible while being faithful to the meaning of the original. Kline wrote in 'A Note on the Translation' in *Selected Poems*: 'All of these translations preserve Brodsky's meters, but they use rhymes and slant-rhymes sparingly, and only in those cases where the rhymes can be introduced without "padding"' (Kline 1973). For further discussion of this, see Kline (1973, 1977) and Ishov (2015; 2018). In the end, Brodsky was pleased with Kline's translations but with some reservations, including some rhymes, as he wrote in a letter to Kline in Easter 1969 (JBP, S.I, GC, George L. Kline, outgoing, Box19 Folder 50). This letter was written on margins of a manuscript of the English publication: 'Joseph Brodsky, Six New Poems, translated by George L. Kline'. Just before the publication of the book, Brodsky also consulted his friend and a translator Alan Myers on Kline's poems. In his letter to Brodsky of 15 July 1972, Myers reassured the poet that the translations were 'of a very high standard' and that Brodsky was 'lucky in Mr Kline', adding:

> If I didn't know your poems in the original at all, I would feel, like Auden, that a very powerful talent, complex and subtle, was before me. [. . .] effects are almost magical (John Donne), and sometimes are splendidly witty (2 *chasa*) and always reflect the spirit of the original. [. . .] This volume would do you enormous credit. (JBP, S.I, GC, 'Alan Myers, Incoming, 1972–93, undated', Box 10 Folder 270)

He also comments on some limitations of the translations: 'the rhythm jerks', padding, some lines 'failing to reflect the right tone'. All in all, he fully supports the publication of Kline's translations (Figure 2.1).

Brodsky's initial delight with *Selected Poems* later changed to disappointment. As he was becoming more confident in English, he could see faults in Kline's translations and started looking for other translators. To Kline's regret, he did not commission him as much for his further publications. Kline, however, remained loyal to Brodsky and continued to offer help with translating new poems. Their collaboration lasted until the mid-1980s, although it took other forms. Kline was no longer Brodsky's only translator but was part of his

2. From Solo Writer in Russian to Collaborative Self-Translator in English   69

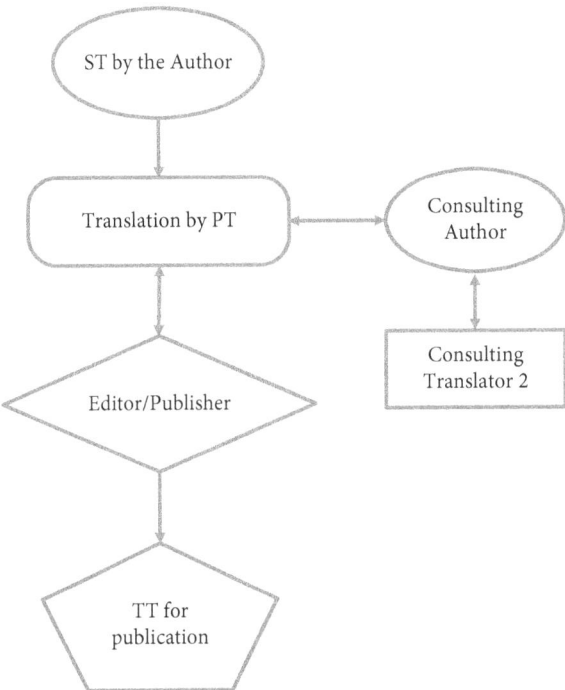

Figure 2.1 Stage one of Brodsky's collaborative translation: Brodsky's collaboration with a poet translator (PT).

translators' network. Figure 2.1 shows the process of translation as it took place when Kline was rendering Brodsky's poems. Brodsky was consulted by the translator but the author's input in the production of TT was limited for two reasons: his lack of fluency in English and the fact that he had a limited amount of time to discuss the poems with the translator. However, this nevertheless was the first stage of Brodsky's collaborative work on the translations of his poems. During this first stage, collaboration was initiated and led by the translator, and the author's contribution was limited.

The book of Brodsky's poems in Kline's translation was timely in introducing the new Soviet exile. In his review of *Selected Poems*, Stephen Spender recognized in Brodsky an original poet who is 'utterly truthful, deeply religious, fearless and pure', but he is less enthusiastic about Kline's translations of his poems:

> Unfortunately with Mr Kline one is never quite allowed to forget that one is reading a second-hand version rather than original poetry. Some lines are jaw-breakers: 'The road's as stubborn as/ the river. / The ash-tree's shadow is/ a fishnet.' But on the other hand the translation has an honesty which enables one to imagine the poetry that always lies just beyond it. (Spender 1973: 11)

After such a review, it is not surprising that Brodsky wanted to explore other translation options for his future book projects.

From remote control to combative collaboration

In the mid-1970s, Brodsky started thinking about publishing his next collection of poems. On 15 December 1975, Nancy Meiselas wrote him a letter with a copy to Kline, which intended to launch the process of putting together a new book of poems. She informed Brodsky that she had received and gone through all the material previously sent to her by the poet and his translator. She added that there was little that she could do until Brodsky found time and energy to 'draw up a list of poems' he wanted to see in a new book. She specifically asked about 'Mary, Queen of Scots' sequence and mentioned that not all of them had been translated (JBP, S.I, GC, Fararr, Straus and Giroux, 1975–95, undated, Box 5, Folder 132). Soon, she received the first draft list of twenty-one poems for inclusion in the new book. Some of the listed poems had already been published in translation and some still needed to be rendered into English. This document was the first indication that Brodsky was going to change his translation strategy. Instead of working with one translator, he decided to employ six different ones: Daniel Weissbort, David Rigsbee, Kline, Richard Wilbur, Carl Proffer and James Scully. The first draft list of poems was soon extended to forty (of which thirty-seven were eventually published in the volume) and the list of translators was also adjusted. This new draft contained a table with four columns: the title of the poem, interlinear version, poet and publisher. Each poem was assigned to two translators who had to be contracted by FSG. One initially proposed translator Scully was no longer on the revised list, while new names were added (JBP, S.I, GC, Farrar, Strauss and Giroux 1975–95, Box 5 Folder 132).[4]

---

4. Ishov further divides Brodsky's 'poetic' translators into those who are 'poets themselves' and '"mere" translators of poetry such as Kline' (Ishov 2008: 137). This division seems problematic to me because it creates a hierarchy of poets and non-poets, in which it is not easy to find a place for such translators as Weissbort, who was both a poet and a translator. It makes more sense to separate all 'poetic translators' into those who do not have a command of the Russian language and have to rely on the interlinear version (Mark Strand, Anthony Hecht, Derek Walcott and Richard Wilbur); and those who can create a poetic translation from the Russian original (Alan Myers, Daniel Weissbort, G.L.Kline, Peter Viereck, Barry Rubin, David Rigsbee, David McDuff). The poet's correspondence with translators demonstrates that he dealt with most translators in a similar way, whether they were established poets like Mark Strand or academics who did not have much experience in poetic translation. Brodsky could propose changes to his translators' English versions even at the final stages when he had the opportunity to look at the galleys. Nobody could be saved from Brodsky's interventions in their renderings (Picture 2.1).

2. From Solo Writer in Russian to Collaborative Self-Translator in English   71

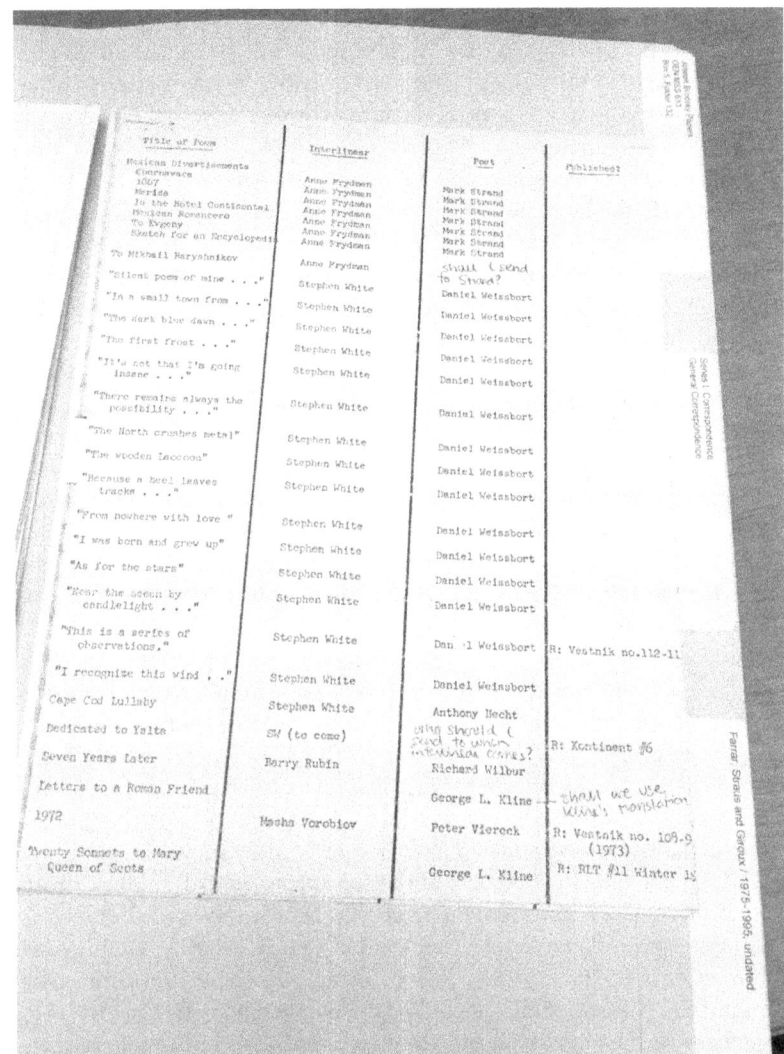

Picture 2.1 FSG's list of interlinear and poetic translators for *A Part of Speech*, page 1 out of 2.

The list of interlinear translators included four contributors: Masha Vorobiov, Anne Frydman, Stephen White and Barry Rubin. The list of poet-translators consisted of six contributors: Mark Strand, Daniel Weissbort, Anthony Hecht, Richard Wilbur, George Kline and Peter Viereck. None of the poems were scheduled to be self-translated at this stage. This was the plan but the result was somewhat different. As the book was shaping up, Brodsky extended his control over the translations by intervening in the work of his translators and beginning to self-translate, although, as becomes evident from a close comparative reading of translations and self-translations in Chapter 3, Brodsky borrowed from his collaborators at this stage.

In March 1976, Meiselas sent out numerous letters to all the involved translators and poets including Richard Wilbur, Mark Strand and Anthony Hecht inviting them to collaborate on Brodsky's translations and reassuring them that the publisher would provide them with relevant interlinear translations (JBP, S.I, GC, Farrar, Strauss and Giroux 1975–95, Box 5, Folder 132). With the help of Brodsky, Wilbur, Strand and Hecht were asked to choose any poems they wished to render in Russian. In addition to the poets who did not speak Russian, Meiselas also contacted a few translators, including Weissbort, Myers and Kline, who were published translators of poetry into English and were fluent in Russian. They did not need interlinear versions but could still have them if they wished to, because every poem to be included in the new book was going to have an interlinear translation and a poetic version in English. So, Meiselas also wrote to four interlinear translators Vorobiov, White, Rubin and Frydman who were contracted by FSG to provide 'literal' translations of poems.

This also meant that the work of all translators including interlinear ones was under contract and would be paid for. The pay rate for interlinear translations was only $1 per line as a one-off payment. In the end, White translated 866 lines, Frydman 674 lines, Vorobiov 128 lines and Rubin 117 lines (JBP, S.II, Poetry, IP, A Part of Speech (New York: FSG) 'List of Translators 1979', Box 47, Folder 849).

Poetic translators were offered a portion of Brodsky's royalties on the trade sales of the book, as well as some of the subsidiary rights [. . .] on a pro-rata basis', as there were many more than one translator involved ('Letter by Nancy Meiselas to Daniel Weissbort, 12 October 1977, FSGI, M&AD, NYPL, Brodsky, *A Part of Speech*). In response to the invitations, some translators replied promptly and enthusiastically, including the poet Anthony Hecht. Others took longer because they were away or busy involved in other projects. For example, Peter Viereck, professor at Mount Holyoke College, was away when the letter from FSG arrived and his student gave him a gist of it on the phone. He was asked to translate two poems anew: '1972' and 'On Death of Friend'. In his letter to Brodsky from 7 October 1976, Viereck wrote that it would be 'a pleasure and privilege' for him to collaborate on Brodsky's volume and he would be able to complete, at least, one poem by the deadline. He explained that he was generally a very slow translator and that translating twelve lines by Heym for his article on Heym took him several years (JBP, S.I, GC, Viereck, Peter, Incoming 1975–95, Box 16, Folder 417). Viereck also wrote directly to Masha Vorobiov, who was mentioned in the letter as his interlinear translator, explaining his approach to translation (maintaining rhyme and rhythm) and taking up her offer to meet in

South Hadley, Massachusetts, United States. He requested the Russian versions of the poems along with line-by-line or interlinear translations.

In her letter to Hecht from 11 March 1976, Meiselas set the provisional deadline for the book to be published in the spring of 1977, but she was aware that this was dependent on how translations were going to shape up. A month later, she shared with Barry Rubin her concern that there were 'bound to be conflicts' (12 April 1976) after she had lunch with Kline who was a bit 'perplexed' and 'hurt' because everybody else but him had been asked to do the translations of the 'Cape Cod' poem (see the discussion of this in Chapter 4) (Letter from Meiselas to Barry Rubin, 21 April 1976, FSGI, M&AD, NYPL, Brodsky, A Part of Speech, 1976–7). The complexity of the book project involving so many contributors inevitably led to the extension of the first deadline. On 14 March 1979, Meiselas still missed the poetic translations of the 'Mary, Queen of Scots' sequence, two poems from the cycle 'In England', the translation of the poem '1972' as well as some final versions of other texts, for which she expected to receive revisions.

Meanwhile, there were further complications awaiting Meiselas. FSG planned to include the long poem 'Gorbunov and Gorchakov' in *A Part of Speech*, which was previously translated by Carl Proffer and published by Ardis. Meiselas asked Proffer for his permission to include the poem. On 25 October 1979, Proffer agreed to have 'Gorbunov and Gorchakov' reprinted but only on the condition that FSG would pay $17 per page (thirty-six pages in total) with the note that the poem would be reprinted 'with the permission of Russian Literature Triquarterly' (1971) by Ardis (JBP, S.1, GC, Farrar, Straus and Giroux, 1976–95, undated, Box 5, Folder 133). FSG found this offer 'ridiculous' and unacceptable and, eventually, decided against including it in the book. Other poems which had previously been translated and previously published in journals, including *The New Yorker*, *The Iowa Review*, *The New York Review of Books*, *Mademoiselle*, *Kontinent 1*, *Kontinent 3*, *Vestnik*, *The Massachusetts Review*, *Bananas*, *Vogue*, *Confrontation*, *The Kenyon Review* and *RLT*, found their way into *A Part of Speech* after publishing rights had been cleared.

The contract for the book was signed between Brodsky and FSG in December 1976 (FSGI, M&AD, NYPL, Brodsky, *A Part of Speech*, 1976–7). Along with the contract FSG also acquired the publishing rights for all Brodsky's work in the English language, which meant that FSG charged other publishers for printing Brodsky's poems which have appeared or were to be published in FSG. For example, in 1977, Weissbort who translated the poem 'Part of Speech' sent it to the journal *Modern Poetry in Translation* without realizing that the publishing rights were already with FSG. When FSG charged the journal a fee for publishing the poem, Weissbort felt obliged to pay the fee himself because he offered the poem for publication to the journal on his own initiative (Weissbort's letter to Meiselas, 4 October 1977, FSGI, M&AD, NYPL, Brodsky, *A Part of Speech*, 1976–7). FSG supported and encouraged the publication of poems in journals prior to their appearance in book form, as they also profited from this. Overall, FSG published the following books of poems by Brodsky: *A Part of Speech* (1980), *To Urania* (1988b), *So Forth* (1996a), *Collected Poems in English* (2000), *Discovery* (1999), *Nativity Poems* (2001). They also published his two collections of essays: *Less Than One* (1986) and *On Grief and Reason* (1995), an essay on Venice in *Watermark* (1992a), a play titled *Marbles* (1989) as well as few other miscellaneous books, such a book with essays by Brodsky, Walcott and Heaney *Homage to Robert Frost* (1996), *An Age Ago: A Selection of Nineteenth Century Russian Poetry*, translated by Alan Myers and with a foreword by Brodsky (1988a).

Roger W. Straus of FSG became a good friend and supporter of Joseph Brodsky and his work. Straus repeatedly offered help and advice, especially when the poet needed financial support which happened on a few occasions. In September 1978, when Brodsky's health deteriorated and needed money, Straus helped him generate some cash and find a temporary teaching job at Columbia University, so that the writer did not have to teach at Michigan in the Midwest, which was at the time inconvenient for him. Further evidence is Straus's letter to Dr Klaus Piper dated 22 September 1978, in which Straus requests an advance for the publication of Brodsky's book in German (Letter from Roger Straus to Klaus Piper, 22 September 1978, FSGI, M&AD, NYPL, Brodsky, *A Part of Speech*, 1976-7). Brodsky's short occasional poem dedicated to Roger Straus sounds rather tongue-in-cheek in the light of the publisher and poet's interdependent financial and commercial arrangements:

> Meet Roger W. Straus
> He runs a publishing house
> He's so gentle at that
> that were he a cat
> I'd gladly serve as a mouse.
>
> Joseph Brodsky (JBP, S.II, Poetry, IP, Meet Roger W Straus, copy of a holograph draft produced in New York magazine 1987, Box 61, Folder 1289)

As a result of having many translators involved in the production of *A Part of Speech*, the book ended up having a number of distinct voices, which was seen by the publisher as a having 'patchwork' quality about it. In a letter from Leslie Faust, Contract and Copyright Department of FSG, dated 31 August 1979 (Letter from Leslie Faust to Barry Rubin, 1979, FSGI, M&AD, NYPL, Brodsky, *A Part of Speech*, 1979), Barry Rubin was contracted to do editorial work on the book as a whole, so it was his responsibility to edit out some differences in tone, to make some final changes and to bring the poems closer together in tone. Some translators felt that 'certain small corrections' were made by him 'unilaterally', without being consulted (Letter from David Rigsbee to Meiselas, 30 July 1979, NYPL, FSGI, M&AD, NYPL, Brodsky, *A Part of Speech*, 1979). These corrections were made after Brodsky had gone through all the poems himself introducing changes with and/or without translators' consent. (Brodsky's engagement with poems is discussed in the following paragraphs and in Chapter 3.) Brodsky much appreciated Rubin's translation and editorial work for him, as he wrote in a letter on 8 November 1995 to the president of Queens College to support Rubin and protect him from being fired due to the college's financial difficulties, suggesting that Rubin (and presumably other loyal translators) helped Brodsky to win his Nobel Prize:

> I won't bore you with my assessment of Professor Rubin's credentials. Professional opinion, colored or not by personal sentiments, cuts little ice when one is beset by budgetary pressures. All I would like to say here is that twenty-three years ago I was impressed enough with Professor Rubin's expertise in matters of Russian literature to entrust him with the translation of my work into English. That's what he did, and that's what won me the Nobel Prize in Literature in 1987. (JBP, S.I., GC, Queens College, (New York: N.Y.), 1973–95, Box 12, Folder 321)

Kjellberg recollects that Rubin, Walcott and Brodsky went through the entire volume at Morton Street and made last changes (Kjellberg 2020). However, it was not only Rubin who proposed changes to the English versions of Brodsky's poems. Kline found it hard to stay out of the editorial process, commenting on other translations. For example, in a letter to Meiselas from 27 July 1979 (Letter from Kline to Meiselas, 27 July 1979, FSGI, M&AD, NYPL, Brodsky, *A Part of Speech*, 1979), Kline criticizes the indentation in Howard Moss's 'Plato Elaborated', which was first published in *The New Yorker*, referring to his conversation with Brodsky about this poem in Cambridge. In another letter a few days later, dated 30 July 1979 from Goose Pond, Kline writes that he wrote to Meiselas telling her that the 'conditionals' needed to be restored in 'A Part of Speech'; this is after Kline heard that Brodsky had not approved changing the conditionals in the last two stanzas of 'Plato Elaborated' (JBP, S.I, GC, Incoming letters and copies of outgoing letters, 1972–94, Box 1 Folder 3).

The project was further complicated by the fact that Brodsky himself became actively involved in reading and revising the translations as the book was shaping up. There were many steps that needed to be taken before the final version of the translation was complete. All translators either sounded or sent their queries to the author. Poetic translators with no command of Russian also contacted interlinear translators. Brodsky returned his extended comments on translators' queries along with his own suggestions. Translators often directly responded to the author with further comments on his suggestions. Finally, translators sent him or FSG their final versions, in which Brodsky sometimes made further changes with or without the translators' consent. Kline's meticulously recorded correspondence with Brodsky is the best evidence of the ongoing conversations between the poet and his translators. For example, in his letter to Meiselas of 24 June 1979, Kline notes that Brodsky found his translations of the 'Sonnets' too 'positive' and lacking the 'self-disgust' that permeates the tone in the Russian original. Kline carried on working hard on improving his translations and incorporating Brodsky's suggestions, although he eventually admitted that some of Brodsky's demands, such as 'triple rhyme', were impossible to bring to fruition in English (Letter from Kline to Meiselas, 24 June 1979, FSGI, M&AD, NYPL, Brodsky, *A Part of Speech*, 1979). The production of translations for the book *A Part of Speech* in English was complex, multidimensional and collaborative.

Figure 2.2 summarizes the process of translation of Brodsky's poems for *A Part of Speech*. Although in most cases there was only one interlinear translation commissioned and delivered, there was at least one case when the poet translator (Anthony Hecht), having been dissatisfied with the interlinear text (by White), ordered another one to be done by his friend and colleague who was also one Brodsky's friends (James Rice). Many poems were attempted by several poetic translators and all translations were subsequently read and edited by Brodsky himself. Some translations were also read and commented on by yet other translators. (Kline made suggestions on poems translated by others.) In the end, all the translations were read and edited by Rubin before they were finalized for publishing.

As the work on *A Part of Speech* was taking place, collaboration reached its peak in Brodsky's English-language career in the mid-late 1970s. The published book contains thirty-seven poems (the number of poems of each kind is given as they are published in *Collected Poems*): of them, there are twelve poems translated with the author or subsequently changed by the author, twenty-three by individual translators, one self-translation and one written by Brodsky in English. Brodsky's following books continued to be collaborative but each of the following contains more and more poems self-translated by Brodsky. *To Urania* (1988b) contains forty-five poems, of which twenty-three are self-translations, nine translated with the author, two translated by individual translators and eleven poems were written originally in English. *So Forth* (1996a) consists of sixty-four poems: thirty-five self-translations, twenty-one poems written in English, seven poems were translated by translators with the author and one translated by a translator (Alan Myers). The first person to notice and comment on the increasing involvement of the poet in his publications in English was Weissbort in *From Russian with Love* who repeatedly clashed with the poet over the authorship and ownership of his translations. However, his numbers do not agree with the above-mentioned figures because Weissbort may have counted the poems as they were published in the individual volumes, and the above figures are given according to the posthumously published *Collected Poems in English*, the volume, which has been verified by Kjellberg who provides detailed comments on each poem.

Somewhat blinded by the upset caused by Brodsky's interventions in his translations while working on the 'A Part of Speech' sequence, Weissbort could not at the time see his relationship with Brodsky as a collaboration but more

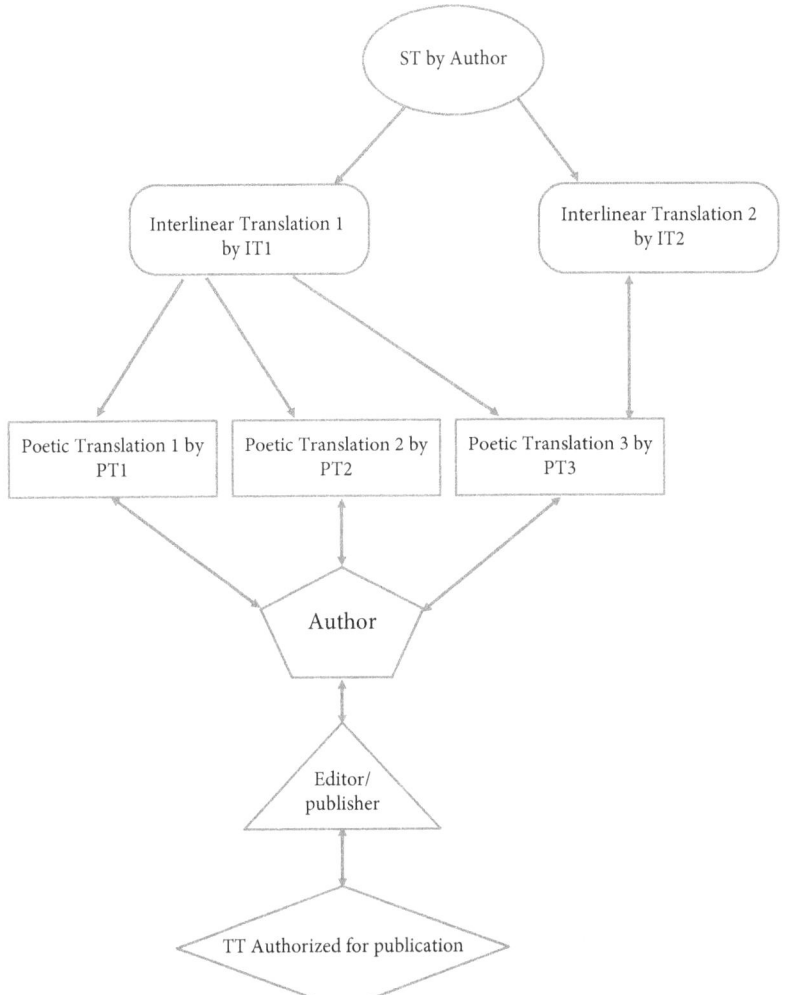

Figure 2.2 Stage two of Brodsky's collaborative translation: Brodsky's collaboration with a network of interlinear translators (IT) and poetic translators (PT), editors and publisher.

as an attack on his liberties and rights as a translator. Nevertheless, Weissbort carried on working and collaborating with Brodsky. The poet's collaboration with his editors and publishers has also had a significant effect on his English-language work, especially when editors, such as Howard Moss at *The New Yorker*, invested in Brodsky's English-language work.

Collaboration with Brodsky was not always easy and, at times, it was more similar to combat. Reflecting on his working with the poet, Weissbort describes Brodsky's 'combativeness', the 'zealousness (over-zealousness perhaps) of a man with a mission' (Weissbort 2004: 50). Brodsky's 'mission' was to promote his uncompromising view of a mimetic poetic translation in English: 'To sum up, he was a stickler for meter and rhyme (while making increasingly bold forays across the conventional borders of English prosody and syntax)' (Weissbort 2004: 50). Despite disagreements about poetic form and hurt personal feelings, Weissbort carried on working with Brodsky and valued his friendship. Of all translators, Weissbort felt this aspect of working with Brodsky most acutely. To describe this sort of collaboration, I have coined the term 'combative collaboration', drawing on a practice called 'Collaborative Combative Drawing (CCD)', which is based on the understanding 'that collaboration is messy' and collaborators have to negotiate 'their personal or professional relationships' as they bring their own ideas to the project they are working on. Their ideas may 'fuse' or 'clash', or both. CCD 'utilizes the energy created by the inherent pushing and pulling in human relationships as a method of (art) production'.[5]

The practice of commissioning multiple translators who were approached independently was employed by Brodsky on numerous occasions. Weissbort was not the only translator who felt upset by it. Kline, another devoted translator and admirer of Brodsky, writes about a similar experience in his letter to Kjellberg from 7 August 1998. Kline remarks on Harry Thomas's translation of 'Odysseus to Telemachus' ('Oddissei Telemaku'): it is not in 'any way improvement on my 1973 version – or for that matter Carl Proffer's version of the same period' (A letter from G. L. Kline to Kjellberg, 7 August 1998, FSGI, M&AD, NYPL).

The way in which Weissbort describes collaboration with Brodsky is reminiscent of this drawing practice: the poet and one (or more!) translator(s) are involved in the production of one translation to be published. Their ideas and approaches to poetic translation may clash and they may disagree with each other. The significant difference between CCD and Brodsky's combative collaborative translation is that, in the latter, the involved parties – the poet, his translators, editors and publishers – have unequal influence on the final product. As the author of the original, the living bilingual poet tends to call the shots and make a final decision on the translation; he exercises the ultimate authorship having signed a contract with the publisher. As Brodsky's confidence in English was growing, he was becoming more combative and was intervening in the translations after they had been completed by his translators.

So, it is evident that there are several shifts that occur in the process of translation during this period: (1) from a singular text (the original, or ST) to multiple target texts (TTs); (2) from the solo author to multiple authors; translations could be written by several translators working independently, either with or without the author and, with or without each other's drafts;

---

5. See the website at https://collaborativecombativedrawing.com/about/.

(3) from the author's working alone to co-authors' writing independently and collaboratively.

Brodsky's poems have been translated into many other languages: German, Bulgarian, Danish, Polish, Norwegian, Swedish, French and some others, but in no other language did Brodsky take part in translation to the extent to which he did in English. Kjellberg recollects that Brodsky participated in his translations in Italian but his Italian was rudimentary. The poem 'Vertumnus' is dedicated to his Italian translator. He was also close friends with Veronique Schtilts, who translated his work in French. He was also close to his Swedish translator Bengt Jangfeldt, who consulted the poet, and his Polish translator Stanisław Barańczak. There were other translators but in 'all these cases they were seeking advice and he did not intervene much in the outcome, and the relationship stayed warm' (Kjellberg 2020). It was only in English, his second, adopted language and the language of his beloved poet Auden that he wanted to carve out a literary space for himself, to shape his own poetic voice, and in order to do this, he had to both collaborate with his translators and combat their 'smooth' translations by making them more 'his own'.

As noted earlier, the more confident the poet was in English, the more he wanted to take ownership of translations. Twenty-three self-translations went into *To Urania* (1988b) were self-translations. However, this did not mean the end of collaboration. In the early 1980s, Brodsky's collaboration on his translations continued but took a different shape from before. Figure 2.3 summarizes the process which is illustrated by the poem known in English as 'Axiom' (see Chapter 3 for an archival analysis of the poem's translation).[6] During this time, Brodsky would translate the Russian poem himself first, and then he would send his translation to two or three readers for feedback, which he could consider and partially incorporate as he saw fit. The fact is that Brodsky continued collaborating on the translation of his texts but his collaboration was initiated and driven by the poet who by then was in control of the process as his own self-translator.

It was during this period that Brodsky developed his own, distinct voice in English. Some critics argued, as was discussed earlier, that he created his own 'binaral or bipolar writing' (Hoffman 1986), an idiolect, a *translationese*, which some found exhilarating and energizing and others dismissed as an odd,

---

6. The poem 'Axiom' is illustrative of the process of how Brodsky sought advice from his collaborators due to the evidence of Brodsky's ST's being faxed to different recipients. One of three collaborators was translator Jonathan Aaron. In an email to Rulyova 5 April 2020, Aaron confirmed that this was indeed how the process had taken place (see further discussion in Chapters 3 and 4). The poem was signed as 'translated by Jonathan Aaron with the author'. This was unusual as most other co-translations by Brodsky with others during this period were published as self-translations, so the contribution of collaborators to English poems was not always as visible as in the case of 'The Axiom'. See further discussion in Chapter 3.

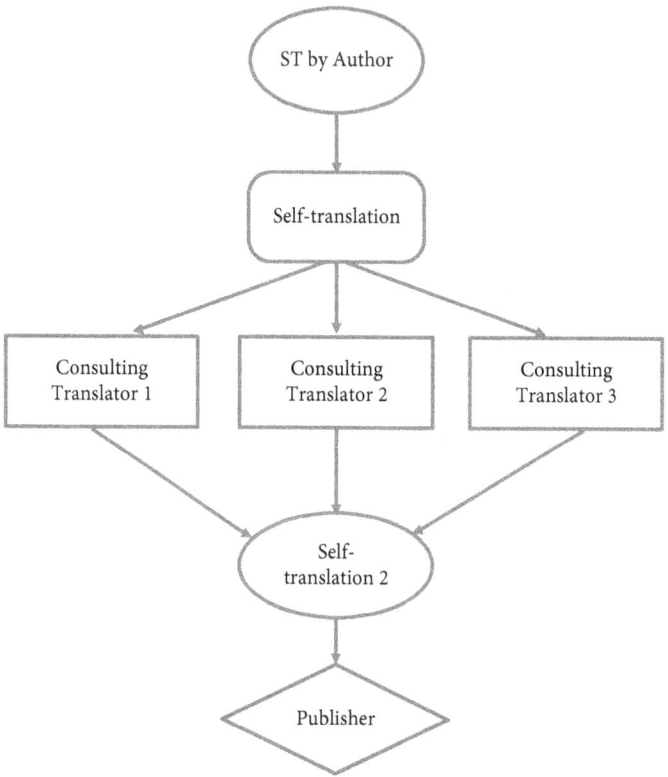

Figure 2.3 Stage three of Brodsky's collaborative translation: The self-translator's collaboration with a network of translators, editors and publisher.

ungrammatical and Russified English. By the early 1990s, Brodsky's idiosyncratic voice became so prominent that critics and scholars tended to focus exclusively on his unique and individual poetic presence in English, on his unique literary persona as if it were something that he had come to English with and forgetting that only a few years previously, in 1972, Brodsky had lacked confidence not only to write in English correctly but to even 'give a running commentary in English', as this became the reason for John D. Duncan, programme chairman of the Poetry Society of Georgia, to withdraw their invitation for Brodsky to do a reading, adding that 'Perhaps when Mr Brodsky's English improves we might have him speak to us if he is still willing' (JBP, S.I, GC, General Correspondence, 1972–94, 4 December 1972, Box 1, Folder 5).

In 1991, Brodsky was appointed the Poet Laureate of the United States and had an overwhelming number of invitations to read and discuss his poetry. His accented voice became part of the American poetic landscape and it is by working with, reflecting on and consciously acting against his translators' advice that Brodsky shaped his idiosyncratic poetic persona in English. Of course, he also learnt from extensive reading in English, using the language on a daily basis, in conversations with his friends, peer poets, students, publishers and members of the public. As Kjellberg notes,

> In considering the effects of his translators' English on his own developing style in English, I would bear in mind that these are balanced against his own very extensive reading in English, particularly of poetry but also of poetry of other languages in English translation and critical prose; his conversations with writers and thinkers he admired; and his participation in American colloquial life (for example, with his students). He was very drawn to learning and using the living language. (Kjellberg 2020)

Kjellberg who worked as Brodsky's secretary in the 1990s observes that his later verse in English (e.g. the poem 'At a Lecture') moved on and readers have not yet appreciated the change in his writing in English. Chapter 3 analyses the making of Brodsky's translations and self-translations throughout the three main periods identified earlier.

Chapter 3

WHAT ARE JOSEPH BRODSKY'S COLLABORATIVE SELF-TRANSLATIONS MADE OF?

This chapter examines what Brodsky's collaborative self-translations emerge from by analysing the draft translations of a few selected poems written and translated at different periods of Brodsky's bilingual career. There is a different story of translation behind each poem, depending on the number of translators and editors involved, on how they felt about their translations and on the level of Brodsky's engagement with their work. However, it is possible to identify, at least, five modes, in which Brodsky's self-translations have come to exist: (1) borrowing, or 'anthologizing' as a form of collaboration; (2) self-translation as a form of reflection on others' translations; (3) commissioning and intervening, or overt collaborative translation; (4) self-translating from Russian ST; (5) from self-translation towards creative writing in English. Brodsky was involved in some simultaneous collaborative translation but this was mostly practised as a playful activity, a form of banter, with his poets-friends, such as Derek Walcott. Nearly all collaborative translation in all those modes listed above usually took place in the form of consequent retranslation, for example, the first interlinear translation would be used in a poetic (re)translation, which could be followed by another retranslation by the author or by a translator with the author. In some cases, translations could be commissioned to two different translators without their awareness of the other's involvement – these translations are not consequent even if they are subsequent. I identify as 'consequent' only the retranslations that were written with the awareness of prior translations. Most Brodsky's translations and self-translations are consequent retranslations because, as Kjellberg points out in the notes on Brodsky's poems in the collections 'To Urania' and 'So Forth' (as they were reprinted in *Collected Poems*), even if the poems were not self-translated they were revised by the author, often subsequently. For Brodsky editing and rewriting prior versions were the ways to ensure the consistency and idiosyncrasy of his poetic voice.

Having established (further evidence is given in the analysis that follows) that most Brodsky's translations and self-translations in English are retranslations, it is worth posing a few questions about the ethics in poetic translation and retranslation. How ethical is it for the translators to use previous translations of poems? To answer this question, Gregary Racz (2013) reviews historical approaches and attitudes to retranslation. He reveals that before the nineteenth century it was customary for translators to quote from previous versions by others. According to Charles Tomlinson, in his translation of Virgil, Dryden 'used up to nine previous editions and their commentaries' (Tomlinson 2003: 79). George Steiner argues that 'the retranslator translates after and against his predecessors almost as much as he translates his source' (Steiner 1975: 391). Racz comes to the conclusion that 'there is no stealing in retranslation' and makes a reference to Donald Frame who compares retranslation with scholarship on the grounds that it is 'a cumulative undertaking' and recommends launching on a retranslation only if the retranslator thinks that they can 'markedly improve on all existing translations, and do that without anthologizing (combining everyone else's best parts)' (Frame 1983: 31–45).

Brodsky would have agreed with Racz's statement that retranslating by using previous translations is not unethical 'as the aesthetic prevails the ethical' (Racz 2013: 12). However, they would disagree on the following point which is that Racz insists that the retranslation should consult 'a prior translation or translation once a TT draft has been finished' as a 'judicious step in the entire enterprise of retranslation' (Racz 2013: 11). As we will see later in the chapter, Brodsky used other translations before he created his own, especially at early stages of self-translation in the 1970s. Brodsky was 'improving' prior versions. In the historical context considered earlier, Brodsky's attempt to improve a translation by consulting previous versions should not be seen as a problem, it seems. However, as Racz explains later this attitude to the (re)translation of poetry changed in the twentieth century, 'the age of free verse'. Racz expands that, in the past, referring back to prior translations was helpful for the translators who applied mimetic or 'analogical' approaches to poetic translation, which, as it happens, Brodsky also employed. Retranslators who took a mimetic approach were looking for the best rhymes and metre patterns to consider for their versions. In the twentieth century, Racz argues that it is unnecessary to study prior translations because contemporary retranslators render only content in the free verse form, or an organic form, which means that a retranslation develops its own form based on the content instead of mimicking the form of the ST. Racz concludes by regretting the disappearance of the practice of mimetic translation and its scholarly referencing of previous poetic versions because, in his view as well as in Brodsky's, form should be considered as an important part of poetic translation.

Racz's observations help us understand how the ethics of poetic translation has transformed as a result of the changes in dominant approaches to the translation of poetry from mimetic (or analogous) to organic (or the use of *free verse*). As I am analysing the translations of Brodsky's poems in English, I will also ponder this and other factors that are related to the issues of ethics in (self-)translation: the period of time between different translations, the involvement of the self-translator in the production of the TT, the role of the author in commissioning translators to conduct poetic and interlinear versions, and will come back to these in the Conclusion.

Mode 1: Borrowing, or 'anthologizing' as a form of collaboration in A Part of Speech *(1980)*

In the 1970s, Brodsky was compiling *A Part of Speech*, a new book of poems in English, for publication at FSG. The sequence 'A Part of Speech', written by Brodsky in Russian in 1975–6, was a crucial part of the book, as it gave it its name. The Russian original sequence contains twenty poems while the published sequence in English consists of fifteen poems (Oslon 2017). In English, the poems are presented in a different order.

In Chapter 2, I discussed how Brodsky and his publisher FSG approached the volume, planning to have one interlinear translation and one poetic translation of each poem. In reality, some Russian poems have up to five English translations by different collaborators. Let us examine a few examples. The sequence 'A Part of Speech' generated multiple translations: (1) Daniel Weissbort's translation published in *Modern Poetry in Translation* in March 1978; (2) Stephen White's typed and undated interlinear translation with the analysis of the poem's metre and rhyme scheme, lexis, references and allusions (see Pictures 3.1); (3) Leslie Simon's typed translation, dated 1980; (4) Two translations by Alan Myers, handwritten and typed,[1] dated 1979 (see Pictures 3.2); (5) a translation by Myers and Brodsky; (6) Brodsky's own translation (JBP, S.II, Chast' rechi, Box 56, Folders 1052, 1055, 1056, 1058). Translators attempted different numbers of poems from the cycle.

As some translations are not dated, it is difficult or sometimes impossible to know exactly in which order they emerged. Moreover, it is tricky to identify the actual authorship of some parts of the texts, especially when they are translated by Myers and/or Brodsky because Myers was happy for the poet to make changes in his translations, as discussed in Chapter 4 (see the section on Myers). At least, three of those translations were published: Weissbort's translation; Brodsky's self-translation, which appeared in *The New York Review of Books* on 20 December 1979; and Weissbort's translation 'revised with the author' published in the posthumous book *Collected Poems* by Joseph Brodsky (2000). To untangle the process of translation of the sequence, I will begin with the translations that have been dated.

---

1. The typed translation is ascribed to Myers on the margins in someone's handwriting: 'Earlier Myers version'. However, this version is in the folder containing translations by Brodsky and Myers. There is little difference between 'Myers earlier version' and the co-translated one by Brodsky and Myers.

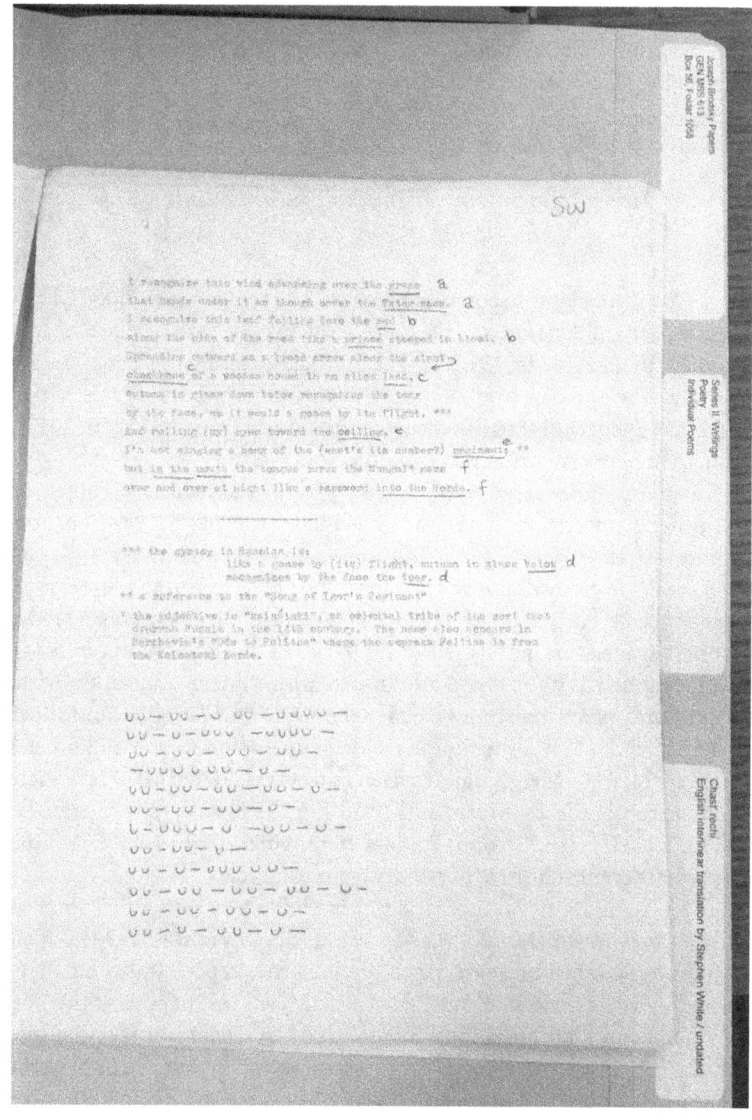

Picture 3.1 'I recognise this wind advancing over the grass' from the sequence 'A Part of Speech' ('Chast' rechi'), English interlinear translation by Stephen White.

First, Brodsky commissioned Weissbort to translate the sequence 'A Part of Speech'. Ishov (2018) discusses in some detail Brodsky and Weissbort's tumultuous relationship regarding these translations, but his article does not present the full picture because it does not mention all the translations commissioned by Brodsky. Having not been satisfied with Weissbort's version

3. What Are Joseph Brodsky's Collaborative Self-Translations Made of?   87

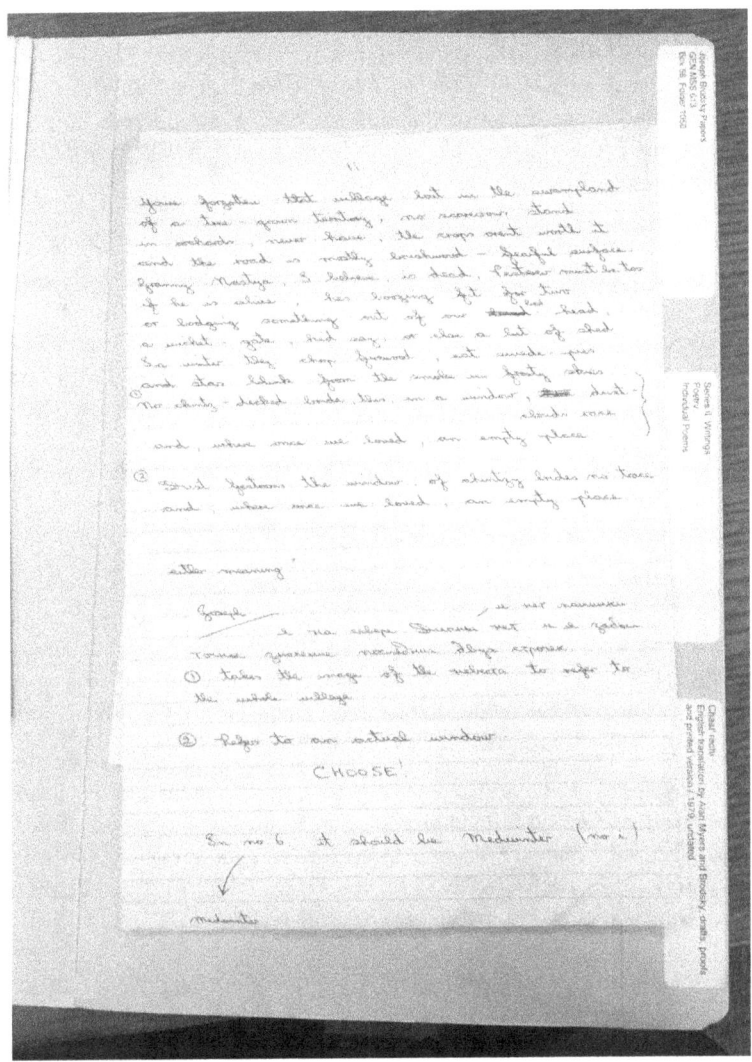

Picture 3.2 Stanza 11 'You've forgotten that village lost in the swampland' from the sequence 'A Part of Speech' ('Chast' rechi'), English translation by Alan Myers, draft.

and, without consulting him, Brodsky asked Myers to translate the sequence. In a letter dated 4 November 1978, Brodsky wrote to Myers:

> would you consider translating the cycle that gives the book its title – A Part of Speech. You see, Danny did it but it came out bloody leaden. Or wooden. If you'll set fo [sic] doing so, please doublecheck [sic] every – there are not so many of them in the cycle – line with Diana. (JBP, S.I, GC, Myers Alan, Outgoing: 1974–87, Box 10, Folder 272)

Myers was happy to oblige and sent his handwritten translation of the sequence to Brodsky in a personal and friendly letter. His translation was a draft which gave Brodsky a couple of English variants of one line and contained some questions about one bit which Myers had found 'troublesome'. Brodsky's first reaction to Myers's version was recorded in the poet's letter from 7 January 1979:

> Got the second half of the shorts. Some of them are really superb. No.12, I think, is better to take out, for it rests in the original on punning replete with paraphrased Russian proverbs. Besides, for all the beauty of your handwriting, I failed to make out the first line. [. . .] So, don't you dare to crack up. Hang on: that's what the fingernails are for. (JBP, S.I, GC, Myers Alan, Outgoing: 1974–87, Box 10, Folder 272)

Myers was delighted to receive Brodsky's approval of his translations. Unlike Weissbort, he was completely committed to Brodsky and accepted the poet's ownership of the translations. In his letters he wrote:

> Dear Joseph,
>
> Thank you for your kind remarks about Часть речи; it's [. . .] almost worth cracking up to hear the words: 'really superb' from you. So speaks the translator [. . .] I'll be glad to hear their fate. (JBP, S.I, GC, Myers Alan, Outgoing, 1974–87, Box 10, Folder 271: 13 January 1979)

> You know, Iosif, I'm far more interested in producing versions that please you than in anything else. So there! I got great pleasure in reading and re-reading your work. The debt is mine. If you think my versions are good enough for the book, fine. If not, DON'T HESITATE TO LEAVE THEM OUT. (JBP, S.I, GC, Myers Alan, Outgoing: 1974–87, Box 10, Folder 270: 21 September 1977)

Despite the initial approval – 'really superb' – Myers's version did not fully satisfy Brodsky either. With the permission of the translator and the full authorial licence on this occasion, Brodsky made some changes to the translations and published them under the author's name, without mentioning Myers even as a co-translator in *The New York Review of Books* on 20 December 1979 on page 15. It is not entirely clear why Myers was not acknowledged in this publication. As a rule, Brodsky acknowledged his translators and co-translators, at least, so that they could be paid for their work. Brodsky was aware of meagre payments to translators and justified publishing his poems in 'well-paying magazines' by the fact that his 'translators should have some sort of incentive' (Letter from Brodsky to Myers, 4 November 1978, JBP, S.I, GC, Myers Alan, Outgoing: 1974–87, Box 10, Folder 272).

A few years later, Leslie Simon translated, at least, three poems from the sequence: 'Oceanside, in candlelight, hemmed around' ('Okolo okeana, pri

3. What Are Joseph Brodsky's Collaborative Self-Translations Made of?   89

svete svechi'),[2] I have known this wind swooping over the grass' ('Uznaiu etot veter, naletaiushchii na travu') and 'From nowhere with love, Marchember the nth' ('Niotkuda s liubov'iu'). In her rather formal letter (which shows that their relationship was purely professional) to Brodsky on 20 July 1980, Simon wrote:

> Dear Mr Brodsky,
>
> here are three more translations from your collection, 'A Part of Speech'. I have tried to keep the levels of diction equivalent and imagery coherent, but it seems just as important to keep the translations breathing like the originals, with principal stress falling on key words and images. (JBP, S.II, Poetry, IP, Chast' rechi, English translation by Leslie Simon, draft, 1980, Box 56, Folder 1055)

Simon added a few footnotes to her translation, which explained her choices for the translation of some idioms and phrases in the poem 'From nowhere with love' ('Niotkuda s liubov'iu').

In addition to the above translations, there are White's interlinear translations of all the twenty Russian poems (not just fifteen that appeared in English) which were part of the sequence 'A Part of Speech' in Russian. These typed translations are not rhymed but key rhyming words in Russian are underlined. Rhyme schemes are specified by hand against each line of the poem. Underneath each poem, there is a metre scheme for each line. White also explained some cultural, historical and literary references, such as a reference to a Russian folk song 'Travelled the whole world over, etc.' He identified and expanded on the use of puns (such as 'sredizimnee' translated as 'medihibernian'), some sonic features of the Russian original, such as the difference between 'ulitsa' ('street') and 'litsa' ('faces') and the importance of the sound 'u' in this context. (For further discussion of his approach to interlinear translation see Chapter 4.)

To gain a better understanding of differences and similarities between translations and of the process of how Brodsky arrived at the version that was approved by him for publishing, it is instructive to compare several translations of a few different poems from the sequence 'A Part of Speech'. In the tables provided in this chapter, different fonts (bold, italic), colour (grey and black) and underlining (single and double) are used to code different English translations for comparative analysis of the used lexis. In some tables, there are several versions translated prior to Brodsky's self-translation. Each version is in a different font/colour. The Brodsky self-translation of the same ST appears in several fonts/colours to identify the words and phrases that the poet borrowed from the translations finished prior to his version. The borrowed words appear in the font/colour of the relevant prior translation.

---

2. Leslie Simon's translations were considerably different from other versions, including the first lines of each poem. Here Simon's first lines are quoted.

In Table 3.1, Leslie Simon's translation was completed after Brodsky's self-translation. Brodsky's self-translation in *The New York Review of Books* (*NYRB*) was published in 1979. It is evident from Leslie Simon's letter to Brodsky which is dated 20 July 1980, that her translation was made about a year after the publication of the self-translation. However, I have still added Simon's translation to the table. The fact that Simon's translation is so different from the others demonstrates that the translator was translating it independently, without consulting prior versions and that doing so leads to rather different lexical and poetic choices. It also confirms that the similarities between Brodsky's self-translation and the three other translations prove that the poet drew considerably on his collaborators' work.

In Table 3.1, there are five translations (Stephen White's, Daniel Weissbort's, Brodsky and Alan Myers's, Leslie Simon's and a self-translation by Brodsky). Each translation in the table is visually distinguished from the others by being printed in a different font (italic, grey bold, underlined) or colour (black or grey). Three of the four translations (White's, Weissbort's, and Brodsky and Myers's) appeared prior to the publication of Brodsky's version published in 1979. It is evident that Brodsky's version borrows from all three prior translations. The borrowed words in Brodsky's version are printed in the font or colour of the translation from which they were taken. If a word was used in more than one prior version, it may appear in several different fonts or colours. The words that have not been used in prior versions appear in the same black font as the main body of the book.

The 1979 published version by Brodsky is a retranslation based on the three prior versions. It borrowed from Weissbort (see lines 1, 3, 4, 5, 6, 8, 9, 10, 12) and Myers (see lines 1, 2, 3, 4, 7 and 9), and took some ideas from White throughout (see lines 1, 6, 8 and 11). The two lines, which Brodsky changed considerably and wrote mostly anew, are 5 and 11. Further, less significant changes were made in lines 6 and 10. As has already been discussed, Brodsky intervened in the existing translations because he wanted to 'fix' the rhyme scheme and the metre where possible, according to his mimetic approach to poetic translation. However, he did not come up with all new rhyming words, accepting four words chosen by Myers and one by Weissbort and introducing seven new rhyming words.

Brodsky's rhyming words:
farms / clover / arms / lover / down / a second / town / happened / profile / to bulk at / Meanwhile / blanket.

Brodsky and Myers's rhyming words:
farms / clover /arms / lover /mouse / groan / house / alone / wall / net / fall / bed

Weissbort did not follow a strict rhyme scheme; his rhyming words were as follows:

Table 3.1 Five English Translations of 'Near the Ocean, by Candle Light. Scattered Farms' ('Okolo okeana, pri svete svechi; vokrug…') from 'A Part of Speech' ('Chast' rechi') by Joseph Brodsky

Stephen White, interlinear, undated	Daniel Weissbort, *Modern Poetry in Translation*, March 1978	Alan Myers and Brodsky; undated	Leslie Simon (1980)	Joseph Brodsky, 20 December 1979, *The New York Review of Books*
Near the ocean by candlelight; all around (a)	'Near the ocean', by candlelight, all around –	Beside the sea, by candle-light; farms,	Oceanside, in candlelight, hemmed around	Near the ocean, by candle light. Scattered farms*
is a field overgrown with clover, sorrel and alfalfa. (b)	A field, lush with clover, sorrel and alfalfa.	fields overrun with sorrel, lucerne-grass and clover.	By fields, overgrown with clover and with sourgrass.	Fields overrun with sorrel, lucerne, and clover.
At eveningtide the body has, like Siva, (so many) arms (a)	In the evening, like Siva, the body grows arms	Towards nightfall the body, Shiva-like, has arms	An evening at my body's, like Shiva's, many-armed,	Towards nightfall, the body, like Shiva, grows extra arms
longing to attain the priceless (one). (b)	that yearn to reach out and touch the beloved	all reaching out, desiring, to a lover.	All trying to reach out and touch the priceless.	reaching out yearningly to a lover.
Falling into the grass an owl overtakes a mouse; (c)	An owl drops into the grass, onto a mouse,	Falling into grass, an owl lands on a mouse,	Hovering, dropping the owl gets his mouse.	A mouse rustles through grass. An owl drops down.
the rafters creak without cause. (d)	and rafters creak for no reason.	the beams give out an unexpected groan.	There's pointless creaking up in the rafters.	Suddenly – creaking rafters expand a second.
In a wooden city sleep is deeper (c)	in a wooden city you sleep more sound.	One sleeps more soundly in a wooden house,	Sleep is sounder in wooden seacoast towns,	One sleeps more soundly in a wooden town,

(Continued)

Table 3.1 (Continued)

Stephen White, interlinear; undated	Daniel Weissbort, Modern Poetry in Translation, March 1978	Alan Myers and Brodsky; undated	Leslie Simon (1980)	Joseph Brodsky, 20 December 1979, The New York Review of Books
because dreams now contain only **what has happened.** (d)	because these days dreams contain only what has happened.	the dreams you have are of the past alone.	Where you only dream of what is past and over.	since you **dream** these days only of things that **happened**.
There's the smell of fresh fish; to a wall has stuck (e)	There is a smell of fresh fish. The silhouette	A fresh fish smell pervades and on the wall	It smells raw fish, a naked chair clings	There is a smell of fresh fish. An armchair's profile
the profile of a chair; thin gauze listlessly (f)	of a chair is sticking to the wall	an armchair's profile, curtains of thin net	In profile to the wall, at the window the netting	is glued to the wall. The gauze is too limp to bulk at
moves in a window; and the moon with a ray straightens the **bay** (e)	Limp gauze stirs in the window, and in the bay the moon's beam	stir feebly at the window; the moon [moonbeams][14] adjusts the tideway's rise and fall,	Limply rustles, and the moon keeps stretching out a beam	the lightest breeze. And **a ray of the moon**, meanwhile,
like a sliding **blanket**. (f)	pulls up the tide, like a blanket that has slipped.	like a blanket slipping off a bed.	To straighten the bay, like loose, slipping bedding.	draws up the tide *like a slipping blanket*.

*The first line in Weissbort's translation is identical to White's first line apart from differences in punctuation.
Source: JBP, S.II, Poetry, IP, 'Chast' rechi'; Box 56, Folders 1052, 1055, 1056, 1058.

around / alfalfa /arms / beloved / mouse / reason / sound / happened / silhouette / wall / beam / slipped

Another poem from the sequence 'I was born and grew up in the Baltic marshland' offers a slightly different story of collaboration. Just like in the above case, the Russian original poem was first translated by White who produced an interlinear English version. Then, Weissbort rendered the poem into English but Brodsky was not entirely satisfied with his poetic version for similar reasons, as in the above case. The third version is by Brodsky. Table 3.2 contains these three English versions of the poem (Stephen White's, Daniel Weissbort's and a version by Brodsky). White's and Weissbort's versions are presented in a different font each. In the version by Brodsky, the words borrowed from the two prior versions (White's and Weissbort's) appear in the font and colour of the translation from which they were borrowed. If a word appears in two different fonts, it has been used in two previous versions.

The authorship of the published translation, which appeared in the *NYRB* on 20 December 1979, is, like in the example above, multiple, as seen from Table 3.2. Weissbort's contribution to the translation is overt, as his name has been acknowledged and kept as the main translator of the whole sequence in *Collected Poems* despite significant changes done to his 'original' version, which made his text almost unrecognisable. Weissbort's own first translation published in *Modern Poetry in Translation* in March 1978 was subsequently replaced by Brodsky's version, which the author had completed, drawing on the interlinear version by White. By comparing all three versions, it is evident that Brodsky has considerably reworked Weissbort's version having borrowed some individual words and phrases from Weissbort's translation in all lines but the last two. A comparison of lexical choices in all three versions shows that both Weissbort's and Brodsky's translations drew on the prior interlinear translation by White.

Rhyming words in the original Russian version by Brodsky, whose English equivalents are underlined in White's translation: near to / in duo / voice / hair / an elbow / a mumur / a tea kettle / seagulls / falseness / further / a barrier / an echo

Rhyming words in Weissbort's version: by the edge of / up the ledge of / as well / at all / elbow / only / a kettle / seagulls / the heart / stand out / check on / an echo

Rhyming words in the version by Brodsky: marshland / marched on / voice / moist / elbow / rumble / a kettle / metal / region / vision / lack / back

Table 3.2 Three English Translations of 'I Was Born and Grew Up in the Baltic Marshland' ('Ia rodilsia i vyros v baltiiskikh bolotakh') from 'A Part of Speech' ('Chast' rechi') by Joseph Brodsky

Stephen White, interlinear, undated	Daniel Weissbort, *Modern Poetry in Translation*, March 1978	Joseph Brodsky, 20 December 1979, *The New York Review of Books*
I was born and grew up in the Baltic marshlands **near to** (a)	I was born and grew up in the Baltic marshes, by the edge of	I was born and grew up in the Baltic marshland
gray zinc waves which always came rolling shoreward **in duo**; (a)	zinc-grey breakers, always coursing in twosome up the ledge of	by zinc-grey breakers that always marched on
and from this come all rhymes, from this comes that faded **voice** (b)	the shore, and from here all rhymes derive, that wan voice as well,	in twos. Hence all **rhymes**, hence that wan flat **voice**
that weaves in and out among them like wet **hair**, (b)	winding between them, if it does at all,	that ripples between them like hair still moist,
if it weaves at all. Supporting itself on **an elbow** (c)	like moist hair. Propped on a crooked elbow,	if it ripples at all. Propped on a pallid elbow,
the helix will discern in them not just a **murmur** (c)	the helix will unwind from them not a rumble only,	the helix picks out of them no sea rumble
but the clap of canvas, of shutters, of palms, **a tea kettle** (d)	but the clap of canvas, of shutters, of hands, a kettle	but a **clap of canvas, of shutters**, of hands, a kettle
boiling on an oil stove, at most the cries of **seagulls**. (d)	boiling on the oil-stove, at most – the cries of seagulls.	on the burner, boiling – lastly, the seagull's metal
In these flat lands what delivers the heart from **falseness** (e)	In these flat lands, what keeps the heart	cry. What keeps hearts from falseness in this flat region
is that there's nowhere to hide and you are visible **further**. (e)	from falseness, is there's nowhere to hide, you stand out,	is that there is nowhere to hide and plenty of room for vision.
It's only for sound that space is always **a barrier**. (f)	and it's only sound space puts a check on:	Only sound needs echo and dreads its lack.
The eye's not going to lament the lack of **an echo**. (f)	the eye does not regret the lack of an echo.	A glance is accustomed to no glance back.

Source: JBP, S.II, Poetry, IP, Chast' rechi, Box 56, Folders 1052, 1055, 1058.

Rhyming words carry extra meaning for Brodsky, so it is worth noting that the three rhyming words that he has kept from prior translations are the ones that were rhymed in the Russian original: voice, elbow and a kettle. Kjellberg (2020) explains some of Brodsky's choices in this particular case:

> Brodsky 'preserved the alternating masculine/feminine rhyme scheme. Patterns of intentional feminine rhymes are rare in English and were hard for translators to produce. [. . .] He was particularly interested in effects that

produced monotony and a sense of diminuendo, particular to feminine rhymes. [...] here is the emphatic masculine rhyme of "lack" and "back". He wanted to get that finality. Interesting that the Russian original ends in a feminine rhyme, "pomekha" / "ekha", which emphasizes the "echo" aspect rather than the "lack" aspect. The sonic shift fits the meaning but in a different way.'

The poem 'From nowhere with love', which is also part of 'A Part of Speech' sequence, represents a similar pattern of collaboration but with some differences (Table 3.3).

The first published translation of the above-mentioned poem is by Weissbort (1978). This translation was consequently 'revised with the author' before it was published in the *NYRB*, like the previous poems of the sequence (20 December 1979). The *NYRB* translation became the authorized version that was subsequently re-published in *A Part of Speech* and in *Collected Poems*. This 'revision with the author' produced a retranslation, which draws on Myers's draft translation as well as Weissbort's and White's. In Table 3.3, I have identified the words and phrases borrowed from Myers and Brodsky's and Weissbort's translations, acknowledging the borrowings from White's version only if they were not subsequently used by Weissbort and Myers and Brodsky. This is because I wanted to focus on the influence of Myers's translation on the version co-authored by Weissbort and Brodsky, as Myers's contribution has not been acknowledged at all. White's contribution was acknowledged as that by an interlinear translator, in general, that is, not to each individual poem that he had translated. Kjellberg who edited *Collected Poems* did not know that Myers's version even existed. This implies that Brodsky wanted to keep the translation process in his own hands; he did not always inform his editors about all the existing translations of his poems, while exercising the author's privilege to interfere in his translators' versions and using them if he found appropriate. This translation published in *Collected Poems* is a collaborative self-translation by Brodsky rather than a version by Weissbort with the author, as stated in the book, especially as Weissbort struggled to agree with all the changes introduced by Brodsky (further discussion of this in section on Weissbort in Chapter 4).

Weissbort's translation published in *Modern Poetry in Translation* does not follow a strict rhyme scheme:

> the enth / it doesn't / features aren't / nor anyone / salutations / continents / angels / both of them / deep / snow / the sheets / below / mumbling 'you' / limits / anew / mirror

Brodsky and Myers's translation attempts to recreate a rhyme pattern similar to the one in the ST:

> Martember / signify / remember / profile / anyone / of five / then / above / of them / floor / the glen / I say no more / moaning 'you' / finite ocean / room / motion

Table 3.3 Five English Translations of 'From Nowhere with Love the Nth of Marchember Sir' ('Niotkuda s liubov'iu, nadtsatogo martobria') from 'A Part of Speech' ('Chast' rechi') by Joseph Brodsky

Stephen White, interlinear, undated	Daniel Weissbort, *Modern Poetry in Translation*, March 1978	Alan Myers and Brodsky, undated†	Leslie Simon (1980)	Attributed to Weissbort in the *Collected Poems* but different from Weissbort's first published translation, as has been changed by Brodsky
From nowhere with love on the Nth of Marchember (a) dear honourable sweetheart but no matter (b)	From nowhere with love, Marchember the enth, my dear respected darling, but it doesn't	From nowhere, then, with love, this nth day of Martember, my dear, respected, sweet – does it really signify	From nowhere with love, Marchember the nth, Dear Sweetheart My darling, but by now it hardly matters	From nowhere with love the enth of Marchember sir sweetie respected darling but in the end
even who for already there is no way speaking (a) frankly to recall the face's outlines not yours yet (b) no one else's either faithful friend* greets you from one (c)	matter who, since to be frank, the features aren't distinct anymore, neither your nor anyone else's everloving friend, salutations	who, even? Since offhand I can't remember for the life of me your face, or even profile – so, no 'true friend' to you or anyone,	Even who, for your face, to tell you the truth, Is already past remembering, best wishes, not yours Truly, but nobody else's either, from someplace on the globe	it's irrelevant who for memory won't restore features not yours and no one's devoted friend greets you from this fifth last part of earth
of five continents which rests on cowboys (d)	from one (on the backs of cowboys) of the five continents,	I send a greeting from that continent of five	Where the buffalo may roam, a cowboy continent;*	resting on whalelike backs of cowherding boys
I loved you more than the angels and than Him Himself (c)	I loved you more than himself or his angels,	propped up by cowboys; I loved adored you then	Since once you were more to me than Heaven above,	I lov*e*d y*o*u better *than* ang*e*ls and Him Himself
and because of that am further now from you than from both of them (d)	and so now am further from you than from both of them,	more than angels, more than Him above	Am I further from you now than from the Infinite?	and *a*m *farther off* due to *that* from *you* t*h*an I am from b*o*th

late at night in a sleeping valley on the very bottom (e) / in a small town buried in snow up to the door handle (f)	late at night in the sleeping valley, deep / in a small town up to its doorknobs in snow,	and so am farther off from you than both of them; / in the small hours, deep down on this sleeping valley's floor	Late at night, in the depths, in a valley fast asleep, / In a little town blanketed door-knob high with snow,	of them now late at night in the sleeping vale / in the little township up to its doorknobs in
writhing at night on the bed sheet (e)	writhing on top of the sheets,	– the township dreams as snow fills up the glen –	Tossing and turning all night on the sheets –	snow writhing upon the stale sheets for the whole matter's skin–
as not noted below to say the least (f)	which, to say the least, isn't stated below,	I writhe upon the sheet (of just how – I say no more)	At the very least, not as referred to below –	
I beat up the pillow mumbling 'you-u' (g)	I pummel the pillow, mumbling 'you'	and wrestle with my pillow, moaning 'you'	Ramming the pillows I bellow out 'you',	deep I am howling 'youuu' through my pillow dike
beyond seas uncharted and limitless (h)	across the seas which have not bounds or limits,	beyond the bordered, bounded, finite ocean,	Here in the dark, from beyond the vast seas,	many seas away that are milling nearer
in the darkness with the whole body like (g) [the rhyming word is 'features' below]	in the dark, my whole body repeating anew	repeating with my body in the darkened room	Out of sight out of mind^, but my body isn't through	with my limbs in the dark playing your double like
a crazy mirror repeating your features (h)	your features, as in some crazy mirror.	your features, a mad mirror's frozen motion.	Repeating your body like a mirror gone crazy.	an insanity-stricken mirror.
* – faithful friend – a standard closing of a letter.				

*The adapted cliché, 'держащегося на ковбоях', is meaningless in English. Better to separate it into tone and cliché and translate them separately. 'Someplace on the globe' and 'a cowboy continent' convey the ironic preposterous sense of dislocation, while 'where the buffalo roam' is a ready-made cliché for America, based, like the Russian one, on an animal image. (It comes from the well-known cowboy ballad 'Home on the range' – Nixon's favourite tune.)

^In place of the untranslatable abbreviation for remoteness (которым конца и края) I have introduced an English idiom from the language of separation. It summarizes the painful truth of the preceding lines and sets off the bizarre fact of love's memory which follows.

†This translation is ascribed to Myers and Brodsky in the description of the folder's content in the Brodsky archive but there is an extra note in handwriting on the sheet of paper with this version stating 'Earlier Myers version'. The version is not dated. It is likely that this version was produced by Myers and then it may have been changed by Brodsky.

Source: JBP, S.II, Poetry, IP, Chast' rechi, Box 56, Folders 1052, 1055, 1056, 1058.

The translation attributed to Weissbort in *Collected Poems* has a different rhyming pattern, closer to the Russian ST:

sir / end / restore / friend / earth / boys / Himself / both / vale / in / stale / skin / dike / nearer / like / mirror

A comparative analysis of rhyming patterns in all three translations reveals that the choices made in the authorized translation attributed to Weissbort are much more reminiscent of Brodsky's poetic style than Weissbort's. Weissbort did not choose to follow the ST's rhyme scheme strictly in any of his poems of the sequence published in *Modern Poetry in Translation*. However, Brodsky consistently highlighted the semantic importance of the rhymed words in the poem and of retaining the rhyme scheme.

As we know from Weissbort's own recollection of working on 'A Part of Speech', he was happy with his first published translations in *Modern Poetry in Translation*. We also know that Brodsky did not find them satisfactory and commissioned other translators (Myers and Simon) to produce their versions. Brodsky was aware that Weissbort was unhappy about this but they managed to talk this through and remain friends. Later Weissbort translated further poems by Brodsky in the years to come. From all the above, it is possible to deduce that the versions of 'A Part of Speech' published in *Collected Poems* are collaborative retranslations driven and authorized by the poet himself based on the prior translations by White, Myers and Weissbort.

Although at the time of putting together the book *A Part of Speech*, Brodsky already had a strong idea about a mimetic approach to poetic translation from Russian to English, he was not yet confident enough to self-translate independently. By studying multiple translations of his poems and by intervening in them, Brodsky was searching for greater formal equivalence between his Russian original poems and their English translations. He was shaping his voice by reflecting on his translators' versions of his poems, by borrowing certain 'blocks' from different versions, as he pointed out himself: 'Although I'm perfectly capable of writing decent, readable poetry in English, to me it is a bit like a game. Like playing chess or building with blocks' ('Interview with Brodsky', Glad 1993: 110). This is how he started to 'self-translate'. In other words, he was constructing the English versions out of his Russian originals by liberally drawing on prior translations. As a result of this, his translations and self-translations produced for *A Part of Speech* should be seen as texts of multiple authorship and constructed in the process of a collaborative work led by the poet.

Mode 2: Self-translation as retranslation drawing on prior translations

The translations of 'December in Florence'

'December in Florence', the Russian manuscript of which is dated 1976, first appeared in English, translated by the author, in the *NYRB* on 1 May 1980. This translation represents a step towards the author's growing confidence in his own ability to self-translate. Berlina begins her interpretive reading of Brodsky's self-translations with this particular self-translation primarily because 'it was the first self-translation Brodsky accomplished on his own'. Quoting Ishov, she writes that Brodsky abandoned three versions by four native speakers (Berlina 2014: 9).

My archival study of manuscripts reveals that there have actually been five translations of this poem in addition to Brodsky's published self-translation, which, I argue, is a retranslation drawing on all the prior versions. First, there is a signed but undated interlinear, word-for-word translation by Barry Rubin with attached notes to the poem detailing its rhyme scheme, metre, allusions, historical, geographical and cultural references and so on (JBP, S.II, Poetry, IP, Box 56, Folder 1075, 'Dekabr' vo Florentsii, English translation by Barry Rubin). Second, there is a 1976 translation by Maurice English and Kline (JBP, S.II, Poetry, IP, Box 56, Folder 1072, 'Dekabr' vo Florentsii, English translation by Maurice English and Kline). Having finished their translation, English and Kline sent a letter to Brodsky in which Kline, writing on behalf of both, explained that the translators had listed a few variants for some lines in the poem and would like Brodsky to choose his preferred version. Some of the choices that they gave him are relatively minor such as using either 'the' or 'a' before 'door' in 5.7. Other variants, on the other hand, differ much more from each other. In particular, they offered several versions of the final line:

> 'in the language of a man long written off as dead'
> (would apply to Dante but not so clearly to JB);
> '... of a man who's been listed with the dead'
> (but this misses the nice irony of 'written off');
> '... of a man whose memory already fades'
> (an exact rhyme with 'arcades', but perhaps too elaborate for '... человека, который убыл');
> '... of a man whose remembered voice already fades'
>> (has the advantage of the above variant, and is more precise, but probably too long, as well as too elaborate). (JBP, S.I, GC, Box 8, Folder 210, Kline, George / 1972–95; letter dated 4 November 1978)

At the bottom of the letter, Kline promises to call Brodsky over the weekend to discuss these matters. Kline was working collaboratively with Maurice English on this poem.

Third, there is a 1977 translation of this poem by Robert Lowell (JBP, S.II, Poetry, IP, Box 56, Folder 1073, 'Dekabr' vo Florentsii, English translation by Robert Lowell). His translation is typed and has some corrections made by hand (not by Brodsky). It has been shown that Brodsky was influenced by Lowell's poetry (Bethea 1994) and greatly respected his work. Lowell and Brodsky met on many occasions, including the first time which was in England after Brodsky had just arrived from the USSR, and discussed poetry. Brodsky particularly enjoyed talking about Dante's *Divine Comedy* with Lowell, to which there are various allusions in 'December in Florence' (Berlina 2014 and Ishov 2017). Brodsky dedicated to Lowell one of his first English-language elegies, having found out about Lowell's unexpected death upon his return from England, in a taxi on the way from Kennedy airport. It was Lowell's death that did not allow the poet to complete his translation of Brodsky's 'December in Florence', on which he was working at the time. As becomes clear from Brodsky's conversation with Tom Vitale, Lowell himself offered to translate the poem about Florence which Brodsky initially referred to as 'Wind in Florence'. According to Brodsky, Lowell 'did several versions of the poem' and they 'had arguments' about them. Then, Lowell went to England, returned to New York, 'landed at Kennedy, and he was dead when the taxi arrived at the door' (Vitale 2014). A hint of what Lowell and Brodsky might have disagreed about can be found in Weissbort's book:

> while I did not much care for Robert Lowell's radically individualistic approach to translation, I concurred with what he had to say in the introduction to his *Imitations* (1962), when he called translators who followed the path of formal mimesis, 'taxidermists not the poets [whose] poems are likely to be stuffed birds'. The trouble with Brodsky was that he simply wouldn't understand that he was asking for the impossible, for the Russian text to be *imported* into English wholesale, English having to be Russianized to accommodate it. (Weissbort 2004: 31; emphasis in original)

It is likely that Brodsky's and Lowell's opposing views on poetic translation caused arguments between the two poets.

Fourth, there is also one unidentified translation of the poem in the archive, which also has numerous corrections and queries by the poet (JBP, S.II, Poetry, IP, 'Dekabr' vo Florentsii, English translation by unidentified translator, draft, Box 56, Folder 1076). Fifth, there are three copies of the 'unapproved' 1978 translation by Alan Myers. It is not known whether Myers had access to Lowell's translation of the same poem but it is unlikely. There are at least two English versions of the poem by Myers; one of them has Brodsky's handwritten comments on it, identifying some mistakes, for example, in stanza 4 where Myers wrote: 'How often eyebrows leap beneath the pen!' Brodsky comments: 'WRONG: How often pen stumbled and strayed to draw eyebrows.' This is just one example where Brodsky rejected the translation of some lines. See Brodsky's further comments on stanzas 1 and 9 in Table 3.4. Brodsky also suggests rephrasing some lines, such as the opening line of stanza 6 where it is proposed that Myers's translation 'A dusty coffee house' be changed to 'In a dusty café'. Brodsky is also unhappy with the 'ruined' beat in this stanza. In the VII stanza, Brodsky identifies a lost reference to Cornelia. Myers's translation is as follows: 'love can't direct the moon much less the sky' but Brodsky insists that there should be 'stars' in this line and refers Myers to the last line of Cornelia. In a similar way, in stanza 9, where Myers translates, 'they stay shut in face of wealth and learning', Brodsky remarks that 'the idea of gold is crucial there' and needs to be reflected in translation. He is also dissatisfied by the rhyme in the bottom lines of this stanza.

Clearly, after all these years and several attempts at having 'December in Florence' translated, Brodsky was still displeased with all the existing versions. Brodsky's letter to Myers dated 4 November 1978 clarifies this:

> Speaking of 'December in Florence', I haven't made any corrections as yet, for I thought there is rather a lot for me to tackle. Look, Alan, you shouldn't get disturbed by my opinions on this or that poem. Good as my ear is for the Russian, I am the last one to make pronouncements in English. Still, there are some nuances that are missing from the English version of 'December', and also something happens here and there to the beat. The drama is that there is noone [sic] around who'd be capable [sic] to check the meter without resorting to counting fingers. Nobody hears anything nowadays! Poets, yjob their mom!' (JBP, S.I, GC, Myers, Alan, Outgoing, Box 10 Folder 272)

So great was Brodsky's frustration that he not only used a Russian swear word in the letter but also finally produced his own translation of the poem in 1980 (JBP, S.II, Poetry, IP, 'Dekabr' vo Florentsii, English translation by Brodsky, drafts and printed version, 1980, Box 56, Folder 1071).Table 3.4 follows the same coding principles as the ones used in the Tables 3.1–3.3. Four translations (Barry Rubin's, Maurice English and G. L. Kline's, Robert Lowell's, Alan Myers's) were made prior to Brodsky's version published in 1980. The words borrowed by Brodsky from prior translations are given in the same font/colour that these words appear in a relevant prior translation. If a word appears in more than one prior translation, it is printed in several relevant fonts/colours.

Berlina observes that Brodsky's English version of the poem is more straightforward and less suggestive than his Russian original. References to Mandelshtam disappear and those to Dante become more pronounced (Berlina 2014: 14, 15). Brodsky was delighted with his rhymes in the Russian version, he states:

> The formal features of 'Dekabr' which recall Dante are recreated self-translation: not only are the triplets reminiscent of *terza rima*, the nine nine-lined strophes also recall the nine circles of hell and the nine spheres of heaven. The only aspect to disappear is the rhymes' femininity – a feature which would have gone unnoticed by most readers, being of little importance in anglophone prosody. (Vail' 1995: 16–17)

In the Russian original, there are compound rhymes. Berlina suggests that in English some slant rhymes may have sounded to Brodsky's Russian ear like exact rhymes: 'indeed' and 'bit' / 'it' (Berlina 2014: 17). Stanza 1 has inexact rhymes in triplets ('won't', 'kind', 'bend'), despite the advice he gave Weissbort

Table 3.4 Five English Translations of 'December in Florence' ('Dekabr' vo Florentsii') by Joseph Brodsky, Stanzas I and IX

Barry Rubin, interlinear	Maurice English and G. L. Kline (1976. Revised on 3 November 1978)	Robert Lowell	Alan Myers, 1978	Joseph Brodsky (published in the NYRB, 1 May 1980)
[The] doors inhale [the]air and exhale steam [vapor]; **but**	The doors inhale air and exhale steam;	The doors take in air, exhale steam,	The doorways inhale air and exhale steam,	The doors take in air, exhale steam; **you**, however, **won**'t
you won't come back here, where paired off **in twos**	but you will not return here. Breaking into pairs,	yet you won't come back here, see the populace stream	but you wont [sic] be back where the people teem	be back to **the shalloed Arno** where, like a new kind
the populous strolls above the shoaled/ shallowed **Arno**,	the crowds go strolling by the/ Arno's failing stream	in couples, in twos, in [and] twos, along the shallow Arno –	in pairs, close by the shoaling Arno's stream,	of **qua**druped, idle **couples** follow the river bend.
calling to mind new* quadrupeds. [The] **doors**	like the new breed of quadruped that's strayed.	new quadrupeds. The doors slam,	like some new kind of beast. The heavy doors	**D**oors bang, **b**easts hit the slabs. Indeed,
slam, **wild animals*** come {go} out onto the pavement.	doors slamming behind them, down the pavement.	wild beasts emerge on the pavement from their hollow [old borough].	slam shut. They pad the pavement on all fours.	the **atmosphere of this city** retains a bit
There really is something from the forest* in the atmosphere	Truly, there is something of the forest glade	This city still has the tang of the forest.	The air's alive with forest noise and claws!	of the dark fo**r**est. It
of this city. This is a beautiful city,	about this handsome city. Yet at a certain age	Truly, it is a beautiful city;	Here in the city, beautiful, no doubt.	is **a** beauti**f**ul **c**ity where at a **c**e**r**tain **a**ge
where at a certain age* you simply avert your gaze from	you simply turn up your collar.	one i.e. of [at a certain] age to [one can] turn from those who follow,	reaching a certain age, you don't look out	one simply raises the collar to disengage
a person and raise your collar.	shutting out its people from your gaze.	and lift [to **raise**] his collar.	for people – raise your collar, shut them out.	from passing humans and dulls the gaze.

Notes	Original	Revision	Brodsky's corrections
line 4: 'new' is an allusion to to Dante's Vita Nuova. It is ironic and suggests a destructive newness. lines 5–6: 'wild animals' and 'forest' – reference to beginning of Divine Comedy. line 8: 'at a certain age' alludes to the first line of the Inferno. 'avert your gaze' implies that since you can't stand people, you look at the city.			Brodsky's corrections: line 3: (shallowed) line 6: it's a paraphrase of Dante's 'Selva oscura' line 9: too imperative
There are cities to which there is no return.	There are cities in this world to which one can't return.	**There are cities to which one cannot return,**	There are cities one won't see again. The sun
The sun beats against their windows, as if they were smooth mirrors. That	The sun beats on their windows as though on polished mirrors.	the sun beats on a window, as if it were a mirror –	Cities there are to which there is no returning. [Cities there are to which there's no returning.] The sun beats on their mirror windows, windows learning [The sun beats on their mirror windows, a sign to the discerning] throws its gold at their frozen windows. But all the same
is, there is no penetrating them – not for any amount of gold.	And no amount of gold will make their hinged gates turn.	that is, there's no penetration, yet money to burn .	entry here's privilege worth earning. [that they stay shut in face of wealth or learning] there is no entry, no proper sum.
There a river always flows under six bridges.*	Rivers in those cities always flow beneath six bridges.	There six bridges always arch the a local river, [clean?]	There six bridges span a running river. [There six bridges span a running river.] There are always six bridges spanning the sluggish river.

(Continued)

Table 3.4 (Continued)

Barry Rubin	Maurice English and G. L. Kline (1976. Revised on 3 November 1978)	Robert Lowell	Alan Myers, 1978	Joseph Brodsky (published in the NYRB, 1 May 1980)
There are places there where there was occasion to press lips*	There are places in those cities where lips first pressed on lips	**there are places where lip first pressed against a lip,**	There those places where myself a lover [There those places where lips touched lover's]	There are places where lips touched lips for the first time ever
against other lips and pen to [sheets of] paper. And	and pen on paper. In those cities there is a richness	and a pen first marked a piece of scrap – [ghost]	pressed lip to lip, likewise pen to paper. [lips and pen pressed paper in a fever.]	or pen pressed paper with real fervor.
there there is a blur of arcades, colonnades, iron scarecrows;	of scarecrows cast in iron, of colonnades, arcades.	a blur of arcades there, collimades [sic], scarecrows –	Arcades, cast iron tyrants down below [The eye is dazed, arcades, columns, cast-iron bugbears.]	There are arcades, colonnades, iron idols that blur your lens,
there the crowd speaks, as it besieges the trolly corner,	There the crowds besieging trolly stops are speaking.	there a crowd speaks as it besieges the trolly-top,	waver in water; there crowds speak, presto, [there the populace surging round the tramcars]	There the streetcars' multitudes jostling, dense,
in the tongue of a person who has departed.*	in the language of a man who's been written off as dead.	*in the tongue of a person departed elsewhere.*	the language of a man gone long ago. [speak the tongue of one long since departed.]	speak in the tongue of the man who departed thence.
line 4: 'six bridges' – the river is the Neva in Leningrad. There is also a parallel with the Arno.			Brodsky's comments on version 2 given in square brackets: line 1: Should have a trifle more epic swing	
line 5: In Russian, the subject of the verb meaning 'press' is not explicit for deliberate slight vagueness.			line 3: The idea of gold is crucial: implies seen insult.	
line 9: The final word of the poem, here rendered as 'departed', has a slightly bureaucratic overtone, as might be attached to the phrase 'arrival and departure'.			lines 7–9: it should rhyme better than that.	

Source: IBP, GEN MSS 613, S.II, Poetry, IP, Box 56 'Dekabr' vo Florentsii. English translations by Robert Lowell (Folder 1073), by Alan Myers (Folder 1074), by M. English and G Kline (Folder 1072), by Barry Rubin (Folder 1075), by Joseph Brodsky (Folder 1076).

several years earlier about rhyming exactly the first and third lines. Additional adjectives in the English version must have been added for filling, but some of them become 'key' words in the English version of the poem: for example, 'idle' is added to the description of couples and again in stanza 7: 'idle fears', 'dark'. In stanza 2, Brodsky chooses 'pupil' over 'eye', prefers the adjective 'raw' to 'damp' or 'moist'.

In stanza 3, 'biustuet' – a neologism in Russian. Berlina makes a reference to a parallel translation of the Russian poem by Kline and Maurice, as they find 'an interesting solution, in which not the bust but the bridge become active', and then Berlina underlines the positive effect of having one poem translated by different translators: 'multiple translations could be the blocks of which a poem's perception outside its country is built. Even if the self-translation happens to be superior overall (which is not automatically the case), a poem still consists of details; even a single interesting solution (like the thrusting bridge) makes the reading of an alternative version worthwhile' (Berlina 2014: 23). While Berlina welcomes, at least, one alternative solution in 'Dekabr' by Kline and English, she criticizes their version for departing from the original's rhyme scheme. She approves of their choice of *terza rima* in the first three stanzas because it is justified by the Dantesque theme. In stanza 4, the rhyme scheme disintegrates. She also criticizes Kline for thinking of 'withering/thing' an exact rhyme despite the difference in stress. In stanza 4, Berlina discusses the choice of a 'pen' over a 'quill' in English, suggesting that a quill takes it closer to Dante while a 'pen' brings it over to Brodsky's times. She also comments on the disappointing choice of the first and last words in this stanza, while in Russian they are 'man' ('chelovek') and 'paper' ('bumaga'), in English, the last word is 'shade' (Berlina 2014: 28).

What escapes Berlina's perceptive close reading is that Brodsky's version is a retranslation of prior translations, from which Brodsky borrows words and phrases in order to 'improve' the formal features of the English poem (see Table 3.4). In stanzas 1 and 9, there is not a single line in Brodsky's retranslation that does not use at least one word or phrase from a prior translation. For example, the beginning of the first line is taken from Lowell's version: 'The doors take in air, exhale steam.' Some of Brodsky's choices for his translation first emerge as a result of his reflecting on his translator's versions, that is, in dialogue with his translators. For example, Brodsky's choice of 'shallowed' first appears in his note to Myers's translation. By the time Brodsky wrote his own version of the English text, he was intimately familiar with all the other versions, so his retranslation emerges from his covertly collaborative work with his translators' prior versions of the poem.

Another interesting example of how Brodsky drew on his translators' work in self-translations is the poem 'Eclogue IV: Winter' (it was first written in Russian in 1977), which was completed about a year earlier than 'Eclogue V: Summer'. The latter was self-translated in 1980 and published in *The New Yorker* in 1982. In the Brodsky Archive, there is an undated interlinear translation of 'Winter

Eclogue' (the title is used interchangeably with 'Eclogue IV: Winter') by Masha Vorobiov, which may mean that Brodsky intended to commission a poetic translation of this poem. Comparing Vorobiov's interlinear translation and Brodsky's self-translation, it is evident that the poet used Vorobiov's interlinear version while working on his poetic self-translation (in Table 3.5, Vorobyov's interlinear translation is given in a different font from Brodsky's version. The words borrowed by Brodsky from Vorobiov's version are given in the same font as Vorobyov's interlinear translation).

A draft of Brodsky's self-translation was sent to Hecht for some feedback (see section on Hecht in Chapter 4). It is not clear whether Vorobiov completed her interlinear translation or did only the first six stanzas (quoted earlier), which are handwritten. Either way, many words and expressions from this part of the poem have been borrowed by Brodsky from the interlinear translation, and his English version emerges as a result of covert collaborative translation. This type of co-authorship is reminiscent of some English-language authors analysed by Stillinger (see Chapter 2), as Vorobiov takes part in the creative process and contributes to the final and authorized English-language version. At this stage, it is worth asking why she was not acknowledged as a co-translator. It is likely that it was because, as a rule, interlinear translators were not mentioned as co-translators. She herself would not have considered herself a co-author either. An interlinear translator did the ground work, which usually remained invisible to the reader.[3] However, hers as well as White's and Frydman's input into Brodsky's English version of his poems should not be underestimated.

Mode 3: Commissioning and intervening – overt collaborative translation

'Eclogue V: Summer'

Even when Brodsky began to self-translate, he continued to commission translators, mostly for pragmatic reasons, such as to save time on translation or to focus on a new poem instead of returning to an old one. Nabokov listed both of these reasons for using translators in English (Anokhina 2017). In 1981, Brodsky commissioned Kline to translate 'Eclogue V'. Having done the first draft translation, Kline sent it to Brodsky for some feedback. Routinely, he accompanied it with a warm letter dated 2 July 1985, containing a list of queries and explaining how he tried to recreate the formal qualities of the poem. Kline mentioned the rhymes that he was particularly proud of, such as 'the slant rhyme of "*khrushchev*" with "jugs of" and "dusks in"' (VI.1.1–3). Kline also noted the weaknesses of his translation, such as one padding, which

---

3. For a discussion of the use of interlinear trots in the USSR, see Witt (2011).

Table 3.5 Two Translations of 'Eclogue IV: Winter' ('Ekloga 4-ia (zimniaia)') by Joseph Brodsky: An Interlinear Translation by Masha Vorobiov and a Self-Translation by the Author, Stanzas I, II and III

	Masha Vorobiov, interlinear	Joseph Brodsky, self-translation
I	In winter dark/dusk comes right after lunch (At this time it's not hard/It's not hard then) to mistake the hungry for the fed	In winter it *dark*ens the moment lunch is over. It's *hard then* to tell starving men from the sated.
	A yawn chases/pursues a simple phrase into the/a lair	A *yawn* keeps *a phrase* from leaving its cozy *lair*.
	(There is) a dry condensed shape to light – the snow dooms the alder thicket, having covered it up,	The *dry*, instant version *of light*, the opal *snow*, dooms tall *alder*s – by having freighted
	to insomnia – (to accessibility) to the eye	them – *to insomnia*, to your glare,
	in the dark. The rose and the forget-me-not come up in conversation less & less. The dogs ~~dash~~ rush	well after midnight. *Forget-me-not*s and *roses* crop *up less* frequently in dialogues. *Dogs* with languid
	(off on) a trail with lazy / sluggish enthusiasm, since they themselves	fervor pick up the *trail*, for they, too, leave traces.
	leave a trail. The night enters the city as	*Night*, having *entered the city*, pauses
	into a nursery, finds the child under its blanket,	as *in a nursery, finds* a baby *under a blanket*.
	and the pen ~~scrabbles~~ creaks, like someone else's sled.	And the pen creaks like steps that are *someone else's*.
II	My life has gone on / is dragging / has prolonged / has dragged (itself) out. In the snowstorms recitative	My life has *dragged* on. *In the recitative* of a blizzard
	the sharpened hearing makes out the theme of ~~freezing~~ turning to ice. Every [empty space] in the garden	a keen ear picks up the tune of the Ice Age. Every 'Down in the Valley' is, for sure,
	is merely a frozen 'boogie-woogie.'	a chilled *boogie-woogie*. A bitter, brittle
	A powerful frost is the revelation to the body Of its impending temperature.	cold represents, as it were, a message to the body of its final *temperature*
	Or – the Earth's sigh for its rich galactic past, where everyone would freeze;	or – the *Earth* itself, *sigh*ing out of habit *for its galactic past*, its sub-zero horrors.
	Even here the cheek grows crimson like a raddish [sic]	*Cheeks* burn *crimson like radish*es *even here*.
	the cosmos is always / at all times shot through with (indistinct) agate	*Cosmic* space *is always shot through with* matte *agate*,
	And the morse that has returned home beeps quietly not finding the radio operator.	and the *beeping Morse, return*ing *home*ward, *find*s no ham *operator*'s ear.
III	In February, the KRASNODAL thickets become lilac,	*In February*, *lilac* retreats to osiers.
	The carrot, unavoidable in the profile of a snowman,	Imperative to a *snowman*'s *profile*,
	grows more expensive. Limited by the eyebrow a glance at a cold object, at a hunk of metal,	*carrots* get *more expensive. Limited by* a *brow*, *a glance at cold*, *metallic objects*
	is [empty space] than the metal itself, lest it prove necessary to tear / pull it with meat.	is fiercer *than the metal itself*. This, while you peel eyes from objects, still may allow

(Continued)

Table 3.5 (*Continued*)

Masha Vorobiov, interlinear	Joseph Brodsky, self-translation
away from the object. Who's to know whether it wasn't how the God surveyed his labor (?) on the eight day and after.	no shedding of blood. The Lord, some reckon, was reviewing His world in this very fashion on the eighth day and after. In winter, we're
In winter, instead of gathering berries	
They plug up cracks with bits of oakum	not berry pickers: we stuff *the cracks with oakum,*
They dream more readily of the common [word not clear]	praise the common good with greater passion,
And objects become a year older.	and things grow *older* by, say, *a year.*

Source: JBP, S.II, Poetry, IP, Ekloga (IV–VI): Ekloga IV-ia Zimniaia, English translation by Brodsky, proof, printed version, 1982–5 (Box 57, Folder 1103), English translation by Masha Vorobiov, draft/undated (Box 57, Folder 1104).

he described as 'a result of desperation', and mentioned the places he was not sure about, such as an erotic reference to Simonides'[4] line that Kline was not aware of in line IV.6.1. Kline failed to see what could be erotic about ankles and assumed that focusing on the bones of the ankles helped not to be distracted by a woman's beautiful face or her breasts. Kline was pleased to tell Brodsky that he had managed to keep the same number of lines: '241' and that he had attempted a 'relaxed *dolnik* meter' having not managed to keep exactly the same length of lines. He added: 'In general, this, like the original, tends to be trochaic rather than iambic, though an occasional iambic fragment may also have slipped in.' His queries had mostly to do with lexis, that is, the meaning of certain words, such as 'obscene language' ('materkom', a diminutive from *mat*), a Russian folk song ('"chizhik" as in "chizhik-pyzhik"') and a 'sunflower' ('podsolnukh'). Kline struggled with Brodsky's colloquialisms and the double meaning of some words. He was also wondering what 'barmalei' meant. The word is usually capitalized and used in singular 'Barmalei', which is the proper name of a villain from Kornei Chukovsky's 'Doctor Aibolit', a popular story for children in Soviet Russia. In the end of the letter, Kline complements Brodsky on the poem, saying that the more he studied it, the more he admired it (JBP, S.II, Poetry, IP, Ekloga (IV–VI): Ekloga V-ia Letniaia, English translation by Kline and Brodsky, drafts and printed version, 1985–7, Box 57, Folder 1110). He also notes that he consciously left more space in between lines in his translation for Brodsky to make comments and suggestions.

In his comments on Kline's translation, Brodsky reminded Kline that rhymes 'should be awfully good to entice the reader' and 'feminine throughout', adding that if Kline wanted to break it, he should do it 'only for compound or hyphenated nouns, or adjectives like "iron-clad"'. He also suggested changing

---

4. Simonides of Ceos (*c.* 556–468 BC) Greek lyric poet.

the opening lines to 'Here you go again, mosquito hymn of summer' or 'I discern you again, mosquito hymn of summer' (which Brodsky notes as his preferred version), or 'I hear once more' or 'Once more, I am hearing you' (JBP, S.II, Poetry, IP, Ekloga (IV–VI): Ekloga V-ia Letniaia, English translation by Kline and Brodsky, drafts and printed version, 1985–7, Box 57, Folder 1110). However, none of these variants were used in the published version in which Kline's opening lines were kept intact.

Nearly two years after the first letter, Kline wrote his second letter dated 30 March 1987 to Brodsky in response to the poet's corrections and suggestions to the translation. This letter was different in tone from the first one, which had contained mostly queries about lexis and explanation of how Kline had tried to recreate the form. The second letter had a 'teacherly' tone, for which Kline apologized at the end of the letter, explaining that he had recently been marking students' translations. His queries are mostly related to Brodsky's changes. He is puzzled that Brodsky changed his feminine rhymes which he 'had been at such pains to use [. . .] throughout'. He was also unhappy about using 'about a dozen rhymes' repeatedly in the poem. He was disappointed by the loss of the strong final words 'the power of

Table 3.6 A Draft Translation of Joseph Brodsky's 'Eclogue V: Summer' ('Ekloga 5-ia (letniaia)') by G. L. Kline with/and the Author, Stanzas I, II and III

Comments on G. L. Kline's draft translation by Joseph Brodsky		G. L. Kline with/and Joseph Brodsky
These rhymes are showing the strain	I	I hear you again, mosquito hymn of summer! In the dogwood tepee, ants sweat in slumber. A botfly slides off the burdock's crumpled epaulet showing us that it always ranked just a private. And caterpillars show us the meaning of 'lower than grass'. The rose-bays'
Nearness?	II	overgrown derricks, knee-deep or ankle – deep in the couch-grass and bind-weed jungle, shine blue, due to their proximity and their angle to the zenith. The praying mantis' little rakes shutter the hemlock's brittle colorless fireworks. The scruffy, whittled
The off rhymes work better than the full rhymes	III	thistle's heart looks like a land-mine which is only half-exploding its ruddy riches. The cowbane resembles a hand that reaches for a carafe. And, like fishermen's wives, a spider patches its trawl, strung out between the bitter wormwood and hedge-mustard's golden miter.

Source: JBP, S.II, Poetry, IP, Ekloga (IV–VI): Ekloga V-ia Letniaia, English translation by Kline and Brodsky, drafts and printed version, 1985–7, Box 57, Folder 1110.

China' ('moshch Kitaia') as well as the reference to crucifixion 'crucified by bitter wormwood' ('raspiatyi terpkoi polyn'iu' in I.3). Kline asked whether they could restore the reference to both. Kline also pointed to a few words and expressions used by Brodsky which Kline found puzzling and unclear, such as 'oval' referring to a face.

It has generally been accepted by scholars that Brodsky insisted on 'mimetic' translation, ensuring the faithful rendering of formal qualities of the original, and that he was therefore prepared, to a certain extent, to change meaning at the expense of form. However, in the above-mentioned letter it is Kline who lamented the loss of the feminine rhyme which was in the Russian original and which he was trying to keep in English at Brodsky's request at the beginning of

Table 3.7 Translation of Joseph Brodsky's 'The Bust of Tiberius' ('Biust Tiberiia') by Alan Myers and/with the Author, Selected Lines

	Alan Myers	Alan Myers with the author (quoted from the draft available in the Brodsky Archive)
Line 1	Salutes to you, two thousand years too late.	All hail to you, two thousand years too late.
Line 2	I too once took a whore in marriage.	I too once took a whore in marriage.
Line 3	We have a few things in common. Plus,	We have some things in common. Plus,
Line 28	Nor, in its own turn, your observant eye	Nor, in its turn, does your observant eye
Line 29	appears to rest on anything before it:	appear to rest on anything before it:
Line 30	neither on any face, nor on	neither on someone's face, nor on
Line 31	an antique landscape. Ah Tiberius!	some classic landscape. Ah Tiberius!
Line 34	of your great cruelty? There are no causes in	for your great cruelty? There are no causes in
Line 41	is to have really no part of truth:	is really to have part of truth:
Line 43	Caesars especially. And at any rate	caesars especially. And at any rate
Line 60	were quite a monster, yet perhaps more monstrous	were surely a monster, yet perhaps more monstrous
Line 72	harsh tongues is like defending lime-trees	harsh tongues is like defending oak-trees
Line 73	from leaves rapt in their meaningless but clearly	from leaves wrapped in their meaningless, but clearly
Line 74	insistent rumbling of majority.	insistent, clamour of majority.
Line 87	Can't this be also that acceleration	Can't that be also that acceleration
Line 92	Should one recant then? rearrange the fate?	Should one recant then? rearrange the dice?
Line 99	and egg-like? Probably. But having hit.	and yoke-like? Probably. But having hit.

In Table 3.7, words underlined by Rulyova to highlight changes.
Source: JBP, MSS 613, S.II, Poetry, IP, Biust Tiberiia, English translation by Brodsky and Alan Myers, drafts and printed version, undated, Box 55, Folder 1034.

the translation process. As the author of the original, Brodsky had the liberty to move away from some formal aspects of the Russian original while recreating others.

As seen in Table 3.6, Brodsky was critical of Kline's rhyme scheme. He was also dissatisfied with some lexical choices, for example, in stanza V, against which Brodsky wrote 'Nope'. In the final published version, Brodsky kept some of the choices that Kline had had concerns about. For example, the masculine rhymes in II.3 are kept, 'square' and 'somewhere' remain, and the reference to crucifixion in I.3 is not restored. However, Brodsky acted on Kline's other criticisms. He got rid of the repeated rhymes, such as 'slumber' in II.3 and III.7 and 'gentle', which was changed in IV.7. But the poet decided to keep the 'even' / 'given' rhyme in II.1 and IV.7.

As a result, it was published in English in 1987 as translated by Kline with the author. This mode of overt collaboration with his translators was characteristic of Brodsky's many translations. The published version of this poem is the product of co-authorship which is fully acknowledged in all subsequent publications. The mode of translating this poem was collaborative, where collaboration takes the form of exchange of letters and drafts as well as conversations in person and on the phone, which Kline referred to in his letters. Although Kline produced most of the translation, Brodsky made some decisive authorial changes to his translation, some of which were disappointing to the translator.

Another example of overt collaborative translation of the poem is a rendering of 'A Bust of Tiberius', which was published as 'The Bust of Tiberius' in 1981. It was translated by Myers. Brodsky was generally satisfied with the translation but made some minor changes. The changes introduced by Brodsky are underlined in his authorized translation, which is in the second column in Table 3.7, while the first column contains Myers's prior translation.

The typed draft translation was signed as 'translated from the Russian by Alan Myers and the Author' (JBP, S.II, Poetry, IP, 'Biust Tiberiia', English translation by Brodsky and Alan Myers, drafts and printed version, undated, Box 55, Folder 1034). However, it was later changed to 'translated by Alan Myers with the author', which is a more accurate acknowledgement of the contribution by the translator. It was first published in the *NYRB* on 25 June 1987.

Mode 4: Self-translating from Russian

In the late 1980s, Brodsky started to self-translate more regularly and with more confidence. The production of self-translations at this stage was a different process. Brodsky chose to self-translate some poems from Russian instead of retranslating them based on prior commissioned translations. In other words, he was more proactive and less reactive, which indicated his growing self-confidence in English. Brodsky's approach to self-translation by then was more independent.

Table 3.8 Two Translations of 'Dorogaia, ia vyshel segondnia iz domu pozdno vecherom', Known in English as 'Brise Marine' by Joseph Brodsky

Unidentified interlinear	Joseph Brodsky
Darling, I've walked out of the house late this evening to take some fresh air blowing from the ocean. The sunset was smouldering like a Chinese fan at the gallery and the cloud was building (itself) up like a lid of concert piano.	Dear, I ventured *out of the house late this evening*, merely for a breath of *fresh air from the ocean* not far away. The sun *was smouldering* low *like a Chinese fan* in a *gallery* and a *cloud* reared up its huge *lid* like a Steinway.
A quatercentury ago you were partial to kebab and dates, sketched in the pocket pad, somewhat sung, entertained with me but later merged with a chemical engineer and judging by letters grew stupid drastically.	A *quarter century* back you craved curry and dates from Senegal, tried your voice for the stage, scratched profiles in a sketch-*pad*, dallied *with me – but later* alloyed *with a chemical engineer and, judging by letters, grew* fairly stupid.
These days they say you are seen in the churches of the capital and in the provinces at the services of mutual friends going now non-stop, one after another. And I am glad that there are distances in this world more incomprehensible than the one between you and me.	These days you've been *seen in churches* in the *capital and in provinces*, at rites for our friends or acquaintances, now continuous; yet *I am glad* after all that the world still promises *distances* more inconceivable *than one between us*.
Don't get me wrong. With your voice, body, name nothing is connected any longer. Nobody has destroyed them, but to forget one life, a man needs as a minimum (to spend) another life. And I have done that portion.	Understand me correctly, though: *your body*, your warble, your middle name now stir practically nothing. Not that they've ceased to burgeon; *but to forget one life, a man needs* at *minimum one more life. And I've done that portion.*
You've got lucky as well. Where else, save perhaps a photograph, you remain forever wrinkle-free, young, cheerful, odious? That is, time colliding with memory learns about its impotence. I smoke in the dark and inhale the rot of ebb tide.	*You got lucky as well: where else, save* in a snapshot *perhaps*, will *you forever remain free of wrinkles*, lithe, caustic, vivid? Having bumped into memory, time learns its impotence. Ebb-tide; I smoke in the dark and inhale rank seaweed.

Source: JBP, S.II, Poetry, IP, 'Dorogaia, ia vyshel segondnia iz domu pozdno vecherom', English Interlinear by unidentified translator, draft, undated, Box 56, Folder 1088; English translation by Brodsky, drafts, proof and printed version, 1989–91, undated, Box 56, Folder 1089.

This, however, does not yet mean that he self-translated in the same solo way as he was writing in Russian. He still relied on some editing and feedback by native English speakers. Kjellberg who worked as his secretary was also working as editor at FSG. An example of such a self-translation is the poem 'Kelomäki' ('Kellomyakki') which was written in Russian in 1982 and self-translated in 1987. Brodsky typed the English draft of the poem and, judging by the few remarks in the margins, he asked an English speaker to look at it. The reader made a few remarks but the overall verdict underneath is clear: 'Is only good frankly.'

Another example is 'May 24, 1980', the self-translation of the 'Ia vkhodil vmesto dikogo zveria'. It was originally written in Russian in 1980 and then self-translated in 1987, the same year as 'Kelomäki'. This poem has been analysed and commented on by scholars and critics who seem to diverge on the quality of Brodsky's English self-translation. No critics, however, have commented on the production of this self-translation. In the concluding section of Chapter 1, I mentioned one particular finding from my archival research that sheds light on how Brodsky approached self-translation at that time. The poet translated every Russian word that he used in this poem into English. So, instead of having an interlinear translation, he created something like a vocabulary list or a glossary (see Picture 1.1). This is a unique example of Brodsky writing a vocabulary list before attempting a self-translation, but having interlinear translations continued to be a helpful practice.

In 1989, Brodsky wrote the poem in Russian 'Dorogaia, ia vyshel segondnia iz domu', which is known in English as 'Brise Marine'. Just like in the case of 'Winter Eclogue', there is an interlinear English translation of the Russian poem, which is likely to have preceded the poet's self-translation but, unlike in the case of 'Winter Eclogue', this typed-up interlinear translation is unidentified and undated. Like Vorobiov's interlinear translation of 'Winter Eclogue', this one does not have any comments on the meaning of words or the poem's structure. The only extra comment on the typed translation is the rhyme scheme noted to the right of stanza 1. It is not known whether Brodsky intended the poem to be translated by a peer poet. Anyhow, there are no further translations of this poem in English apart from Brodsky's self-translation, which is first written by hand and then typed up. Brodsky's self-translation draws on the interlinear text in a similar way to that in which his 'Winter Eclogue' referred to Vorobiov's translation. In Brodsky's self-translation, the borrowed words and expressions from the interlinear version are in the same font as the interlinear itself (see Table 3.8) (JBP, S.II, Poetry, IP, 'Dorogaia, ia vyshel segondnia iz domu pozdno vecherom', English Interlinear by unidentified translator, draft, undated, Box 56, Folder 1088). In Table 3.8, there are two translations: an interlinear version by an unidentified author and Brodsky's self-translation. The former is given in a different font to the latter. The words and phrases borrowed by the author from a prior interlinear translation are presented in the same font as they appear in the prior interlinear version. After the poet typed his English self-translation, he faxed it to Kjellberg for some feedback.

The poem 'So Forth', which is Brodsky's self-translation of the Russian poem 'Konchitsia leto. Nachnetsia sentiabr' (1987), was published in 1992. The self-translation shows how much Brodsky's approach to self-translation had changed by the early 1990s. He felt sufficiently confident to write his self-translation without any prior translation to draw on. Neither did he need a glossary like when he did in 1987. However, Brodsky still relied on editing feedback. Some drafts of this self-translation were sent to Margo Picken, Brodsky's friend and neighbour along with Masha Vorobiov, who read through his various drafts. The poem returned with a few corrections: six definite articles were changed for indefinite articles in lines 4 and 5 of stanza 2. Brodsky agreed with the changes and then showed it to someone else for another round of editing. This time, another article was corrected in the third line from the bottom of stanza 3: 'a silhouette' was changed for 'the silhouette' and a typo was noted in the word 'silhouette', in which 'h' was missing (JBP, S.II, Poetry, IP, 'Konchitsi leto. Nachnetsia sentiabr'. Razreshat otstrel', English translation by Brodsky, drafts, proof and printed version, 1987–92, Box 60, Folder 1240). This shows that by now the poet primarily was seeking only an editor's intervention to check his draft translation for errors and typos.

Mode 5: From self-translation towards creative writing in English

The sequence of four poems Centaurs I–IV[5] represents a step from self-translation towards creative writing in English. The Russian original poems are typed in the top half of the page. Each poem is short and the bottom half of the page is blank. By hand, Brodsky wrote the first draft of his self-translations in the bottom half of the page. His writing appears free-flowing and confident in the choices that he makes. (See Picture 3.3.)

Only in a few spaces, he included some optional phrases, such as 'in vernacular [sic]' and 'according to papers' in the first line of 'Centaurs I'. In the same line, he added 'ravishing' before 'beauty'. Then he typed an English self-translation but he was not yet satisfied with one part of the self-translation, specifically, the definition of catastrophe in brackets in lines 3–4. His first translation of it is the literal one from Russian: '(after all a catastrophe / is something in whose outcome it's hard not to undergo some changes)'. Later, Brodsky comes up with a shorter version: '(is something the outcome of which is only changes)'. On the same sheet, under a shorter version he wrote the third version which moves away from the Russian original: 'Ogles the guises a lull refuses.' He evidently spent some time thinking about this line and, on a piece of paper headed 'The Stanford Courts', he started typing his latest version of the poem in English but stopped after the two lines. (See Picture 3.4.)

---

5. For discussion of the poems' content and form, see Berlina (2014).

3. What Are Joseph Brodsky's Collaborative Self-Translations Made of?   115

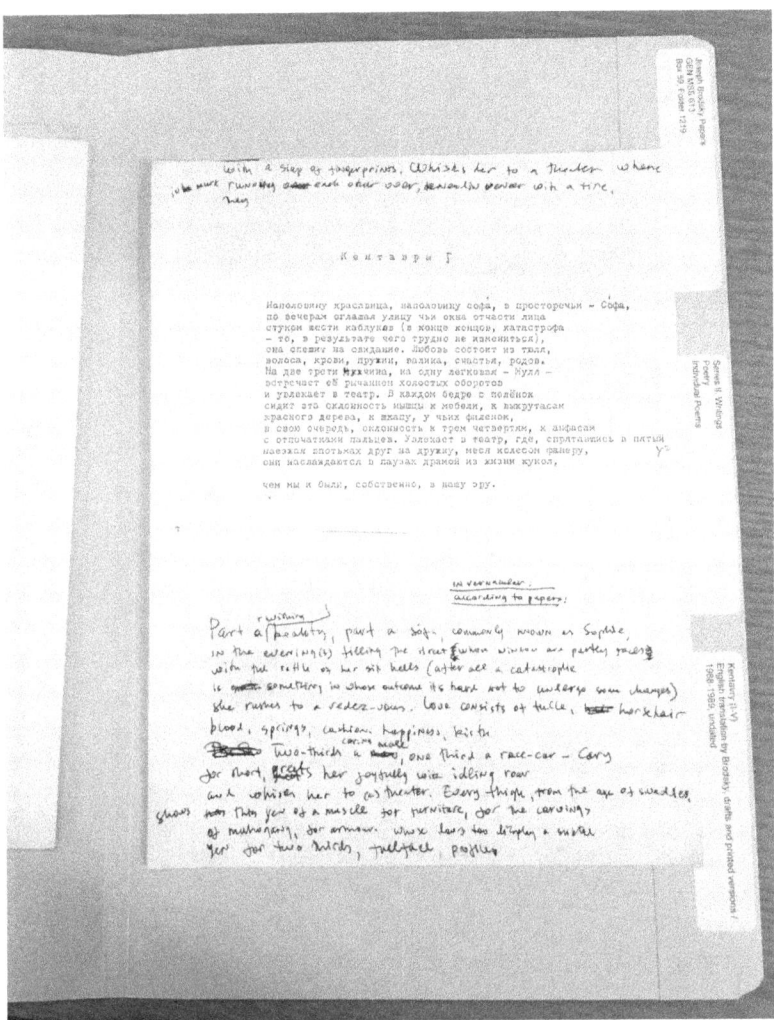

Picture 3.3 'Centaurs I' ('Kentavry I'), English translation by Brodsky, draft, 1989, page 1.

Below, in handwriting, he noted: 'Is keen on developments a lull refuses / Ogles the guises [underneath: outfits] a lull refuses.' Underneath these lines written in pen, there are two more lines in pencil: 'Whose windows are faces too / Always leaves change as an afterglow.' The bottom lines were not used in the final version of the self-translation. Comparing how Brodsky had co-translated *A Part of Speech* (1979) with how he approached his self-translation of the sequence *Centaurs* (1988), the change is undeniable: the poet is now much more at ease writing in English. At this stage, he self-translates creatively and independently, with only minimal editing help. He still made

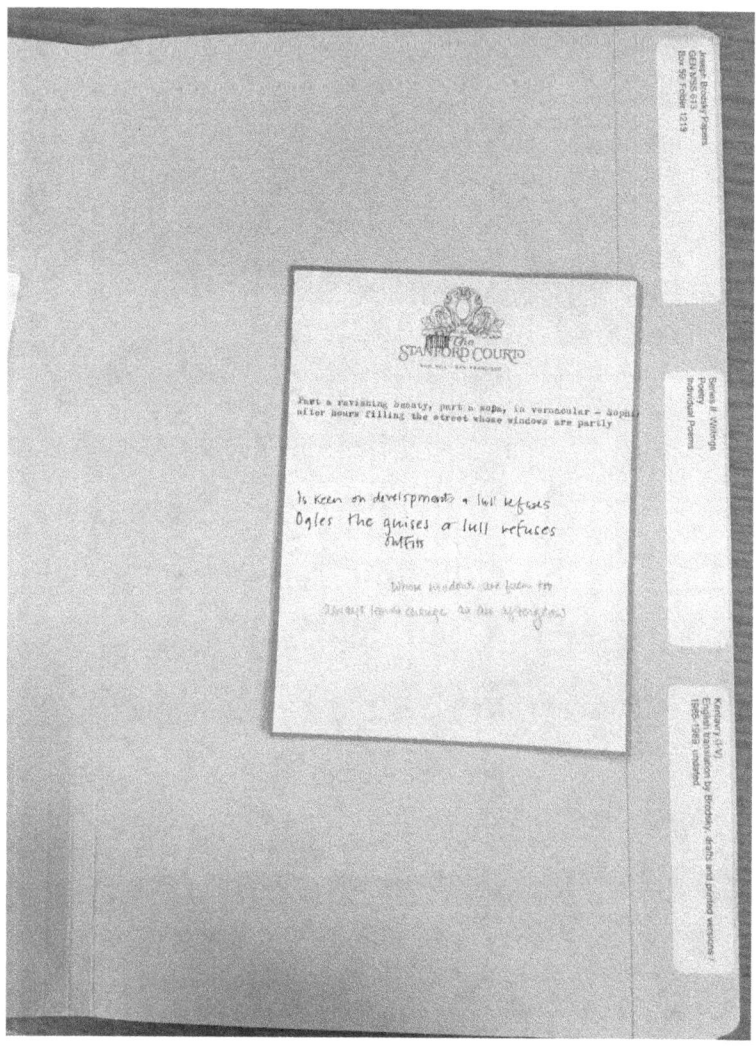

Picture 3.4 'Centaurs I' ('Kentavry I'), English translation by Brodsky, draft, 1989, page 2.

minor grammatical errors, especially when it came to the use of articles. This is because Russian does not have articles and it is therefore particularly difficult for a Russian speaker to use them.

'Angel' is also a self-translation (1993) with minor editing corrections made most likely by Margo Picken, according to Kjellberg, after the poet completed the first draft. The definite article 'the' was replaced by 'a' before 'metallic hanger' in line 3. In line 5, 'has' was added before 'ever happened'. In line 9, 'but' was replaced with 'just' (JBP, S.II, Poetry, IP, 'Angel', English translation by Brodsky, drafts, proof and printed version, Box 55, Folder 1001).

There are several versions of Brodsky's self-translation 'Daedalus in Sicily'. Kjellberg recollects that Brodsky dictated it to her, and she wrote it by hand and then typed it to work on it further (Table 3.9).

Early drafts have a few corrections made by hand on them by Kjellberg or by her with the author.[6] Some grammatical and stylistic changes are made, for example, two definite articles are deleted in line 13 before 'land' and 'water', the verb 'has' is changed for 'had' in line 9, 'those' is replaced with 'his' before 'constructions' in line 5 and 'had' is added before 'already' in line 14. Kjellberg worked closely with Brodsky on this text, making her own suggestions and adding Brodsky's changes: 'trying so hard to supply himself with work' was changed for 'so busy/busily getting himself commissions'; 'to run' was replaced with 'to flee' in line 16; 'loom' was used instead of 'stand' after 'behind' in line 19; 'tusks' or 'molars' were suggested to be used instead of 'teeth' in line 19. Brodsky incorporated all these changes and the poem was retyped afterwards. The typed second draft also has further handwritten comments by Kjellberg and by the author himself in between lines and in the margins.[7] For example, he changed 'when young had already invented the seesaw' for 'had already invented when he was young' in line 21. A later draft went through further changes, such as replacing 'perished in flight from falling' for 'perished in flight by falling' in line 9. Other changes were lexical: it was proposed that 'extremely old man' be changed to 'deeply old' or 'really ancient' in line 12. Interestingly, it was suggested that 'his constructions' be changed back to 'these constructions'. It was also proposed to add 'from these inventions' to replace 'and inventions' so as to create repetition in line 15. 'Repeatability' was replaced with 'replication' in line 19. It was proposed that line 21 be rewritten 'has already invented when he was young'. The two final lines were rewritten. Brodsky's last two lines in the third version are as follows:

He bends down and ties to his ankle a thread
to return himself from the land of the dead.

It was suggested that 'to return to' be changed to 'to lead him back'. Underneath, two new lines were proposed to replace the above:

He bends down, and having tied a lengthy thread to his ankle
so that not to get lost takes the first step towards the land of the dead.

Incidentally, Brodsky partially incorporated this change in his following version, which was faxed to the *NYRB* where Kjellberg worked at the time on 9 July 1993:

---

6. The first round of corrections by Kjellberg is in the second column in Table 3.9. Her deletions are shown in strikethrough font and her additions are underlined.

7. In Table 3.9, the second round of corrections by Kjellberg show her additions and suggestions in capital letters.

Table 3.9 Joseph Brodsky's Draft Translations and a Printed Version of 'Daedalus in Sicily' ('Dedal v Sitsilii'), including Ann Kjellberg's Corrections

Joseph Brodsky's first typed draft	Corrections and suggestions by Ann Kjellberg (underlined and the deleted words are crossed over)	Joseph Brodsky's second draft	Further corrections by Ann Kjellberg in bold and in brackets	Published version
All his life he was building / constructing something, inventing something.		All his life he was building something, inventing something.		All his life he was building something, inventing something.
Now an artificial cow for the Cretan queen,		Now an artificial cow for the Cretan queen,		Now, for a Cretan queen, an artificial heifer,
for cuckolding the king. Then the labyrinth –	to cuckold the old king / his boss, the king	to cuckold his boss, the king. Then the labyrinth –	to cuckold his boss, the king. Then the labyrinth – **NOW (TO PREVENT FOR . . . FOR)**	so as to cuckold the king. Then a labyrinth this time for
this for the very king himself, so the latter could hide from idle glances	this for the **very** king himself, so the latter could to hide from idle glances	for the king himself, to hide from idle glances		the king himself, to hide from bewildered glances
an unseemly / awkward offspring. Now a flying contraption (when the king finally realized who at court	infelicitous / inconvenient	an inconvenient offspring. Now a flying contraption (when the king finally realized who at court		an unbearable offspring. Or a flying contraption, when the king figured out in the end who it was at his court
was so busy supplying himself with work / busily rustling up commissions / trying so hard to supply himself with work)	drumming so busy / busily getting himself commissions	was trying so hard to drum up commissions)	**BUSY ALL DAY DRUMMING / WORKING**	who was keeping himself so busy with new commissions.
to save his head from the scimitar		to save his head from the scimitar		The son on that journey perished falling into the sea,

of the royal conclusions. A son has perished in flight from falling	A son had perished in flight from falling	of the royal conclusions. A son had perished in flight from BY falling	like Phaeton, who, they say, also spurned his father's
into the sea like Phaeton – who also at one point neglected his father's instructions. On the hot sand of Sicily there sits an extremely old man capable of moving			orders. Here, in Sicily, stiff on its scorching sun, sits a very old man, capable of transporting himself through the air, if robbed of other means of passage.
through air when he can't on the land or the waters.	through air when he can't on the land or the waters.		
All his life he was building something, inventing something.			All his life he was building something, inventing something.
All his life from these constructions / buildings and inventions	All his life from these his constructions / buildings and inventions	All his life from his THESE constructions [,] FROM THESE and inventions	All his life from those clever constructions, from those inventions,
he had to run. As though inventions	he had to flee.	he had to flee. As though inventions	he had to flee. As though the inventions
and constructions strive to get rid of their blueprints,	and constructions strive to get rid of their blueprints,	and constructions [strive to get rid of] SHUN their blueprints,	and constructions are anxious to rid themselves of their blueprints
childishly / like children ashamed of their parents, out of fear, presumably,	childishly ashamed of their parents, presumably,	presumably, ONE IMAGINES / IT WOULD SEEM	like children ashamed of their parents. Presumably, that's the fear
of repeatability. Waves are running onto the sand,	of replication. Waves are running onto the sand,		of replication. Waves are running onto the sand;
			behind shine the tusks of the local mountains.

(*Continued*)

Table 3.9 (*Continued*)

Brodsky's first typed draft	Corrections and suggestions by Kjellberg (underlined and the deleted words are crossed over)	Brodsky's second draft	Further corrections by Kjellberg in bold and in brackets	Published version
behind loom the blue teeth of the local mountains. He, however,	behind stand the blue teeth tusks / molars of the local mountains.	behind shine the tusks of the local mountains. He, however,		Yet he had already invented, when he was young, the seesaw,
already when he was young invented the seesaw,	had already (when he was young) invented the seesaw,	when young had already invented the seesaw,	HAS ALREADY INVENTED, WHEN HE WAS YOUNG,	using the strong resemblance between motion and stasis.
making use of the strong resemblance between stasis and motion.		making use of the strong resemblance between stasis and motion.		The old man bends down, ties to his brittle ankle –
He bends down and ties to his ankle the thread	He bends down and ties to his ankle the a thread	He bends down and ties to his ankle –	HE BENDS DOWN, AND HAVING TIED A LENGTHY THREAD TO HIS ANKLE SO THAT NOT TO GET LOST, TAKES A STEP/THE FIRST STEP TOWARDS THE LAND OF THE DEAD.	(so as not to get lost) a lengthy thread,
		to his ankle a thread,	A THREAD TO HIS ANKLE	
in order to return / to lead him back from the realm of the dead.	in order to return himself / to lead him back from the realm of the dead.	to return himself from the land of the dead.		straightens up with a grunt, and heads out for Hades

Source: JBP, S.II, Poetry, IP, 'Dedals Sitsilii', English translation by Brodsky, drafts and printed version, 1993, undated, Box 56, Folder 1068.

> The old man bends down, ties to his brittle ankle –
> so as not to get lost – a lengthy thread,
> straightens up with a grunt, and heads out for Hades.

This version became the final one but with one change – brackets were used instead of dashes, in the published version, which came out on 10 July 1993, the following day after Brodsky faxed it to the *NYRB* (JBP, S.II, Poetry, IP, 'Dedals Sitsilii', English translation by Brodsky, drafts and printed version, 1993, undated, Box 56, Folder 1068).

The poem 'Ischia in October' ('Iskiia v Oktiabre') was translated by the author and dated roughly 1993–5, the time when the poet felt confident to self-translate and write in English. The two drafts of the English version available in the archive reveal a different and more confident approach to the germination of this text. The first draft was typed in English either by Brodsky or by Kjellberg. At this stage, Kjellberg worked closely with Brodsky on his self-translations. Reflecting on this, Kjellberg says that she would not say so much that she was 'proposing changes':

> We were working on it together. I identified problems – with rhyme or grammar – and suggested some way to solve them, and then Joseph came up with his own solutions. My notes are kind of drafts or ideas that I sketched out as possible options. [. . .] At the time I was a junior editor. I had worked at *The New York Review of Books* and *FSG* and studied English poetry and had some experience, and I was working for him as a secretary and typist. I approached it as a helper and supporter rather than from a position of authority. [. . .]
>
> I considered myself an editor – mostly addressing the problems of grammar and usage – not a translator or a person with my own reputation or literary presence. Joseph was paying me at the time to type his correspondence and manuscripts and stuff and I helped him with this sort of thing. I was also a young person, thirty-one, in 1993. I was learning from Joseph and considered myself more of a pupil than an authority. But like a few other people who were helping him, we were aware of the criticism of *To Urania* and wanted to support his reputation and readership in English by helping him arrive at solutions that were true to the complexity of his thinking as well as English usage; there were no single right answers. [. . .] I loved it. Working with Joseph on his poems was its own kind of very deep experience of involvement in the creative process. To have a person working on that level – but also needing real help – it's a rare confluence. (Kjellberg 2020)

Kjellberg hugely valued her experience of working with Brodsky. Despite proposing changes to his drafts, correcting certain mistakes and later making some bolder suggestions, she would not see herself more than an editor and a secretary. Her contribution is evident in the draft of 'Ischia in October'. She made various minor corrections or suggestions mostly involving the use of definite and indefinite articles, especially in stanzas 4 and 5 (in square brackets). She also made a few lexical suggestions, such as in line 2 of stanza 2, proposing that 'prices are higher and longer bills' be replaced with 'the higher prices fill longer bills', and in the following line that 'all these changes' be amended to 'the many changes'. Kjellberg also suggested rephrasing two lines in stanza 2.

In this case, Brodsky accepted the proposed changes in line 2 and further amended the third line in the published version. There is a sheet with a few drafted stanzas typed up but not in the proper order of the poem; these stanzas are scattered on the page. It looks like, having received feedback on his draft, Brodsky was now fine-tuning them; he was now retranslating his own self-translation, which could be seen as another step towards writing in English. It is almost possible to see Brodsky's thought process: he was clearly dissatisfied with the first line of stanza 9 'Too few people' and kept looking for other options: 'The faces so rare to use pronouns' or '[The] faces are rare; and so are [the] pronouns.' Eventually, he dropped all these variants for 'Almost no people; so that pronouns [. . .]' (JBP, S.II, Poetry, IP, 'Iskiia v Oktiabre', English translation by Brodsky, drafts, proof and printed version, 1993–5, Box 59, Folder 1204).

The story of 'Axiom'

Despite gaining confidence in self-translation, Brodsky still needed advice and feedback not only from Kjellberg but also from others. The story of the rendering of the poem 'Axiom' shows how a self-translation may turn into a co-written translation as a result of the self-translator's turning for some advice. The Russian original of the poem does not have a title and is known as 'Mir sozdan byl iz smeshen'ia gryazi, vody, ognia'. In the archive, there are four copies of the poem and they are all typed. Brodsky self-translated the poem from Russian first and sent several copies of his text to collaborators for feedback.

The first copy was faxed to Jonathan Aaron on Tuesday, 30 May 1995 at 4.12 pm (Fax Number 3517856) and was returned on 1 June 1995 at 11.49 pm (MT Holyoke College LRC 413 5382635). Jonathan Aaron made the following corrections in the poem:

Line 2: 'encrusted into' is underlined by the reader – suggestion in the margin 'embedded in'
Line 4: 'won't' is encircled – suggestion in the margin 'wouldn't'
Line 6: 'tenor's for busted lungs' where 'tenor's for' is crossed out – suggestion in the margin 'singer's'
Line 7: 'came' is encircled – suggestion 'broke'
Line 8: 'the' added before 'birds'
Line 10: 'is too' is encircled and '?' put next to it; another question mark is at the end of the line

3. What Are Joseph Brodsky's Collaborative Self-Translations Made of? 123

Line 11: 'singing' is encircled – suggestion to replace it with 'music'; 'a screeching is underlined' is to be replaced with 'the howling', according to a suggestion in the margins

Line 13: 'In bellowing beaks' is encircled with a '?' next to it – the suggestion is hardly readable: 'cl's call'

Line 15: 'sounding' is taken into square brackets

Line 16: 'numerous stone-cold suns' is taken into round brackets; 'the' is added before 'addressless'

Line 17: 'Scram' is encircled; 'Amscray' is suggested instead

Line 18: ';' is added after 'lost!'

Line 19: 'the' is encircled to be replaced with 'an'

Line 21: 'But' is added at the start of the line; 'still' is crossed over to be replaced with 'when'

Line 22: 'hums' is encircled at the start of the line; a comma is added after 'huge'; at the end 'still hums' is added to the line

Line 24: the whole line is crossed out; on the margin '(image?)' is added; in 'depleated', 'a' is underlined as a misspelling.

Underneath the poem: Line 25: 'exhaustless' is written and then crossed out

Line 26: 'Is exhaustless, where deposits multiply' is added by the reader, then 'exhaustless' is crossed out and something like 'endless' added

There are several lines added in handwriting underneath:

'There, in its bowels, looms ... wrinkle-spinning wheel which runs'

'On raw material whose supply won't be depleted as long as deposits still multiply' (this line is underlined)

'depletes at the rate of deposits'

The second copy of the first draft translation by Brodsky was also sent for feedback and came back with fewer corrections by somebody else:

Line 4: 'won't' is encircled and 'wouldn't' is suggested; 'is' is encircled and 'was' is suggested

Lines 6–7: against the two lines in the margins 'present intrudes' is added underneath 'was' – it is not entirely clear where 'present intrudes' should be added

Line 10: the whole line is encircled; there is a remark next to it: 'seems labored'

Line 13: two last words at the end of the line are encircled: 'none, see'

The third copy returned with only a couple of corrections:

Line 4: 'won't' is crossed out and replaced with 'wouldn't' in the margins

Last line: 'a' is crossed out in 'depleated'

Having reflected on all the suggestions and corrections, Brodsky finalized the translation. His revised 1990 copy had the following changes incorporated:

Line 2: 'embedded in' accepted (see copy 1)

Line 4: 'you'd never presume' (see all corrections in all copies)
Line 6: 'the tenor's for busted lungs' is left as was originally written by the author
Line 7: 'broke into' is accepted (see copy 1)
Line 9: 'the' is added as suggested in copy 1
Line 10: the whole line is rewritten after being questioned by the reader in copy 1: 'is' is taken out at the beginning; 'astray' is incorporated into the line, as suggested by the reader in copy 1
Line 13: 'bellowing' is taken out as suggested in copy 1 and is replaced with 'shrieking'
Line 15: 'sounding' is taken out as suggested in copy 1; 'either' is added instead
Line 16 is rewritten as suggested in copy 1 'addressless stone-cold suns' has replaced 'numerous stone-cold suns'
Line 17: 'Amscray' is accepted as suggested in copy 1
Line 18: a comma is added instead of ';' which was suggested in copy 1
Line 19: 'the excess' is taken out and replaced with 'a surfeit' – the article was suggested in copy 1
Lines 21–24: partially rewritten following the suggestions made in copy 1: 'still' is replaced with 'looms', and, not entirely as suggested, 'still' is taken out. Instead of the suggested 'still hums' at the end of line 22, 'its roots' is added
In addition, Brodsky rewrote the last two lines:

'Plugged into a raw material whose supply
We, the deposits, eagerly multiply.'

As Brodsky incorporated most of the changes proposed by Aaron, he added his name as a co-author. Moreover, he was named as the main translator. The translation by Aaron with the author first appeared in *Queen's Quarterly* (Canada) (102:2) in the summer of 1995.

Writing in English

'Anthem' was written by Brodsky in 1995. In the archive, we find a draft of this poem written in English with some pencil marks by Kjellberg who was Brodsky's primary English-language editor at the time. After Brodsky had revised his draft based on Kjellberg's suggestions,[8] he sent it to an unidentified person for further feedback. There is a faxed copy with marks and comments in the margins, containing a few corrections and suggestions in the archive[9] (GEN, S.II, Poetry, IP, 'Anthem', drafts and printed version, Box 55, Folders

---

8. In Table 3.10, Kjellberg's deletions are in strikethrough font and her suggestions are in capital letters in column 2.

9. In Table 3.10, the second, unidentified reader's suggestions are in regular font in column 4.

Table 3.10 Poem 'Anthem': Joseph Brodsky's Drafts in English, Including Corrections by Ann Kjellberg and an Unidentified Reader

Stanza	Joseph Brodsky's first draft	Ann Kjellberg's corrections in capital letters	Joseph Brodsky's second draft	Second reader's corrections	First published in *Queen's Quarterly* (Canada), 102:2, summer, 1995
2	Of all prisons The Four Seasons has a better diet that foils a riot.	has THE BEST diet FOR SQUELCHING a riot.	Of all prisons The Four Seasons has the best diet for squelching riot.	*'Squelching' - is this the best verb?	Of all prisons The Four Seasons has the best diet and welcomes riot.
6	Climate's permanence is caused by prevalence of nothingness in its texture, and atmospheric pressure.	THE climate's permanence is caused by THE prevalence	The climate's permanence is caused by the prevalence	A(?) climate's . . .	A climate's permanence is caused by the prevalence of nothingness in its texture, and atmospheric pressure.
8	Using the mercury more accurate than the memory which also is mortal climate is moral.	SINCE THE ACCURACY OF MERCURY BEATS THAT OF MEMORY	Since the accuracy of mercury beats that of memory (which is also mortal) the climate is moral.	a(?) climate . . .	Since the accuracy of mercury beats that of memory (which is also mortal), climate is moral.
9	Thus, when it exhibits its bad habits, it blames not the parents but the ocean currents.	it blames not the parents but the ocean currents.	Thus, when it exhibits its bad habits, it blames not parents but ocean currents.	Thus, When it exhibits	When it exhibits its bad habits, it blames not parents but ocean currents.
10	Or if charged with tedium and meaninglessness of its idiom, it seeks no legal help but grows local.	Or if charged with THE tedium it WON'T SEEK legal help but GO local.	Or if charged with the tedium and meaninglessness of its idiom, it won't seek legal help but go local.	help but goes local.	Or charged with the tedium and meaninglessness of its idiom, it won't seek legal aid and goes local.

Table 3.10 (Continued)

Stanza	Joseph Brodsky's first draft	Ann Kjellberg's corrections in capital letters	Joseph Brodsky's second draft	Second reader's corrections	First published in *Queen's Quarterly* (Canada), 102:2, summer, 1995
11	Keen on history, it also enjoys the mystery of the Hereafter being their author.	THOUGH keen on history, it's VERSED IN the mystery BUT WON'T NAME THE author	Though keen on history it's versed in the mystery of the Hereafter but won't name the author.	Also, keen on history but won't name And looks like their [refers to what?] author.	Keen on history it's also well versed in the mystery of the hereafter and looks like their author.
13	Likewise, the main feature I share with the future mutants is curious shapes of the cumulus.	mutants is THE curious	Likewise, the main feature I share with the future mutants is curious shapes of the cumulus.	... the future's mutants ... (?)	Likewise, the main features I share with the future's mutants are those curious shapes of cumulus.
14	Praised be the entity incapable of enmity and equally finicky when it comes to affinity.		Praised be the entity incapable of enmity and equally finicky when it comes to affinity.		Praised be the entity incapable of enmity and likewise finicky when it comes to affinity.
15	Yet if one aspect of this very abstract thing is its gratitude for finding a latitude.	for finding a latitudes.	Yet if one aspect of this very abstract thing is its gratitude for finding latitude.	of this very highly abstract	Yet if one aspect of this highly abstract thing is its gratitude for finding latitude,
15	then a rational anthem sung by an atom to the rest of the matter should make both feel better.	to the rest of the matter should PLEASE THE LATTER.	then a rational anthem sung by an atom to the rest of the matter should please the latter.		then a rational anthem sung by one atom to the rest of matter should please the latter.

*The second reader adds at the bottom: 'I think there may be a problem of sense in stanza 14: "equally finicky" is syntactically [not clear] to mean the same thing as "incapable of enmity". But I don't get how the two phrases actually relate to or connote with each other.'

Source: JBB, S.II, Poetry, IP, 'Anthem', drafts and printed version, Box 55, Folders 1003 and 1004.

3. What Are Joseph Brodsky's Collaborative Self-Translations Made of? 127

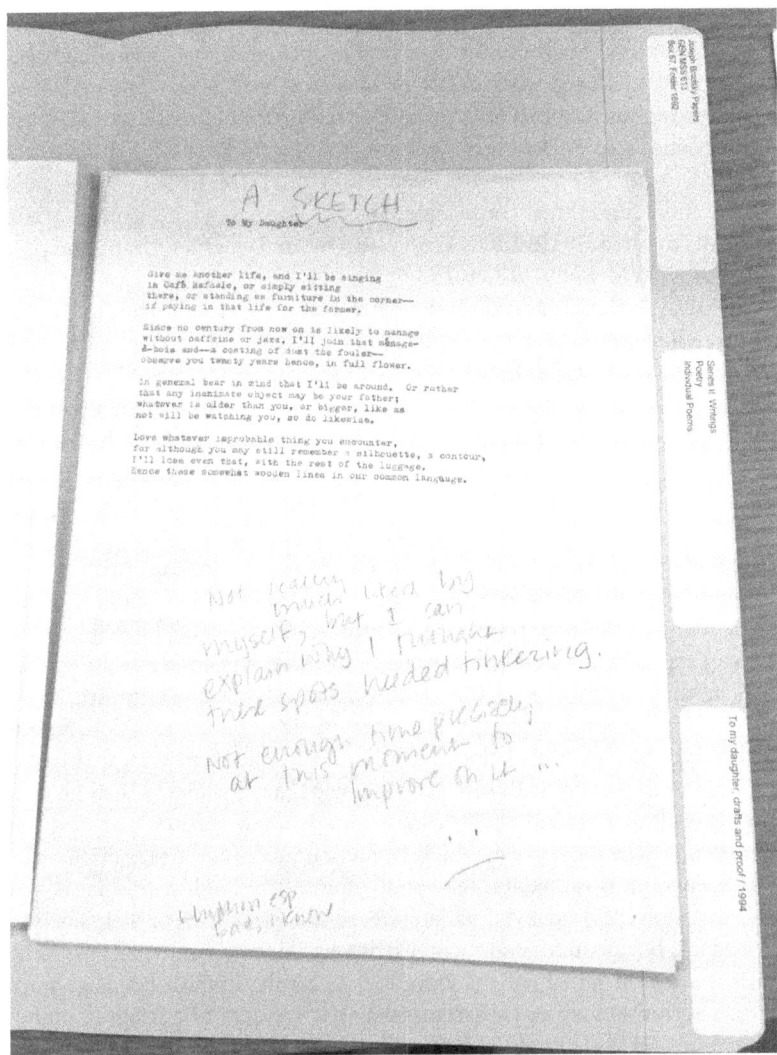

Picture 3.5 'To My Daughter', a draft poem written in English by Brodsky.

1003, 1004). In Table 3.10 I quote only the stanzas that have been changed as a result of this editing process.

Interestingly, the second reader questioned a few suggestions by Kjellberg which had been incorporated into the second draft: 'squelching' in stanza 2, the choice of the definite article 'the' before 'climate' in stanzas 6 and 8, the addition of 'Thus' at the beginning of stanza 9, 'Though' added by Kjellberg at the beginning of stanza 11, the proposed ending of stanza 11 'but won't name' which was changed by the second reader to 'And looks like their author'. Fewer corrections were proposed by the second reader to change Brodsky's phrasing, but it is likely this is because the awkward or incorrect parts had already been identified by Kjellberg whose choices may not have been approved by the second reader but they certainly pointed to the problematic parts of the poem.

The poem 'To My Daughter' was also written by Brodsky in English and published in *The Times Literary Supplement* on 2 December 1994.[10] In the archive, there are three consecutive drafts, one of which contains some comments by a reader (JBP, S.II, Poetry, IP, 'To My Daughter', drafts and proof, 1994, Box 67 Folder 1692) (Picture 3.5).

One of the drafts contains the first two complete typed quatrains and the first three lines of the third quatrain, also typed up. The last line of the third quatrain and the last quatrain are drafted by hand by the poet. The following draft has all four stanzas typed up with some corrections and suggestions by Kjellberg in red. Some corrections are stylistic or grammatical but there are also some suggestions for rhyming words: instead of Brodsky's rhyming 'manage' with 'damage', she added some further rhyming words: 'marriage', 'menage-/a-bois' and 'melange'. Then, there is a typed-up draft which incorporated some of Kjellberg's suggestions including the one to rhyme 'manage' with 'menage – / a-bois' and the grammatical corrections. This draft has another reader's feedback in pencil, and it is not very positive: 'Not really much liked by myself but I can explain why these spots needed tinkering. Not enough time precisely at this moment to improve on it . . . [this is followed by a small drawing of a sad face emoji].' The word 'tinkering' is characteristic of the kind of collaboration that Brodsky had with his helpers, mostly in the role of editors, at this stage. He would draft a poem with some editing help from Kjellberg. Then he would send his draft to a second reader who would do some further 'tinkering' with the text, after which the poem would be revised by the author for publication.

As seen from this chapter, the production of the English translations and self-translations of Brodsky's Russian poems underwent several stages between the mid-1970s and mid-1990s but there was one constant quality about it, which was that it remained collaborative. As a rule, English-language poems were the retranslations and self-retranslations produced as a result of multiple authorship and collaboration between the poet, his interlinear and poetic translators as well as editors and publishers. Brodsky curated his English-language voice in the process of interactions with all his helpers, by borrowing from their versions, by reflecting on their and his own choices, by asking for feedback on his self-translations. In Chapter 2, I proposed three main stages in Brodsky's bilingual writing, which are summarized in Figures 2.1–2.3. In this chapter, a close comparison of different English versions of the same Russian original shows that there are further differences in the modes of collaborative

---

10. The date given in the Brodsky Archive (written by hand) is wrong; the correct date is given in *Collected Poems*: 2 December 1994 (*TLS*, 4783: 4).

translation. Most of Brodsky's translation work was done in the form of consecutive collaboration and retranslation, that is, in stages. For instance, poems were first rendered by an interlinear translator who may have worked in collaboration with the author; then they were retranslated by a poetic translator, checked by the author a few times in the process, then read and corrected by an editor and finally proofread by a publisher. The number of times that a translation might be changed and/or corrected in the process could vary a lot, depending on various factors. Brodsky never considered any translation an end product. He looked at them as work in progress. Some translations changed even after the first publication and appeared with corrections in consecutive publications. As the author of the originals, Brodsky had the author's privilege to shape the final translation as he thought appropriate, usually based on his mimetic method of poetic translation but not exclusively.

Translators' contribution to Brodsky's texts may be overt or covert depending on what they were contracted to do. Interlinear translators' contribution was covert or implicit because they were not fully acknowledged as co-translators. Poetic translators' contribution was more likely to be overt, although it also depended on various factors, such as the number of translators involved in the production of the published translation and the number of times the text has been changed and whether it was done in consultation with translators or not. In some cases, translators' actual input into a translation (especially that of interlinear translators) was significant but not fully acknowledged. Editors' contribution to the production of Brodsky's English-language texts was also considerable at times but was not acknowledged as co-authorship. Overall, there has not always been consistency in the way in which Brodsky's collaborators were acknowledged partly because his own contribution to finalized English versions changed a lot throughout the 1970–90s.

Chapter 4

'MICROHISTORIES' OF JOSEPH BRODSKY'S TRANSLATORS

While the previous three chapters primarily focused on Brodsky as a self-translator and his translation practices, this chapter shifts attention from the poet to his translators, or from the centre to the periphery of Brodsky's translation networks. The purpose of this is threefold: to contribute to a history of poetic translation from Russian to English in the second part of the twentieth century, to reveal the role played by individual translators in the poet's networks and to create the 'microhistories' of the translators, some of whom have been little known and hardly acknowledged. The comparative analysis of translation drafts by different translators in Chapter 3 has already revealed how Brodsky's collaborative self-translation practices changed throughout his English-language career. In this chapter, I focus on the people who are behind those multiple translation drafts by considering their correspondence with Brodsky, interviews, notes in the margins, handwritten corrections and other archival documents. These archival papers and other documents help us understand translators' motivation and the cognitive process of collaboration with Brodsky. The chapter is underpinned by Jeremy Munday's concept of translators' 'microhistories' (Munday 2014). The stories of translators are usually difficult to trace, as Munday puts it: 'When it comes to the study of translation, until recently exclusion seems to have been the norm. Traces of the translator are generally hard to find in many collections and require some excavation' (Munday 2014). This is particularly true in relation to interlinear translators whose background work on the rendering and analysis of the ST was considered as something unfinished (*polufabrikat*), a text that needed further work on poetic form. This chapter is structured to reveal a 'history from below', to use Jim Sharpe's seminal notion, which Munday draws on in his understanding of 'microhistories' (Sharpe 1991: 27). This is why this chapter begins with the stories of 'ordinary' interlinear translators and then moves on to others. This approach allows the reconstruction of the translators' contribution to Brodsky's poetry in English. The facts that we learn from translators' correspondence and other relevant documents tell us about their interaction with the poet, publishers and each other. They also contribute to larger narratives about the practices of collaborative translation and self-translation, the role of institutions and individuals played in the production of poetry in translation.

The chapter is designed like a mosaic of pieces of different size. The length of each subsection depends on how much information I have extracted from archival documents and published sources about each translator. When it was possible I contacted either translators or their heirs to verify the accounts given in this chapter. I am grateful to Jonathan Aaron, Laura Anderson (James Rice's widow), Paul Graves, Chris Hanak (G. L. Kline's daughter), Helen Hecht (Anthony Hecht's widow), Mark Hutcheson, Stephanie Viereck Gibbs Kamath (Pieter Viereck's granddaughter), Juliet McKane (Richard McKane's daughter), Valentina Polukhina (Daniel Weissbort's widow), Sam Ramer, Harry Thomas, Ben Weissbort (Daniel Weissbort's son) and Stephen White for reading through the relevant parts of the chapter, sending me their valuable feedback and permissions to use unpublished correspondence of Brodsky's translators. Some of their stories about working with Brodsky have been added to the chapter with their permission. By no means can I cover all Brodsky's translators and their stories. For example, I have not been able to find enough information about Anne Frydman, an interlinear translator, who was involved in the work on *A Part of Speech*. I discuss the microhistories of two other interlinear translators, Masha Vorobiov and Stephen White, who also contributed to *A Part of Speech* and whose names have not been acknowledged, on a par with poetic translators in published volumes by Brodsky. It was not a malicious attempt to diminish their significance but practice at the time. In the USSR, interlinear trots were an established practice. As discussed by Witt (2011), this remains an under researched area. Revealing the work interlinear translators have put into their literal renderings of Brodsky's Russian poems accompanied by detailed notes on versification patterns and detailed poetic analyses is helpful not only for understanding their contribution to the translation process but also potentially for teaching poetry because they are excellent examples of how to analyse the metre, rhyme schemes and the poem's structure and lexis. My 'history from below' includes not only commissioned translators but also the translators who became involved in Brodsky's collaborative translation networks in other ways, either by other translators' or by the author's invitations, for example. James Rice's account of his interactions with Brodsky, although he was not contracted by FSG to produce interlinear versions in English, is informative, as it adds to the complexity of Brodsky's translation networks.

After discussing the stories of interlinear translators, the chapter turns to Brodsky's poetic translators including Jonathan Aaron, Paul Graves, Anthony Hecht, G. L. Kline, David McDuff, Richard McKane, Howard Moss, Alan Myers, Mark Strand, Harry Thomas, Peter Viereck, Derek Walcott, Daniel Weissbort and Richard Wilbur. These translators are discussed because I have found relevant material about their collaboration with the poet. Their accounts confirm my argument that the English versions of his poems were produced in collaboration with the poet and sometimes with other translators and editors.

Many poetic translators have had at least minor tensions or disagreements with Brodsky about some changes that he proposed. In addition to commissioned translators, Brodsky's poems were rendered by a few enthusiasts who attempted some translations without the poet's permission. As a rule, Brodsky rejected their versions but thanked them for their effort. It is worth saying that all the above-mentioned translators admired his work in Russian whether they could access it in the original language or in prior interlinear renderings. For most of them, translating Brodsky was a privilege, a challenge and a lesson not only in Russian prosody but in patience.

Masha Vorobiov

Masha Vorobiov, a Russian émigré and a tutor of the Russian language and literature at the Vassar Liberal Arts College, was commissioned by FSG to conduct some interlinear translations for the book *A Part of Speech*, as described in Chapter 2. In the end, Vorobiov was paid $128 for having translated 128 lines (JBP, S.II, Poetry, 'A Part of Speech', New York: FSG). However, this rather small remuneration does not reflect the range and breadth of work that Vorobiov has done for Brodsky. Vorobiov was so much more than an interlinear translator for Brodsky. She was his close friend and a neighbour in New York, where she lived above his rented apartment at 44, Morton Street. Brodsky moved there in 1974. Kjellberg describes her as a very close friend of the poet, adding that they lived almost as a family, 'in a way replacing Joseph's family life in communal flat (*kommunalka*) back in Russia (Kjellberg 2020). Vorobiov was born into the family of a Russian professor of history of architecture in Vilnius, the capital of Lithuania. She came to the United States with her family after the war when she was still young. Vorobiov was described by Lev Losev as Brodsky's caring sister (Losev 2006).

In her first letter to Brodsky after his arrival in the United States, on 20 August 1972, she warmly recalled her first meeting with him, which had taken place at Olga Borisovna Eikhenbaum's place in Leningrad in 1967 (JBP, S.I, GC, Vorobiov, Masha, Incoming, 1972–93, undated, Box 16 Folder 424). She recollected how Brodsky had recited his poems, sung songs, how they had talked about Robert Frost and Polish poetry, and how Brodsky had recommended them to read the Russian poet Yevgeny Baratynsky (1800–44). On that occasion Brodsky mentioned that he would be interested in becoming a poet-in-residence somewhere in the West. Upon his arrival in America, she welcomed him to New York, invited him to New York University and offered him a place to stay at her house in Greenwich Village. Once Brodsky rented his own apartment underneath hers, they became even better friends. As Brodsky's visitors recall, sometimes they would pop in Vorobiov's either for a chat or to have dinner together. On one occasion, Brodsky's friend and poet Aleksandr Kushner was treated to a delicious dinner at Vorobiov's (Vail' 1998: 181).

Her letters make clear that Brodsky was the heart and soul of parties and gatherings in Morton Street. On 13 January 1974, she wrote how much they had missed Brodsky during his travels:

> It has got quiet without you in New York but there are many 'Brodsky places', a pile of music cassettes and records making noise in four languages – in the air (or in our ears) there are bits of good poems and an echo of Joseph's Broar (groan + roar), and many other things that are difficult to list. I miss midnight telephone calls. Iosif, I understand that you don't particularly love other people's sofas but just in case if you have a change of heart please be informed that the sofa in my lounge is always yours if need be.[1] (JBP S.I, GC, Vorobiov, Masha, Incoming, 1972–93, undated, Box 16 Folder 424)

Vorobiov repeatedly expressed her admiration of Brodsky's poems, sent him updates on his friends' life in New York during his many travels, reported on his bank statements that came by post in his absence. She addressed her letters to 'Darling Iosif' but always used the formal 'Vy' to express her deep respect and friendly distance. Also, she often used 'we' when she wrote to Brodsky and signed letters as Marya or Masha and 'your NY contingent', as in the letter above from 13 January 1974. Her letters to Brodsky combined brief reports on home administration and warm personal touches, such as in the undated letter quoted below:

> It is indescribably sad without you here, especially as we keep finding things that remind us of you – a piece of string with a paper attached at the end of it for Lis'ka [Vorobiov's cat], a Chinese doggy-bag in the fridge, a jar from Parker Super Quink Ink, an autumnal flower, Barry and Lidia's portraits, a Nescafe tin, etc., etc. Not speaking of the wonderful, non-biting blanket which illuminates the whole room. All this lived-in atmosphere – only the lodger is missing and the lodger is where he should not be. At least, that's how it looks from here.[2] (JBP, S.I, GC, Vorobiov, Masha, Incoming, 1972–93, undated, Box 16 Folder 424)

1. Here translation of the following is mine: 'А в Нью-Йорке без Вас все как-то притихло. Но осталось много "бродских мест", – кипа пленок и пластинок, производящих звуки на четырех языках, – в воздухе (или в ушах) обрывки хороших стихов да эхо of Joseph's Броar (те groan + roar), да еще много чего, что трудно перечислить. И я скучаю по полуночным телефонным звонкам.'
'Иосиф, я понимаю, что Вы не любитель чужих диванов, но все же, на случай, что you have a change of heart, Вы знаете, что диван в моей гостиной всегда готов быть Вашим.'

2. Here translation into English of the following is mine: 'Непередаваемо грустно, что Вас здесь нет, тем более, что все время находим что-нибудь, что про Вас

Brodsky shared personal details of his life with Vorobiov including his health problems. In his long undated letter to Masha (1976?), Brodsky described how, because of his worsening heart problem, he had ended up at a sanatorium in Italy. His letters were intimate, as one might write to a very close friend or a family member. While travelling in the UK, Brodsky sent Vorobiov a couple of letters from England where he felt bored and homesick, desperately wishing to be back in New York (JBP, S.I, GC, Vorobiov, Masha, Outgoing, 1974–94, undated, Box 16, Folder 428). At times, he asked her to deal with some urgent or important issues while he was away, such as an invitation for his parents to come to the United States. Brodsky and Vorobiov travelled together; for example, Brodsky took her to Rome and Venice in winter 1984. After his death, she took part in the founding of the Joseph Brodsky Fellowship Fund.[3]

So, working on Brodsky's interlinears was only an extension of Vorobiov's multifaceted relationship with the poet. As noted in Chapter 3, her rendering of '1972' has scrupulous notes, explaining the meanings of certain Russian words and realities, connotations, intertextual references, allusions and puns (see Picture 4.1).

In her notes on interlinear translations, Vorobiov commented on internal rhymes, rhythm and rhyme patterns. Where appropriate she noted the author's suggestion for the genre to be used in translation, such as 'English ballad crossed with spiritual'. Vorobiov provided lots of nuanced information about the original Russian text, some of which had been added after consulting Brodsky directly. For example, in note 2 on page 4, Vorobiov discussed the two Russian words meaning 'age': *vozrast* (literally meaning one's age) and *starenie* (ageing), explaining that they had different roots in Russian. The first word is related to 'growth', the second to one 'ageing' in the sense of 'growing old'. She also added a note that Brodsky suggested using 'geronteon' [*sic*] in English, which was the title of a T. S. Eliot poem. This suggestion shows that Vorobiov was working in close collaboration with Brodsky himself. Also, there is a typo in the title of T. S. Eliot's poem, which should read 'Gerontion' (1920). This typo and other minor errors in English indicate that Vorobiov's English was still slightly affected by her Russian perhaps.

When Vorobiov provided a literary reference to a well-known Russian poem, such as Pushkin's 'Greetings, Young and Unfamiliar Tribe' (1835) in note 4, stanza 4, she also gave the details of the recommended translation of

---

напоминает – то веревочка с бумажкой для Лиськи, то Chinese doggie-bag в холодильнике, то баночка из-под Parker Super Quink Ink, то осенний цветок на столе, то Барри-Лидины портреты, то банка с Nescafe и т.д., и т.д. Не говоря уже о сказочном, не-кусающемся одеяле, от которого светится вся комната. И весь этот обжитой порядок, – только жильца нет, а жилец там, где ему совсем не место. At least, that's how it looks from here.'

3. http://www.josephbrodsky.org/about

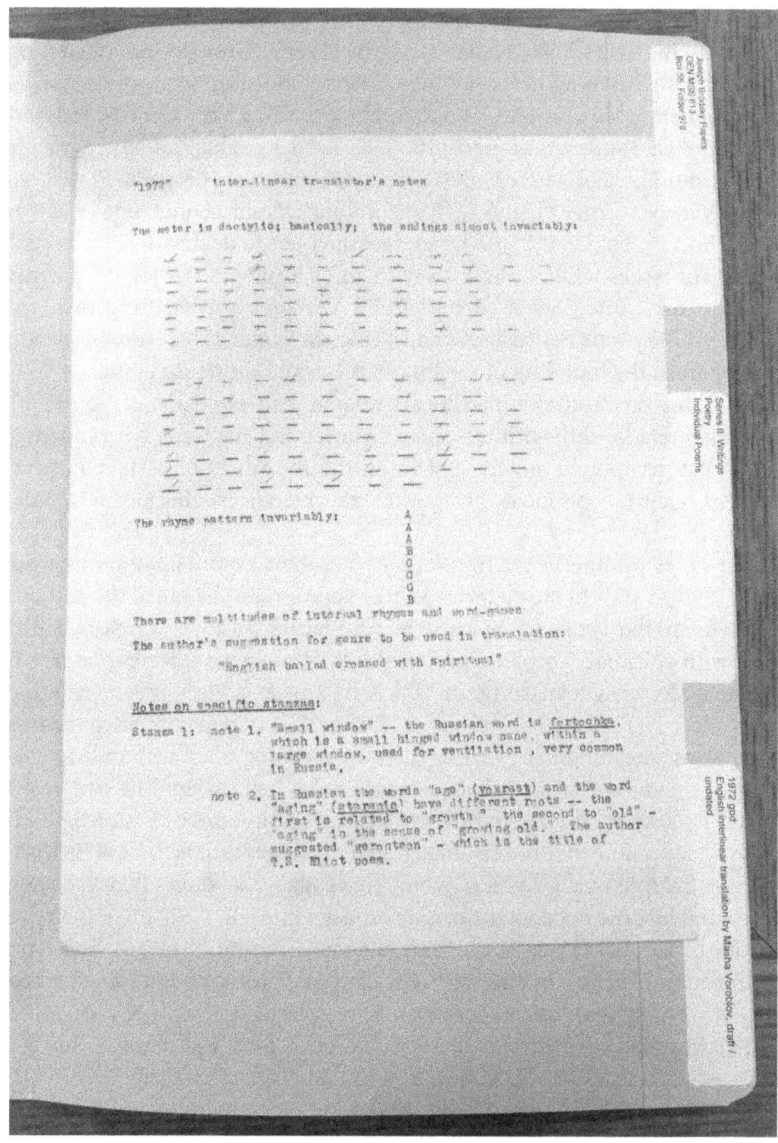

Picture 4.1 Interlinear translation of '1972' and translator's notes by Masha Vorobyov.

the Pushkin poem into English. She explained all Russian set phrases and expressions, which were used to create puns in the original, such as in note 8 to stanza 9: 'Pun is based on two expressions: *Val'at' duraka* to play the fool, literally – to roll the fool around; *durak pod kozhei* – fool under the skin – male sex organ.' In addition, she detailed historical references, such as one to Prince Igor, a legendary Russian prince and his speech in line 6, stanza 11 (JBP, S.II, Poetry; IP; 1972 god; English interlinear translation by Masha Vorobiov, draft, undated, Box 55, Folder 978). Reflecting on Vorobiov's interlinears and notes, Kjellberg suggests that Brodsky and Vorobiov were trying to set a standard of what sort of information should be included in the interlinears (Kjellberg 2020).

Unlike the translation of '1972', Vorobiov's interlinear translation of 'Lagoon' ('Laguna') does not have detailed notes on each stanza, but it has only a few notes, explaining idioms and the use of foreign words. Perhaps, this is because she was not originally commissioned to do this interlinear rendering. According to the table produced by FSG (see Chapter 2), the two poems 'Lagoon' and 'Anno Domini' were not scheduled to be sent to interlinear translators because they had been translated by Weissbort. 'Lagoon' was to be published in *Vestnik* and 'Anno Domini' came out in *The Iowa Review*. In the end, 'Anno Domini' was published in Weissbort's translation and 'Lagoon' came out in Hecht's translation. Vorobiov's interlinear rendering must have been used by Hecht for his poetic version.

Vorobiov's first translation of the fourteen stanzas of the poem 'Lagoon' was handwritten; there were one or two stanzas on each page. Some pages were subsequently written on in pencil. When she came across an idiom she gave both the translation of literal and figurative meaning. For example, Vorobiov translated the idiom 'po gorbu ego plachet' as 'the aspen in the forests weeps for his burden', while providing a literal meaning in the footnote: 'weeps for his humpback'. She pointed out that Brodsky had used the English word 'fish' in Russian transliteration in the original (JBP, S.II, Poetry, IP, Laguna, English translation by Masha Vorobiov, drafts, undated, Box 60, Folder 1255). Vorobiov's knowledge of the original text is so detailed and intimate that it is certain that she worked in close collaboration with the poet.

Later, in the 1980s, Vorobiov continued to help with interlinear renderings, at least one of which ('Eclogue IV: Winter') was used by the poet himself when he self-translated the poem, as discussed in Chapter 3. Brodsky appreciated her help and friendship. In 1995, he dedicated a poem to Vorobiov, whose surname originated from 'vorobei' meaning 'sparrow' in Russian. The poem was written in English on her birthday, dated 8 February 1995 (Box 59 Folder 1170):

Happy birthday, dear Sparrow!
Chirp and sing and never fret!
Dodge a sling and dodge an arrow
(save it points at 'toilet')

Soar above the Hudson's trickle,
see Tackonec, see Mass Pike,
now that this Republic's eagle
finds in you its lookalike.

Stephen White

In his brief email correspondence with me dated 10 March 2020, Stephen White refers to his relationship with Brodsky as 'uplifting and felicitous'. He recalls that they both came to the University of Michigan at the same time: White began his studies as a graduate student, and Brodsky started to work as a professor and a poet-in-residence. In 1977, White completed his PhD and got his first job teaching Russian courses and an introductory course in linguistics, as he wrote to Brodsky in his letter from Mount Vernon in Iowa, dated 15 September 1977 (JBP, S.I, GC, White, Annamarie and Stephen, 1977–87, Box17, Folder 442). White says that he sat in on every class Brodsky offered, warmly adding that Brodsky's 'kindness and strong engagement in all his students has been a bright beacon' to him all his life. White admits that he is eternally thankful that his 'path crossed with his' (White 2020).

In 1976, Stephen White was still a graduate student of Russian when he was commissioned to produce interlinear translations of twenty-four poems for Brodsky's *A Part of Speech* book. He translated more than any other interlinear translator commissioned for *A Part of Speech* by FSG: 866 lines (JBP, S.II, Poetry, A Part of Speech (New York: FSG) 'List of Translators 1979', Box 47, Folder 849). He usually typed his interlinears and then corrected them by hand, with additional comments on some lexical, syntactic and poetic aspects of Russian originals. At the end of each line, White noted the rhyme pattern by hand: for example, 'a,b,a,b,c,d,c,d,e,f,e,f' (see examples of his translations in Chapter 3). He also underlined all the rhymed words by hand. His word-for-word translation of the sequence 'A Part of Speech' was typed in the top half of the page, and in the bottom half he provided the ST's rhythm pattern, or the metre. In footnotes, he explained the use of some lexical units, the specificity of Russian syntax, literary references, such as those to 'Song of Igor's Regiment' and the nineteenth-century Russian folk song 'I've traveled the whole universe over', the usage of rare words and phrases, such as the adjective 'kaisatski' (see Picture 3.1), pointing to intertextual reference to Derzhavin's poem 'Ode to Felitsa' (JBP, S.II, Poetry, IP, Chast' reach, English translation by Stephen White, undated, Box 56 Folder 1058). White explained Brodsky's neologisms, such as 'tikhotvorenie', a silent poem, and the multiple readings of the words, such as 'nemoe' ('mute' and 'not mine' if separated into two words 'ne' and 'moe'), and 'prelomit' ('to break' and 'to break bread'). He expanded on the use of puns and came up with some witty equivalents in some cases. He commented on relevant Russian idioms, such as 'Water does not flow under a lying stone'. Just like Vorobiov and Frydman, White was aware of the importance of poetic form to Brodsky. He underlined the Russian rhyming words in his interlinear translations, including some meaningful rhymes in the middle of the line. As shown in Chapter 3, White's interlinear translations of the poems in 'A Part of Speech' were influential on final poetic versions.

Among other interlinear renderings, White produced an annotated translation of the long 'Cape Cod Lullaby' poem, accompanied by his notes on the poem's rhyme scheme. This version was sent to Anthony Hecht who found it lacking for his poetic rendering and asked his friend and colleague James Rice to make one more interlinear translation, which Rice did in 1977 (see later in this chapter). Hecht's poetic rendering of 'Cape Cod Lullaby' drew on both interlinear translations by White and Rice, claiming both of them were not entirely adequate (see the section on Hecht).

Comparing the two brief microhistories of Vorobiov and White is informative. As a native English speaker and a young scholar at the time, White was gaining valuable experience of translating Russian poetry and making a small amount of money. He was young, deferential, cooperative and hard-working. These characteristics made him similar to Nabokov's young male translators into English (see Chapter 2 and reference to Anokhina 2017). Vorobiov, on the other hand, was a native Russian female translator who was Brodsky's friend and an admirer of his poetry. She was happy to help not only with interlinear translations but also with administrative support as well as being a supportive friend, in general. Like White, she was cooperative, loyal and accommodating.

James Rice and some unidentified translator

James Rice was a professor of Russian literature at the University of Oregon. Rice's main research interests focused on Fyodor Dostoevsky's literary legacy (Rice 1985, 2011). Brodsky met Rice in 1976 when he was visiting the University of Oregon in Eugene, Oregon. Rice recollected warmly that Brodsky had generously given ten talks in a short time. After that, Brodsky and Rice became friends and exchanged a few cards, letters and telephone calls. Rice described their relationship as 'unofficial' and 'fun', with 'no particular academic or serious purpose' (Rice 1998: 19). Rice's widow Laura Anderson notes in her correspondence with Rulyova that Rice admired Brodsky greatly and was delighted to be associated with him (Anderson 2020). But Brodsky was also responsive to Rice's ideas. At his suggestion, Brodsky reread Pushkin's 'A Story of Goryukhino Village' and, in his letter to Rice, he made some insightful observations about the influence of technology on writing, saying that Pushkin's sentences and his writing style were the result of his writing with a feather quill.[4] He also remarked on how sentences had become longer and syntax got more complex in Dostoevsky's writing, arguably, because he had started to dictate his work instead of writing with a pen (Brodsky 1998: 22–3).

---

4. See Berlina's comments on the choice between a quill and a pen in the translation of 'December in Florence' in Chapter 3.

The next change to writing style occurred when typewriters were invented, according to Brodsky. He also noted the difference between the poet and the prose writer, emphasizing that poetic style was more compressed compared to prose. As a Dostoevsky scholar primarily, Rice approached his interlinear translation of Brodsky's poetry with the awareness of this difference.

Unlike Vorobiov and White, Rice was not commissioned by FSG to make interlinear translations of any poems for *A Part of Speech* but approached by Hecht, as discussed earlier. Hecht himself chose the poem 'Cape Cod Lullaby' for rendering into English because poets-translators were given the privilege to pick their favourite poems by Brodsky. Hecht did not speak Russian, so he needed an interlinear translation to work with. Rice's approach to interlinear translation was academic and self-consciously presented as a 'first-stage translation', like a research project, which led to the final stage of the work.

In the translator's note, sent along with his first-stage translation, Rice explained the poem's rhythmic organization and noted the importance of rhyming words and references:

Joseph Brodsky, 'Cape Cod Lullaby' (Kolybel'naia Treskovogo mysa); Xmas(Russian text: Kontinent, No. 7): First-stage translation by J. L. Rice

TRANSLATOR'S NOTE: The basic rhythmic organisation of this poem consists in a long verse line – from six to four essential stresses, syllabically variable – divided by caesura into hemstitches. In almost every strophe the final line truncates this pattern. With only two or, more often, three stresses. In a few instances, where the main body of a given strophe consists of exceptionally short lines (e.g., VI, 1, with lines of four or three stresses), the final line remains distinctly briefer by virtue of syllable count. The only exceptions to this prevailing pattern are stanzas III, 1 and III, 2. In the poet's manner of declaiming, caesura and rhyme are always carefully articulated with pauses, frequently involving a certain tension against syntax; syntactic suspensions are especially felt in enjambments, where rhyme articulation and pause abruptly counter the logical flow across lines.

The following first-stage translation strives to keep the logical integrity of verse lines, and to remain literally faithful to the original, although throughout reference has been made to a 'sort-of bullshit translation' supplied by the poet, by hands unidentified. English equivalents to the original rhymes are underscored, in the hope that a later stage of translation may pull toward this aspect of organisation, so very essential to the proper feel of the verse. For the same reason, original stress-counts and rhyme-schemes are noted. The various 'lullaby' or 'cradle-song' referents become apparent as the poem unfolds. In commentary following a performance of the first section, the poet also referred to a Charlie Parker recording of 'Lullaby of Birdland' with which he was familiar before his emigration. (JBP, S.II, Poetry, IP, Kolybel'naia treskovogo mysa, English interlinear translation by Jim Rice, 1977, Box 6, Folder 1235)

Rice coined the term 'first-stage translations' to refer to 'interlinear ones', emphasizing the same quality of this sort of translation that Myers described as 'polyfabrikat' (the Russian word that refers to something that is half-ready and needs to be further cooked before consumption – see the section on Myers). It is curious that, as Rice was working on his text, he approached yet another person to help him with the rendering. He also wrote to Brodsky while working on his version to inform him that he had been collaborating with Jas. Sullivan who helped him turn Rice's translation into 'something more like poetry' (23 December 1976, JBP, S.I, GC, Rice, Jim, Incoming, 1976–96, Box 12, Folder 334, Box 12, Folder 334). This shows that, in some cases, the translation project was going out of anyone's control, as the commissioned translators, such as Hecht, were involving extra helpers who, in their turn, invited further collaborators. Brodsky was, however, aware of all these layers of translation and the people involved, at least, in this case, because Rice was in correspondence with the poet. Prior to the translator's note, on 31 January 1977, on behalf of himself and Sallivan, Rice sent Brodsky a long list of queries, related mostly to the meaning of expressions in 'Cape Cod Lullaby' (JBP, S.I, GC, Rice, Jim, Incoming, 1976–96, Box 12, Folder 334). Nine and a half months later, on 14 November 1977, Brodsky replied to his letter, providing Rice with detailed answers to all questions, explaining the connotations of queried words, the use of idioms, slang expressions and so on.

One rather curious detail pertains to the story of the 'unidentified translation', of which Rice referred in his letter to Brodsky. Brodsky sent this unidentified rendering to Rice and described it as a 'sort-of bullshit' translation. Although Brodsky had been unhappy with some translations and, at times, had said unflattering things about them, the way he described this translation was different. For example, in his communication with Weissbort about the translation of the sequence 'A Part of Speech', Brodsky was always specific in his criticism pointing to the lack of formal correspondence between the original Russian and Weissbort's translation. But in this case, Brodsky referred to a translation as a 'sort-of bullshit' without giving any specific details. This leads me to think that this was a draft self-translation by the poet himself. It was sent to Rice in 1977 when Brodsky started self-translating but was not yet confident in his skills. This might have been a way for Brodsky to seek some feedback on his work without intimidating his translators and without embarrassing himself if he still felt vulnerable writing verse in English. I have further reasons to believe that the unidentified rendering is a self-translation based on a comparative analysis of three interlinear translations of 'Cape Cod Lullaby'.

Below are the two extracts from 'Cape Cod Lullaby'. I have chosen these from the strophes that Rice had queries about in his letter to the poet because they present particular difficulty to the translator. This is one of the three queries by Rice: 'II,3 – skvoz' 'baraninu tuč: does "mutton" suggest a color, or a shape, or both, or none of the above?' And there are eleven queries from Sallivan, including the following:

VII,1 – "<u>telo sposobno podnjat'</u> vselennuju na roga'

I can't get away from envisioning a bull; whether or not this is what is wanted, it is hard to put into English without some notion of what kind of head (humanoid?) joins the horns to the body. (I sense that this enquiry is rather prying, and probably deserves to be ignored.)

VII,3 – <u>poxoži na slezy syra</u>: Are the <u>slezy</u> drops of moisture (whey), or porous indentations, or emotional outpourings of some particular sad cheese you have known? (31 January 1977, JBP, S.I, GC, Rice, Jim, Incoming, 1976–96, Box 12, Folder 334)

And this is how Brodsky responded:

VII.1 'telo sposobno podnjat' vselennuju na roga'... <u>roga</u> is certainly a bull's feature, and you are quite right. '<u>Roga</u>' also the nickname of punishment (slang), i.e. <u>rog v bok</u> – a horn in a rib. Also '<u>dat' po rogam</u>' (hit his horns) is a kind of a prisoner's abbreviation of that paragraf [Sp] in his verdict which states '<u>poraženie v pravax</u>' (limitation of rights), i.e. being deprived of right to vote, to reside in certain areas. Etymology (if one may call it so) is this: <u>poraženie</u> – <u>porazit' po rogam</u>. 'I've been given five year(s) of limitations in rights' will render in Russian either as '<u>mne dali 5 let porazenija v pravax</u>' or 'mne dali 5 let po rogam'. Hence, '<u>roga</u>' is something which sort of crowns the man's head (not as a mark of his mistress's unfaithfulness) but as a mark of his being stubborn – see '<u>uprjamyj kozel</u>'. Second meaning – which deals with lifting the universe is an echo of Archimedes's saying: 'Give me the spot to rest/base (my instrument – recap) on, and I'll lift the world.' <u>roga</u> = '<u>ryčagi</u>'. (JBP, S.II, Poetry, IP, Kolybel'naia treskovogo mysa, English interlinear translation by Jim Rice, 1977, Box 60, Folder 1235)

As seen from the above, Brodsky gave Rice a lot of food for thought by providing several different connotations of 'horns', some of which – relating to the prison jargon – would not have been known even to all native Russian speakers. This hardly made Rice's job easier. It is not surprising that this poem presented so many difficulties for interlinear translators who, despite all their efforts, have failed to replicate all the nuances and connotations of the poem. It is worth comparing the three available interlinear translations of a couple of difficult parts of the poem mentioned earlier (see Table 4.1).

Comparing these renderings, only the unidentified translator dared to drop any reference to 'horns': 'On finding a fulcrum's leverage can one lift / The weight of the world.' Neither White nor Rice left 'horns' out; the 'unidentified' translator must have had access to the author's intention, which is revealed in Brodsky's response to Rice, explaining the second meaning: 'which deals with lifting the universe is an echo of Archimedes's saying: "Give me the spot to rest/base (my instrument – recap) on, and I'll lift the world." <u>roga</u> = "<u>ryčagi</u>"'. This choice by the unidentified translator is further evidence to support my claim that this secret translator is Brodsky himself.

Another reason to believe that Brodsky was responsible for this unidentified translation is that it includes a few uses of articles that reveal a non-native speaker's command of English. For example, the use of the definite article before 'armies' in II.3 by the unidentified translator stands out in comparison with the other two translations in which the article is not used. If we accept that Brodsky sent Rice a self-translation without telling him, then the production of the English version of 'Cape Cod Lullaby' appears even more complicated. We have encountered three interlinear translations, one of which was a self-translation shared with Rice. In addition, Rice worked on his translation collaboratively with Sullivan and Brodsky himself. Ironically, the poet-translator Hecht found both interlinear translations – by White and by Rice with Sullivan – not entirely adequate because, in his view, neither of the translators fully understood the original. Whether they did or not, it is evident that they certainly tried and invested a lot of work into the rendering of 'Cape Cod Lullaby', none of which was acknowledged in the published version of the poem. In all publications, it states that the poem was translated by Hecht.

Anthony Hecht

When Brodsky's old Russian friend Aleksandr Kushner asked him to describe Anthony Hecht as a poet, Brodsky said: 'Imagine if I were born not in Russia but in the USA and if I lived all my life in America. I would have been similar to him and I would have been writing like him' (Vail' 1998: 174). Hecht, like Brodsky, was hugely interested in Auden, having published *The Hidden Law: the Poetry of W. H. Auden* (Hecht 1993), 'the fruit of a lifelong critical and imaginative engagement with W H. Auden's works', as stated on the book. This perceived similarity between Hecht and Brodsky is a result of their equally deep-seated regard for Auden. Brodsky and Hecht also appreciated each other's work. Perhaps, this helped Hecht's translations of Brodsky's poems to remain intact, with less correction by Brodsky than many other translators' renderings.

In a Charlie Rose film to commemorate Brodsky, Hecht recollected the poems that had particularly moved him:

> There are two poems of his that particularly move me. One is quite long. It is 'Lullaby of Cape Cod'. And it's about getting drunk one night. But getting drunk is mixed up with the fact of his exile. The fact that he is a lone man in a foreign country washed up on a strange shore. And eventually he invites cards to get drunk with him. The other poem is much more dense and dramatic and more moving. It's 'A Hawk's Cry in the Autumn' and it's about his own extinction. Joseph knew as his friends knew that his end was approaching... and this poem is about the sacrifice that is part of the artist's life. (Rose 1996)

Table 4.1 Four Translations of 'Lullaby of Cape Cod' ('Kolybel'naia treskogovo mysa') by Joseph Brodsky, Stanzas II.3 and VII.1

	Stephen White, interlinear	Unidentified	James L. Rice, interlinear	Anthony Hecht (19 June 1978)
II.3	and sailed off through the mutton of clouds. Below rivers meandered, roads gave off dust, haystacks yellowed. Opposing each other, trampling the dew, like the long lines of a still unclosed book stood armies occupied in game and black like roe.	And flew into muttony clouds. Way down below Rivers meandered, roads blossomed with dust, ricks yellowed, Everywhere in balanced opposition, Formal like a print in a still open book, Trampling the dew, the armies rehearsed their game, And cities went dark as caviar.	And glided through the mutton of the clouds. Down <u>below</u> rivers meandered, roads gave up dust, yellow were the <u>threshing-floors</u>. Opposite each other stood – trampling the dew, like long lines of a <u>book</u> not yet closed, – armies engaged in a game, and black as <u>caviar</u> –	And sailed into muttony clouds. Below me curled Serpentine rivers, roads bloomed with dust, ricks yellowed, And everywhere in that diminished world, In formal opposition, near and far, Lined up like print in a book about to close, Armies rehearsed their games in balanced rows And cities all went dark as caviar.
VII.1	Only a corner woven over completely with cobwebs has the right to be called a right corner. Only upon hearing 'bravo' does the actor rise from the floor. Only upon finding a fulcrum is the body able to lift the universe on its horns. Only that body moves whose leg is perpendicular to the floor.	Only a corner preserved by dust and cobwebs Has a right to be called right-angled. Only on hearing 'Bravo' does the actor rise from the floor, and only On finding a fulcrum's leverage can one lift The weight of the world. Only that body moves Whose legs stand at right angles to the floor.	Only a corner all embroidered with cobwebs has the <u>right</u> to be called square. Only when he's heard a '<u>Bravo</u>!' does the actor rise from the floor. Only by finding <u>support</u> is the body capable of lifting the universe on <u>horns</u>. Only that body moves whose <u>leg</u> is perpendicular to the <u>floor</u>.	Only a corner cordoned off and laced By dusty cobwebs may properly be called Right-angled; only after the musketry of applause And 'bravos' does the actor rise from the dead; Only when the fulcrum is solidly placed Can a person lift, by Archimedian laws, The weight of this world. And only that body whose weight Is balanced at right angles to the floor Can manage to walk about and navigate.

Source: JBP, S.II, Poetry, IP, Kolybel'naia treskovogo mysa, English interlinear translations: by Steven White, undated, Box 60, Folder 1236; by unidentified translator, undated, Box 60, Folder 1239; by Jim Rice, 1977, Box 60, Folder 1235.

We know that Hecht had already chosen 'Cape Cod Lullaby' to translate for 'A Part of Speech', and we also know that translation was a long and complex process which involved four interlinear translators: White, Rice, Salliven and an unidentified translator (possibly, Brodsky himself). But it was even more complicated and contested. In addition to the translators already mentioned, Brodsky must have asked Myers and Kline to render the poem too. In fact, this poem was so popular that Kline fought desperately to translate it himself, writing to Hecht, trying to convince him to drop translation in favour of Kline:

> Perhaps, you saw John Russel's piece a couple of months ago in *The New York Times Sunday* 'Arts and . . .' section. It was on 'The Arts in the Seventies' and included a very warm and generous paragraph on Joseph. It also mentioned that I was translating 'Cape Cod Lullaby', which may have come as a surprise. Joseph tells me that you've agreed to do it, working with an interlineal version. I would be delighted to defer to you, but in this particular case the poem is very close to me, and I've already invested a great deal of time and energy in putting it into English (though considerable work remains). If you haven't yet gone too far, woeful you be able to do something else for the Farrar, Straus & Giroux volume? (6 May 1977, JBP S.I, GC, Kline, George, 1972–95, undated, Box 8, Folder 209)

Hecht interpreted his letter as a 'fierce claim' to Joseph's 'Cape Cod Lullaby', and Kline's attitude as 'proprietary', for which Kline apologized in a letter dated 7 June 1977. Later, Kline withdrew his suggestion that Hecht should translate some other poems by Brodsky (JBP, S.I, GC, Kline, George, 1972–95, undated, Box 8, Folder 209). On 4 November, Meiselas wrote to Hecht that having received 'a capsulised version of George Kline's interference', she was 'even more furious' than she was before, stating: 'Kline persists in thinking that he has inalienable rights to the translation of Joseph's poetry, despite the fact that he has been told several times that this is no longer the case' (FSGI, M&AD, NYPL, Brodsky, A Part of Speech, General, 1976–7). In response, Hecht updated Meiselas on his progress, saying that he had nearly completed his translation of 'Cape Cod Lullaby': 'the poem is stunning: not simply as fine as anything of Joseph's that I know, but as fine as almost anything in all modern poetry that I can think of. It is deeply moving, full of tenderness, humour, intelligence, and a wild, drunken freedom that is half sadness and half comic' (28 December 1977, JBP, Hecht, Anthony, 1976–93, Box 6, Folder 170).

Having completed his first translation, Hecht sent it to Meiselas at FSG with a letter in which he said that he had not strictly followed the metre and rhyme patterns:

> In what I am afraid may initially disappoint Joseph I have decided to forego any attempt to render the elaborate rhyme and metrical pattern, or even some sort of English equivalent of my own invention to serve what must

surely be part of the masterful technical pleasures of the original. I decided on this course because I felt that the substance itself of the poem, its richness of braided themes, its suppleness and variety of metaphors, its huge scope, its diversity and homogeneity of matter, all seemed to me so dense and so necessary that I felt throughout that any attempt of mine to mimic the poem's formal features would mean a ruthless sacrifice of many of the most splendidly imaginative features of the poem that make it an astonishing achievement that it is. I have therefore attempted modestly, to work the poem into six-line stanzas of blank verse, taking occasional liberties here and there. (Letter dated 28 December 1977, JBP, Hecht, Anthony, 1976–93, Box 6, Folder 170)

At its conclusion, he added that at times he had not been entirely sure about the meaning in some parts of the poem. So, it is not surprising that when Brodsky read Hecht's translation he made further suggestions and changes. Hecht responded to Brodsky's interventions in a letter dated 26 February 1979:

Dear Joseph,

here are some revisions of various parts of 'Lullaby to Cape Cod'. As I told you on the phone, not all the ones you suggested were possible or even, in some cases, desirable. For example, as you suspected, while 'chordate' means just what you want in V, it is for most American and English readers, far too technical and scientific a term to be grasped without consulting a dictionary. As for bathtub image in IV, I find it difficult to work in because hard to visualise: the canals fill because wind and tide raise the water level, but tubs fill from a spout. As for 'our dim times', as compared with 'the era of friction', dim means both unfavourable and badly lit, and the poverty of the light fits well with the following metaphors about eyesight and the speed of light. Admittedly, things that were possible and powerful for you in the Russian, I have had to tame or sacrifice here and there. But I do feel that now, with these latest changes, the poem as a poem in English holds together, carries a rich burden of pathos and humour, and what the advertisers call 'a reasonable facsimile' of what you intend. Let me only add that I think it might now be useful to include a note on VII which might read – 'Northern Sphinxes': sculptured figures placed along the embankments of the Neva river in St. Petersburg. (JBP, S.II, Poetry, IP, Kolybel'naia treskovogo mysa, English translation by Anthony Hecht, draft, 1978–79, Box 60, Folder 1237)

Hecht did not accept all of Brodsky's suggestions, exercising his privilege as a poet in his own right and a native speaker of the English language. 'Cape Cod Lullaby' in Hecht's translation was first published in *Columbia* 4, Spring-Summer, 1980. Subsequently, the title was changed for 'The Lullaby of Cape Cod'.

Table 4.2 Two Translations of 'Lagoon' ('Laguna') by Joseph Brodsky: Masha Vorobiov's Interlinear Translation and Anthony Hecht's Poetic Translation, Stanzas I and II

Masha Vorobiov, interlinear	Anthony Hecht
I Three old women, knitting in deep armchairs are discoursing in the lobby about the sufferings on the cross; the <u>pensione</u> 'L'academia' together with the entire Universe is sailing towards Christmas, to the rumble of television, the clerk having stuck his ledger under his arm, is turning the wheel.	Down in the lobby three elderly women, bored, Take up, with their knitting, the Passion of Our Lord As the universe and the tiny realm Of the <u>pension</u> <u>Accademia</u>, side by side, With TV blaring, sail into Christmastide, A lookout desk clerk at the helm.
II And ascending the gangplank, the lodger goes on board to his room carrying in his pocket (a flask of) grappa, a complete nobody, a man in a raincoat, who has lost his memory, his homeland, his son; the aspen in the forests weeps for his burden* if indeed anyone weeps for him at all. * <u>po gorbu ego plachet</u> – literally, weeps for his humpback	And a nameless lodger, a nobody, boards the boat, A bottle of grappa concealed in his raincoat As he gains his shadowy room, bereaved Of memory, homeland, son, with only the noise of distant forests to grieve for his former joys, If anyone is grieved.

Source: JBP, S.II, Poetry, IP, Laguna, English translations: by Anthony Hecht, draft and printed version, undated, Box 60, Folder 1254; by Masha Vorobiov, draft, undated, Box 60, Folder 1255.

In addition, Hecht also translated 'Lagoon', which was published in *A Part of Speech*. On this occasion, he worked with the interlinear translation by Vorobiov (Table 4.2).

Comparing Vorobiov's interlinear rendering with Hecht's translation gives fascinating insight into how an interlinear translation can be transformed into a new poem. Hecht's version is so much more laconic and crisp compared to Vorobiov's rendering; the text's transformation is impressive and the meaning is carefully transported.

Brodsky valued Hecht's opinion and sent him his poems when he started self-translating and writing in English. One of them was 'Winter Eclogue' (see the discussion in Chapter 3), which Hecht read with 'mounting pleasure and admiration':

> First of all, it is beautiful and moving in its own right – an eloquent and astonishing poem of sustained plangency and elegiac mood. It moves like a cortège. But in addition it is something of a <u>tour de force</u> in its deliberate violation or contradiction of the Virgil 'Fourth Eclogue' from which it appears to spring. While the Virgil is all forward looking, expectant and prophetic, yours is deeply and darkly retrospective and melancholy. And while the Virgil was famously and shamelessly Christianized, yours seems to me, by virtue of

its backward-looking perspective, and its grave sadness, somehow Jewish in spirit. In other words, what I think you have done is miraculously to relate by contrast and contradiction, the past with the future, the Old with the New Testament, lament with exultation, and all by the suggested Vergilian link in which the Roman poet serves you as he once served Dante. It is a brilliant and highly original work, and moreover, a beautiful one. I am truly grateful to you for sending me a copy of it. (18 May 1982, JBP, Hecht, Anthony, 1976–93, Box 6, Folder 170)

Hecht was at times critical of Brodsky's English and was direct in telling his Russian friend about his reservations. Having read 'Roman Elegies' at Brodsky's request, he wrote on 14 June 1983:

The poems are lovely – moving, and very much your own in clear and resonant ways. But there are real problems about colloquial English idioms and syntax. There are places where your inversions of normal word order make for very unnatural English. There are a few places where I would urge a change of word. In #III you use 'seraphim' as though it were singular, and in a rhyming position, though the singular is 'seraph'. There are, by my count, only half-a-dozen such cruxes that call for attention, along with a few typographical errors. Maybe we can get together over them some mutually convenient time. (JBP, Hecht, Anthony, 1976–93, Box 6 Folder 170)

Having read the published version of Brodsky's collection of essays *Less Than One*, Hecht sent his compliments to the poet:

Your splendid book, LESS THAN ONE, has just arrived, and I have been reading in it, carefully and with limitless pleasure. I can't tell you how delighted and excited I am by everything I've read so far, or how enthusiastically I look forward to the rest. There are very few writers of critical prose who can arouse that kind of electric response. But it seems to me that your writing here has many of the virtues of your poetry: a mind at once witty and tragic in its large view, a mind of uncanny speed, agility and grace, a mind that both by its sinuosity and clarity represents a vision of wisdom. And a range that is imperial in its breadth. (JBP, Hecht, Anthony, 1976–93, Box 6, Folder 170)

Even when Hecht no longer translated Brodsky's texts, he helped his Russian friend by giving feedback on his work in English. In Brodsky Hecht recognized a great poet and a perceptive essayist, first through translation and then, when Brodsky started to write in English, despite the Russian poet's imperfect command of the English language. Hecht's letter to FSG in the early 1990s beautifully summarized his appreciation of Brodsky's talent as a writer: 'Dear Roslyn Schloss, Thank you very much for sending me the uncorrected proofs of Joseph's new book, Watermark. Even an uncorrected Brodsky text is better than a corrected one by most writers' (January 1992, Letter by Hecht, FSGI, M&AD, NYPL, Brodsky, Watermark, General).

Richard Purdy Wilbur

In 1961, Richard Wilbur, an American Pulitzer Prize-winning poet, made a trip to the Soviet Union as part of a cultural exchange programme. At the invitation of Max Haywood and Patricia Blake, who were 'extremely good linguists' and 'extremely good at conveying original tone', he translated the Russian poet Andrey Voznesensky. Five poems by Andrei Voznesensky were soon published in *The New York Review of Books* on 14 April 1966 in translation by Patricia Blake, and Max Hayward, Richard Wilbur and W. H. Auden.

On 9 September 1972, Wilbur wrote to Rhoda Schwartz that he had been honoured to hear Brodsky's feedback on his poetry. Brodsky appreciated that 'technical felicity' was 'a means and a by-product rather than an end' in Wilbur's poetry. Wilbur valued Brodsky's 'concision and clarity' in how he puts this, especially as it was an 'unpopular thing' to say at the time (JBP, S.I, GC, Wibur, Richard, 1972–90, Box 17, Folder 445). In the same letter, Wilbur refers to his first forthcoming meeting with Brodsky in January in Michigan. Later Wilbur attempted to translate Brodsky because he had been told that the best translations of his poems into Russian were by Brodsky. He wanted to express his gratitude by translating Brodsky's poems into English. Also, Wilbur was one of the most admired translators from French to English, so translation was not new to him. In an interview, he says:

> I heard that he was very choosy, very finicky about translation, so I wanted to do something that he would approve of. My first translation from a Brodsky poem took me a month. And the second was done rather slowly too with the help of linguistic council and dictionaries. By then I was trying to teach myself the Russian language. And this was probably the best effort I made in translating a Russian poem. (Wilbur 2017)

Even Richard Wilbur's 'final' translation of the poem '6 Years Later' did not escape Brodsky's criticism and corrections. According to Wilbur,

> The poem of Brodsky called '6 Years Later' (dedicated to M.B. 1968). He [Brodsky] was very approving of this translation although not that sure of the two lines in the latter stanzas. He went down to Oklahoma and on the flight back he and Derek had studied my translation and had decided that one or two tinkering should be made in the latter stanzas. I of course had no business of objecting any change he might make in my translation of his poem but I did cling to my original and perhaps mistaken lines. Joseph publishing it in the book of his own used an improved version. (Wilbur 2017)

Note the slight irony in Wilbur's comment above. First, although he accepted that Brodsky had had the authority to make changes to Wilbur's translation of Brodsky's poem, at the same time, he contradicted himself by referring to his own translation as 'my original'. Second, when he published his 'original' translation in his book of poems, he ironically noted that Brodsky had preferred his own so-called 'improved' version of the last two lines, created by him with the help of Walcott.

On 23 July 1973, Carl Proffer asked Wilbur to translate Brodsky's poem 'The Funeral of Bobò'. In a letter to Proffer of 1 February 1974, Wilbur warned that he was 'a slow worker' when it came to translation and explained how he approached it:

> I have kept the meter, and used a stanza in which the odd lines are rhymed in one or another approximate way, and the even lines are rhymed purely. I hope the translation will move and sound well to Joseph's ears and yours. The tone of the poem I take to be painful, scalding, bitter, sardonic, and I hope not to have struck any wrong notes. The poem also seems to me to be full of hints, nudges, suggestions, and I shall be happy if I have not obscured any such implications irretrievably. (1 February 1974, JBP, S.I, GC, Wilbur, Richard, 1972–90, Box 17, Folder 445)

He added that he had also appended a page of 'alternative notions', which consisted 'of ideas which for the most part struck me as second-best', but if Brodsky preferred them he could revert to them. Wilbur also anticipated that Brodsky would 'jump out of his skin on noting' that Wilbur had added four of his own words and reassured him that he had not done it so much as a 'short ego-trip' but 'an effort to fulfil the form' in accordance with Brodsky's 'drift', as perceived by Wilbur (1 February 1974, JBP, S.I, GC, Wilbur, Richard, 1972–90, Box 17, Folder 445).

As for Wilbur's translation of 'Seven Years Later', as he referred to it in his letter to Meiselas on 13 May 1977 (the original Russian poem is entitled '7 Years Later' as opposed to the published English translation 'Six Years Later' apparently because someone figured out that it had to be six years for 2 January to fall on a Tuesday, according to Kjellberg), he was interested to know which lines Brodsky wished to discuss with him. He wrote that he had had 'numerous alternative versions of many of the lines' and had been prepared to 'amend the translation without too much difficulty'. He carried on to explain the changes he had introduced in the translation:

> I hope you don't mind my failure to reproduce your varying of the stanza-pattern; it was simply more convenient to keep to the form of the first stanza, once I had begun thinking in it. In any case, do be frank, intolerant and insistent in your criticisms. (JBP, S.I, GC, Wilbur, Richard, 1972–90, Box 17, Folder 445)

In the same letter to Brodsky, he politely declined the offer to translate Brodsky's 'December in Florence' because he was 'raging to write some poem' of his own again. He closed his letter with a reference to his only new poem which is about the walk that Brodsky, Jonathan and Wilbur took when Brodsky came to Cummington for the first time and an invitation for Brodsky to visit them there again. The letter also contains the poem entitled 'Forget-me-not' ('Nyezabudka') for Joseph Brodsky, in which Wilbur recollects how Brodsky told him about forget-me-nots growing in the *kolkhoz* where he had done his hard labour in Archangel region. The flowers evoked a conversation about the world, in which 'Some laws, thank God, resist the blear-eyed dogmatist' (JBP, S.I, GC, Wilbur, Richard, 1972–90, Box 17, Folder 445). In his 16 December 1977 letter to Meiselas, Wilbur inquired whether Brodsky had received his letter with the 'Forget-me-not' ('Nyezabudka') poem and whether he would mind for political or personal reasons if Wilbur had it published. He also provided four alternative two-line endings to 'Seven Years Later', as he had heard that Brodsky had liked the poem apart from the last two lines.

For Wilbur, 'translation is not an art in which the translator shows off but a craft (a collaboration, if necessary) in which the original is got across into another language as well as possible,' which he wrote in a letter to Brodsky on 26 April 1982. It was necessary for him to explain his remarks about the translation of 'Six Years Later' because he felt misunderstood by an interviewer. Wilbur made some comments on the fact that Walcott and Brodsky together changed the last two lines in his translation of 'Six Years Later', despite the variety of the options that Wilbur had sent Brodsky. Wilbur added that his comment would amuse them rather than be presented as if Wilbur had been hurt. He adds that he 'had no objection to collaborating in whatever manner with Derek, who is one of the best English poets in operation' (JBP, S.I, GC, Wilbur, Richard, 1972–90, Box 17, Folder 445).

Derek Walcott

Walcott and Brodsky met at Robert Lowell's funeral in 1977. They developed a strong friendship thereafter. Both Nobel Prize–winning poets much admired each other's poetry and both wrote critical essays on each other's poetry. Brodsky's collection of essays *Less Than One* contains a piece on Walcott 'The Sound of the Tide', which was originally written in 1983 as an introduction to Walcott's *Poems of the Caribbean* (for the detailed discussion of the essay, see Hanford 2000). In the 1980s, Brodsky commented that Walcott was the best English-language poet. This statement was widely quoted when Walcott became a Nobel Prize winner in 1992. In an interview given to Petr Vail', Brodsky recalled how he and Walcott had met for a chat in Oklahoma and Brodsky entertained Walcott by translating lines from Mandelshtam's poetry by memory (Vail' 1998: 255). Brodsky also mentioned that Walcott had 'once helped' him to translate Brodsky's own poem. As noted by Wilbur (see the section on Wilbur), it was in a conversation with Walcott that Brodsky came up with 'an improvement' on Wilbur's two last lines in 'Six Years Later'. In playful and informal conversations about poetry, Walcott and Brodsky inadvertently discussed and sometimes 'improved' translations.

Walcott talks about other times when he and Brodsky translated Russian poems together. Once Barry Rubin, Brodsky and Walcott worked on the translation of one poem together for three or four hours, and even then the result did not satisfy them. At some point, Brodsky lost patience and swore in Russian because it was simply impossible to keep the formal structure of the poem: rhyme patters, rhythm, etc. (Polukhina 1997: 410). According to Brodsky, there are Russian poets whose work it is simply impossible to translate into English, including Marina Tsvetaeva and Alexander Pushkin. However, Walcott insisted that Brodsky's poems were translatable thanks to the intellectual element in his work. Walcott identified one important aspect of Brodsky's requirement for a translator: 'The translator should follow the intention of the author instead of copying the original' (Polukhina 1997: 410). This quote from Walcott demonstrates why Brodsky could never be satisfied with any translation fully apart from his own – he was the only one who had complete access to and understanding of his own intention in the original. Having said that, Walcott's contribution to *A Part of Speech*, which was a rendering of 'Letters from the Ming Dynasty', is a remarkable translation in English much appreciated by readers and critics.

Mark Strand

Mark Strand, a recognized American poet, was approached to translate Brodsky's poems but never did so. He also shared his impressions of Brodsky's verse in English. He admitted that he could not fairly characterize Brodsky as a Russian poet because he did not speak Russian but,

> as an English poet, he was an exotic. He did things that no English or American poet born into the language would possibly do. The way he ordered language was so unusual – it was an understatement. He made choices that none of us here would ever make. We are bound by word orders and structures that we grew up with and he wasn't. So, his poetry was at once a flagrant violation of whatever – what we had to do and were coming to terms with in English poetry, – and also a miraculous step forward. I found him unbelievably gifted at invention. There is no poet in England or in America who would take the chances that Joseph took. No-one sounds like him. It is if the English language was his toy. He loved it and he played with it in ways that it was not possible for someone who was born into the language to. And underneath that play of course there is a huge moral dimension to his poetry,

the dimension that draws on his experience as an exile, his experience in the Soviet Union, having been sent to Archangel. [. . .] He would listen patiently to me read my poems over the phone and then tell me correctly almost all the time what was wrong with them and how I might improve them. (Rose 1996)

Strand declined the offer to translate Brodsky's poems. He explained that for him the first impression of the original was the key to creating a good translation. If the poet has to work with an interlinear translation, it means that he only has to be satisfied with the secondary impression received from the first-stage translation, which means that 'the first impression of one is distorted by the first impression of the other' (Polukhina 1997: 385). Strand described Brodsky's English poetry as follows:

> It seemed that it was grown from in a tube, which meant that it sounded artificial. It was metrically shaped (*vyverennoi*) (it was important to him) but it lacked freedom, spoken language. It was neither quite spoken nor formal but it was consistently Brodsky's own. Joseph had original rhymes which were almost always inexact, that is they would rhyme if you pronounce them with a Russian accent. (Polukhina 1997: 386)

In the above quote, Strand summarized the view that many shared, which was that Brodsky's poems in English lacked the spontaneity and fluency accessible to native speakers. It was his *strangership* expressed in an accented English that became his trademark and consistent part of his voice in English.

George L. Kline

Cynthia Haven, whose book of interviews with G. L. Kline is forthcoming in 2020, describes him as follows: 'George was a "square", meticulous scholar, modest, persevering and thoroughly decent in the old-fashioned sense of the word' (Email to Rulyova on 12 January 2020). This impression of him as a scholar and a translator replaced his former identity as a 'professor of combat', a pilot and an army veteran Lt. George L. Kline, 'who was a navigator on 50 bombing missions over Europe' during the Second World War, according to the article in Pueblo Colorado, 1944–5, 'Lieutenant Kline knows Italy, Hungary, Yugoslavia, Austria, Rumania, Bulgaria and Southern Germany almost as well as he knows the palm of his hand. He served eight months with the fifteenth air force and flew fifty missions as a B-24 navigator, bombing enemy targets in most of these countries' (JBP, S.I, GC, Kline, George, 1972095, Box 8, Folder 210).

Kline was Brodsky's first official translator who rendered all the poems for Brodsky's first book, *Selected Poems*, as discussed in Chapter 2. Throughout his life, Kline remained one of Brodsky's most loyal translators. They first met in 1967 during Kline's visit to St Petersburg. Reflecting on his work and relationship with Brodsky, Kline pointed to some parallels in their language acquisition – they both were late bilinguals. Kline was always professional and respectful of his relationship with Brodsky. Unlike Weissbort who took changes to his translations personally – as a challenge to their friendship – Kline never lost his cool. However, in his dealing with other Brodsky's translators, at least, in case of Hecht, Kline nearly overstepped some boundaries, at least once in an incident discussed earlier.

Kline tried to do his best to render Brodsky's poems in the most faithful way in terms of their meaning and form. He showed his drafts to the poet and revised them where necessary. Although Kline appreciated poetic form, he was not a poet himself and at times his renderings were described only as shadows of Brodsky's originals in Russian. In his column in *The American Poetry Review* for January and February 1973, Donald Hall wrote: 'the translations of Brodsky are unsatisfactory. . . . Too many of the translations from a forthcoming Penguin selection are clogged with trite poeticisms, dead metaphors, archaisms, and vapid abstractions,' as quoted in Kline's letter to Brodsky on 31 October 1973 (GLKP, GEN MSS 650, S.1, C, Correspondence with Joseph Brodsky, Incoming letters and copies of outgoing letters (1 of 3 folders), 1972–94, Box 1, Folder 3; Levertov, Brodsky and Hall 1973). Having read this, Kline described feeling as if he had been 'kicked in the stomach' and his first reaction was to 'give up the whole project', leaving the job of translating Brodsky to Wilbur, John Updike and James Scully, whose translations Hall praised. Kline felt particularly hurt because he credited Hall with 'literary judgement and taste'. However, in the same letter, Kline hopes that Hall mistook someone else's translations for his at one of Brodsky's readings. He then suggested that perhaps the criticized translations had been done by Jamie Fuller, whose translations were read in Ann Arbor on 19 September 1972. Overall, Kline's translations in *Selected Poems* received fairly good reviews when the book was published but not without criticism. Both Spender and Auden noted that they could see a great poet despite the translations, implying that translations were only successful enough to give a glimpse at Brodsky's originals.

Kline was a true collaborator in translation. He tirelessly corresponded with Brodsky on corrections and alterations at all times during the preparation of *Selected Poems* and later, when he was commissioned to translate Brodsky's individual poems for his further collections. For example, on 20 November 1976, he sent Brodsky his final version of 'Second Christmas' ('Vtoroe Rozhdestvo'), commenting: 'it is a great improvement over the two earlier versions – thanks mainly to your criticisms and helpful suggestions. As you recall, I am sure, the rhyme on "unfrozen – horizon" – probably the best in the whole translation was yours' (GLKP, S.1, C, Correspondence with Joseph Brodsky, Incoming letters and copies of outgoing letters (1 of 3 folders), 1972–94, Box 1, Folder 1). Another example is in his letter on 30 March 1987; he admitted that Brodsky had 'obviously improved his translation "at many points": I particularly admire such "nakhodki" ("finds") as "naiads/jeremiads" (III.1), "often/. . ./orphan" (III.3), and "moon-spun vowels" (IV.10)'. Kline also reiterated the problems: Brodsky's reintroducing masculine rhymes ('square/somewhere/tear') (III.1) after Kline had been 'at such pains to use only feminine rhymes throughout'. He pointed to the half a dozen rhymes that had been used more than once (30 March 1987, GLKP, S.1, C, Correspondence with Joseph Brodsky, Incoming letters and copies of outgoing letters (1 of 3 folders), 1972–94, Box 1, Folder 1).

Brodsky's interventions in Kline's work increased as the poet's English improved. Brodsky's early letters to Kline were written in Russian. In one of these letters, Brodsky was very appreciative of Kline's work and his translations, and he was grateful that, to use Brodsky's words, destiny brought them together. Brodsky's comments on Kline's translation of 'The Butterfly' ('Babochka') were characteristic of his early interventions: he made very few actual suggestions about how to render specific words and phrases in English; instead, he pointed to the parts of the poem in which the tone had been distorted. For example, he was not satisfied with Kline's overly romantic rendering: in relation to stanza 2, Brodsky wrote: 'This is romanticism, and in the original there is nearly bureaucratism, a non-emotional observation.' When Brodsky made specific points about the use of certain words in English, he translated them back into Russian and compared them to the original Russian words: '"Days are like butterflies" is incorrect. "Days, they are like you."' In every stanza, Brodsky identified misreadings and mistakes in rendering by translating them back into Russian and comparing them to the original (GLKP, S.1, C, Correspondence with Joseph Brodsky, Incoming letters and copies of outgoing letters (1 of 3 folders), 1972–94, Box 1, Folder 2).

In the late 1980s, he treated Kline's translations rather differently: he was more assertive and sure of his choices in English. On 15 February 1987, Brodsky sent a letter regarding the final version of 'Eclogue' translated by Kline:

> Dear George, here's our 'Eclogue', and I think we better consider this version final. I had to redo it largely because most of translations in the forthcoming book are done by my humble self anyway, and the idea is to sustain the diction. As you'll see, a great deal of your version has survived – if not intact, then in a somewhat restructured form. There are, of course, losses – to your version as well as to the original – but the tonality of the poem sustains then better than some of your gains that seemed to me at times a bit dangling and burdensome for its body to carry. [. . .] There is enough of you in this final version to have your name underneath it; of course we can add 'and the Author' so that one would know whom to blame for its infidelities – and so that you know who needs your help (right away!) in correcting them. (GLKP, S.1, C, Correspondence with Joseph Brodsky, Incoming letters and copies of outgoing letters (1 of 3 folders), 1972–94, Box 1, Folder 2)

Kline collaborated with other translators of Brodsky as well as with the poet. As mentioned in Chapter 3, he translated one poem 'December in Florence' with Maurice English. Their collaboration on 'December in Florence' began in 1977. Kline produced an interlinear translation of the Russian original and sent it to Maurice along with his notes on the poem's rhyme and metre scheme ('flexible meter close to the *dol'nik* of traditional Russian folk poetry') (23–24 July 1977, GLKP, S.1, C, Correspondence with Joseph Brodsky, Incoming letters and copies of outgoing letters (1 of 3 folders), 1972–94, Box 1, Folder 13). In the same letter, Kline confirmed that his interlinear translation had been approved by Brodsky who noted the only potentially misleading rendering – memory pills (GLKP, S.1, C, Correspondence with Joseph Brodsky, Incoming letters and copies of outgoing letters (1 of 3 folders), 1972–94, Box 1, Folder 13). On 15 August 1977, M. English sent Kline a clean copy of his translation, along with a list of questions, most of which were lexical and semiotic. M. English, a poet himself, was perplexed by some of the images created in the Russian original and was not sure how best to render them: he was 'bothered' by the imagery of 'the entrance with eyelids', 'waves with fingers', 'face in the darkness', 'words on its surface', and 'the door number ... rough' or 'rough-haired' (GLKP, S.1, C, Correspondence with Joseph Brodsky, Incoming letters and copies of outgoing letters (1 of 3 folders), 1972–94, Box 1, Folder 13). On 7 September, English sent Kline a revised translation, which, in his view, looked less polished after he had made changes. He and Kline had a telephone conversation, which, to M. English's regret, had not answered all his queries regarding the meaning of some of the imagery and expressions (GLKP, S.1, C, Correspondence with Joseph Brodsky, Incoming letters and copies of outgoing letters (1 of 3 folders), 1972–94, Box 1, Folder 13). On 4 November 1978, M. English wrote to Brodsky to tell him that both translators were satisfied with the translation 'en principe' and provided several variants of some lines and phrases (GLKP, GEN MSS 650, S.1, C, Correspondence with Joseph Brodsky, Incoming letters and copies of outgoing letters (1 of 3 folders), 1972–94, Box 1, Folder 3). However, the work on the poem continued: on 5 June 1979, Kline wrote to M. English to congratulate him on his excellent translation but made a few further remarks, suggesting using 'the man' instead of 'people' in stanza 4, reviewing the description of the bell in stanza 5 (it is not silent), and proposing to use 'the' instead of 'a' before 'goldfinch'. M. English supported each suggestion with evidence from the Russian text (GLKP, S.1, C, Correspondence with Joseph Brodsky, Incoming letters and copies of outgoing letters (1 of 3 folders), 1972–94, Box 1, Folder 13).

Another example of Kline's collaboration with Brodsky is in the letter dated 10 January 1987, in which Kline talked about the translation of the 'Fifth Eclogue'. Kline explained that he had discussed the poem with Eric Pervukhin, 'checking for mistakes and misleading renderings' (GLKP, S.1, C, Correspondence with Joseph Brodsky, Incoming letters and copies of outgoing letters (1 of 3 folders), 1972–94, Box 1, Folder 2). However, this did not save the poem from major revision by Brodsky later (see the previous paragraph). Kline also made comments on other translators' versions of Brodsky's poems, acting as an editor at times. For example, he once wrote to Weissbort pointing out the loss of meaning of the word 'wheel' (see section on Weissbort).

Poetic translation is a difficult job. Working with many competing translators and an increasingly demanding poet could make it even harder. Kline shared this feeling in one of his letters in 1972:

> In the last few days, I've had two letters (one from the editor of Partisan Review, the other from a book publisher) praising the translations read at the Donnell Library Centre in general, and the translation of 'Odysseus to Telemachus' in particular. Encouraging; and I sometimes need such encouragement – when the discouraging task of poetic translation begins to get me down. (6 November 1972, GLKP, GEN MSS 650, S.1, C, Correspondence with Joseph Brodsky, Incoming letters and copies of outgoing letters (1 of 3 folders), 1972–94, Box 1, Folder 3)

Kline also recommended, at least, one translator to Brodsky. It was David McFadyen,[5] a bright and very personable postgraduate student who was interested in Brodsky's poetry and had written a piece on 'Kentavry' and wished to translate the 'Novaia zhizn' poem (23 February 1990, GLKP, S.1, C, Correspondence with Joseph Brodsky, Incoming letters and copies of outgoing letters (1 of 3 folders), 1972–94, Box 1, Folder 2). Throughout many years of his collaboration with Brodsky, Kline remained Brodsky's devoted translator. He kept a close eye on Brodsky's publications, offered advice to the poet and his translators, sent Brodsky recommendations and was always there if need be.

Alan Myers

Alan Myers was a noted translator of Russian prose and poetry into English. His major translations include works by Fyodor Dostoevsky (Dostovesky 2008, 2009), Valentin Rasputin, Brodsky and a collection of poems by nineteenth-century Russian poets *An Age Ago* with Brodsky's foreword (Myers 1988). He was married to Diana, a Russian woman whom Brodsky knew from St Petersburg. The Myerses were Brodsky's close friends. The poet visited them in England. On one occasion, the Myerses showed him around the country, and that trip inspired a poetic cycle of six poems 'In England', which the poet dedicated to them. It was included in the book *A Part of Speech*. The poems are published as 'translated by Alan Myers'. Myers rendered many other poems and a play titled 'Marbles' by Brodsky into English, often in collaboration with the author. Myers admired Brodsky's work and shared his view of poetic translation. Their changing working relationship shaped their collaboration strategies over the years.

---

5. Later David MacFadyen published two books on Brodsky's work: Brodsky and the Baroque (1998), and Brodsky and the Soviet Muse (2000).

As Myers was translating the six poems of the cycle 'In England', he exchanged a few warm and friendly letters with Brodsky. Their correspondence was never just 'professional'. Myers's letters contain poems and queries about the publication of some texts and feedback on Brodsky's corrections and suggestions. Myers patiently explained differences between Americanisms and Englishisms (1 September 1977), commented on other translators' versions (Letter dated 15 July 1972 in JBP, S.I, GC, Myers, Alan, Incoming, 1972–93, Box 10, Folder 270) in addition to sharing personal news about his own health and life. Collaboration between him and the poet was a seamless part of their friendship. Myers insisted that he was 'very happy with practically everything' Brodsky did to his translations (Letter dated 25 November 1978). When Myers made suggestions, they usually dealt with word connotations, semantics, ironic undertones that were not obvious to a non-native English speaker. For example, in a letter of 1 September 1977, Myers suggested changing a few things in the poem 'Soho': 'I timidly suggest leaving out the last half-line (Lialia agrees). [. . .] too insistent, even banal. If you insist use "carousel" because the English words have wrong associations (carousel is an American usage).' He made further observations for the poem 'Three Knights', highlighting that no English abbey had 'domes, rotundas or baptisteries'. He proposed replacing these foreign-sounding words with English medieval abbey terms. Myers's hard work and attention to detail paid back. Mark Strand once sent an undated postcard to Brodsky to compliment him on the poem 'East Finchley' in Alan Myers's translation: 'I remember being struck by East Finchley when you showed it to me at the Ressio, but encountering again, this week in *The New Yorker*, it struck me even with greater force. Such as beautiful poem! (Alan Myers should do all work into English.) Beautiful, but with a transcendent authority that very few poets ever achieve these days' (JBP, S.I, GC, Strand, Mark, 1978–95, Box 14, Folder 383).

Myers's tone was always gentle, polite, self-deprecating, loyal and loving. He got only slightly offended when Brodsky told him to consult his Russian wife Diana (for further info about Diana and Alan Myers[6]) regarding the meaning of a Russian word or a phrase. Alan commented in one of his letters:

> I am never annoyed by what you point out; the only thing is when you tell me that 'something is not in the Russian' and refer me to Diana. Unless I've got the meaning wrong it's merely me trying to wring a rhyme out of the English. You recall that English words are on average half as long as Russian – well that means me using twice as many words as you and some of them may not actually be in the original, that's all. Take your amended lines about the parrot in 1967 for example; to get a rhyme you've introduced a new idea altogether (about the bird never lying etc) now if I'd done that you'd have scrawled in thick black pen . . . 'this is a sheer nonsense..!' or have re-written

---

6. see https://bookhaven.stanford.edu/tag/diana-myers/

the line out in literal English! (Letter dated 25 November 1978, JBP, S.I, GC, Myers, Alan, Incoming, 1972–93, Box 10, Folder 270)

Myers is one of Brodsky's translators who persistently reiterated that he was 'more interested in publication than money', which, he jokingly added, showed 'how amateur' he was' (Letter dated 24 October 1978). Brodsky, on the other hand, always made sure that his translator was paid: 'I don't want any fucking Red Cross business around here, understand? Besides, it's crumbs, peanuts' (Letter dated 4 November 1978). Brodsky cared about payments to all his translators and did not want anybody to do this work for free, especially as most of his translators often needed money to make ends meet. However, his good intentions did not always correspond to actions sometimes due to the fact that too many people would become involved in a translation, like in the examples of '1972' and 'Cape Cod Lullaby' discussed earlier. Myers was one of the translators of '1972'. As is evident from the following letter, he sent two English versions of the poem to Mieselas, explaining that he could no longer improve any of them and adding that he had help with one of the versions:

Dear Ms Mieselas,

I am sending, as you see, two versions of Joseph's 1972. The first, unrhymed, is a serious attempt to keep J's insistent rhythm & dactylic line-endings, while keeping the meaning of the words intact & the number of syllables exact. J. grudgingly admitted it was the best version yet, but then began insisting on rhymes all through. This is an old song, I know, J. said syllables, stress, rhythm could all be altered to suit the rhyme. I'd been working on this for weeks and felt a complete retranslation was beyond me. I attempted to refuse but J. (in hospital) insisted and 'helped' with some amazing rhyme suggestions. Sue produced a version which is rhymed in J's sense but Sue [has] been unable to hold a rhythm throughout (Sue not a poet). The versification could be described as irregular! No doubt a fresh eye can choose, or combine, or edit one or both. Sue spent too long (3 months!) to be able to see straight.

Kindest regards,

Alan Myers (Letter 4 April 1978, JBP, S.I, GC, Myers, Alan, Incoming, 1972–93, Box 10, Folder 270)

This indicates how challenging Myers and his collaborators found the process of poetic translation at times. It is practically impossible to disentangle the work of each contributor in the published version of '1972', especially because his translation of '1972' was 'fiercely ripped apart' by Brodsky and, in the final version, which was co-authored, Myers hardly saw any traces of 'his' version (Polukhina 1997: 467). Nevertheless, Myers was acknowledged as the main translator. A note to '1972' in *Collected Poems* states that the poem was translated by Myers with the author and first appeared in *The Kenyon Review*, 1/1 in 1979.

Myers also translated the 'Mexican Divertismento' sequence, following Frydman's interlinear translations and incorporating Brodsky's later interventions. The poems first appeared in the *NYRB* on 10 December 1978; a note to the sequence in *Collected Poems* describes them as translations by Myers with the author. According to Myers, the first poem of the 'Mexican Divertissemento' was translated by him with the exception of the first line of the second stanza. Myers admired the new line added by Brodsky: 'The crystal, be it noted, smashed to sand' (Polukhina 1997: 467).

Myers also felt that the poem '24 December 1971' was actually his translation apart from the last line. However, later, he noticed that Brodsky had nearly completely reworked his 'finished' translation. The poem in English translation by Myers with the author was published in the *NYRB* on 21 December 1978. Myers described Brodsky's approach to poetic translation as 'filling in a crossword'. Increasingly, he found it harder and harder to acknowledge his co-authorship because Brodsky was changing his texts so much. This is when he began to produce 'first-stage' translations for the poet to create a poetic, mimetic version of the original. According to Myers, they did not actually work together at the same time. Their collaboration was consequential, that is, the translator would first produce a translation, whether interlinear or 'poetic', and then the poet would make changes, either minimal or retranslate the text nearly entirely. Eventually, Myers agreed with Brodsky on 'a new modus operandi': Myers would give Brodsky an 'unfinished product' (*polufabrikat*), which, in other words, is an annotated interlinear translation. (Polukhina 1997: 468).

In the late 1970s, Brodsky he felt torn between lacking confidence in English and wanting to 'fix' the formal qualities of his poems in English translation. On the one hand, Brodsky said that he was 'the last one to make pronouncements in English'. On the other hand, he could not help it but complained that 'some nuances' had been missing and the beat had been distorted in some English versions – so working with Brodsky required a combination of skill, patience, admiration and loyalty to the poet (JBP, S.I, GC, Myers, Alan, Outgoing, 1974–87, Box 10, Folder 272).

Brodsky dedicated this occasional poem to Myers upon his birthday. The last stanza of this five-stanza poem is quoted below:

Since you were born before myself
It's hard to choose between to be
or not to be, Mylord, thy serf.
signed (but not sealed alas) J.B. (1974)

Daniel Weissbort

Daniel Weissbort was a poet, scholar and translator. He was a co-founder (with Ted Hughes) and an editor of the journal *Modern Poetry in Translation*. As professor of English and comparative literature at the University of Iowa, he taught literature and ran translation workshops. He was Brodsky's friend as well as his translator. Weissbort examined the complexity of his relationship with the poet in more detail than any other translator. In his book *From Russian with Love* he reflects on many years of working with the poet and reveals Brodsky's approach to translation by the fact that he had 'to stake out territory for himself between languages, a kind of medial marginality' (Weissbort 2004: 36). Brodsky's determination to follow a mimetic approach to translation led to many arguments between the two. At times Weissbort felt violated by Brodsky's interventions in his finished translations, especially the translations of the sequence 'A Part of Speech', which Weissbort was proud of. However, he continued to work with the poet. Their relationship is best described as combative collaboration (see Chapter 2). Unlike Myers, Weissbort defended his versions of Brodsky's poems despite feeling dispirited when he saw his texts changed by the poet. They exchanged many letters which reveal some of the ups and downs during the many years of their collaboration.

In 1976, Brodsky commissioned Weissbort to translate the sequence 'A Part of Speech'. Weissbort agreed and produced a translation that was later published in the *Modern Poetry in Translation*. Brodsky was reasonably pleased with Weissbort's rendering, having sent the translator a card, in which he said that the poems were 'OK' and he wanted Weissbort to do more translations for the book. Despite commissioning him, on reflection, Brodsky unfortunately did not find Weissbort's approach to poetic translation from Russian to English entirely satisfactory because the translator was not as faithful to the formal qualities of the original poem in Russian as Brodsky would have liked to. Without seeking the translator's consent, Brodsky intervened in Weissbort's translation, of which Weissbort was very proud and received a translation prize for. At a public reading of Brodsky's poetry, shortly before Weissbort was supposed to recite his translation of 'A Part of Speech' along with Brodsky's reading in Russian, Brodsky handed him a corrected version of Weissbort's translation. The translator could not believe his eyes: his text had been muddled, with words changed and moved around (see the section on Mode 1 in Chapter 3). Weissbort agreed to read the new version but, understandably, he was cross and upset, and he found it very hard to get over this incident. This led to further disagreements and a heated exchange of letters between the poet and the translator. In one of them, Weissbort wrote:

Dear Joseph,

First, on reflection, it was utterly within your rights to do what you did about the translation. And actually, I almost thank you for it, since your action was among several which highly symbolically finally convinced me that I was wasting my time fucking around with other people's work unless purely for money-making purposes or because there was a direct correlation with my own work. In your case the latter was not so (nor was the former, of course, thou' surprisingly it did actually bring in some sheckels!), because much as I do admire your work, and much as I recognise its importance, it is very distant from me personally (unlike its perpetrator!) My objection to the whole affair has to do with 'friendship'. In my view you acted with a high-handed disregard of pretty basic rules, at least as I see them. First the manner of your telling me, at that ghastly evening in Cambridge. Second, you have not really re-done the translation; you have strung it together – quite effectively – using lines and hints from my versions and, doubtless, from that of other people, who unbeknown to me, you had evidently; (contrary to the quite clear understanding I had from you that I was 'commissioned' to translate this poem) engaged in trying their hands too. The result of your efforts strikes me as rather good finally (with some criticisms which I could but will not, at this stage, make) but there is a simple morality involved here. I feel that you ought to make it clear in your introduction or whatever exactly how you arrived at a version, which though the original poem, the Russian, is obviously yours, does not wholly belong to you. None of this would matter much, of course, except that I feel it shows a cavalier disregard for others' feelings on your part and I do have some trouble with that. (26 November 1979, JBP, S.I, GC, Weissbort, Daniel, Incoming 1972–96, undated, Box 17, Folder 439)

He finished the letter by saying that if Brodsky were to alter his other translations, Weissbort would rather his name were removed. Three days later, on 29 November 1979, Weissbort was even more upset and enraged, having received a letter from Brodsky with 'the emendations' by Brodsky and Walcott. He could not accept the changes to his translations and he did not think that they had improved his texts. He was horrified by some uncolloquial words and phrases that Brodsky introduced, such as 'heartened palms', 'make the two-backed beast'. He insisted that his name should not be used when the translations were published, yet he was also upset because not all the translators' input was acknowledged:

> I would like to make a grand gesture and say that I now forbid the use of any of my versions, untouched or bowdlerised by you and sundry other visitors to your apartment or wherever. However, I suppose I should forego that pleasure and simply say that I do insist you, if you use my version substantially, but have altered it with Walcott or whoever, you put these other names with mine. [. . .] It is my work, subtly (or unsubtly) depending on your point of view, changed. They are only translations but still had a certain dynamic working for them, in their pristine state, which has now been distorted. (29 November 1979, JBP, S.I, GC, Weissbort, Daniel, Incoming 1972–96, undated, Box 17, Folder 439)

He continued the letter by saying: 'For the sake of my own blood pressure, I will not look at the book itself when it comes out.' On 30 November, Weissbort corrected his wish in another letter, saying that after not being able to agree on Brodsky and Walcott's changes to his translations, he would like to withdraw his translations from the book. In the end, the sequence 'A Part of Speech', as was discussed in Chapter 3, was published as a series of co-authored translations: translated by Weissbort with the author, despite the fact that some poems had been practically retranslated by Brodsky.

For Weissbort, it was both an ethical and aesthetic issue; it was a matter of his professional pride and his friendship with Brodsky. He was torn between continuing to work with Brodsky and withdrawing his translations because he could not bear the idea that they would be changed and published without his approval. At the core of the matter for Weissbort was ownership of his work – Brodsky's treatment of translations as extensions of the poet's own originals bothered Weissbort: he felt that translations were the product of the translator's work. Brodsky's reassurance that he treated all translators the same way, which was true, did not appease Weissbort because they fundamentally disagreed about the authorship of translations in principle. In a short letter that followed on 7 March 1980, Weissbort attempted reconciliation with Brodsky. Weissbort appreciated Brodsky's greatness in Russian but attempted to point out that the rules that Brodsky applied to his Russian texts would not work in English:

> Joseph, of course you understand a great deal, more than any of 'us', but finally you must, I think, allow 'us' to have our say. Nor must you decide who we are. This is beyond anyone's power. As an English-Language poet, you are other than you are as a Russian poet. You do not inherit your eminence, as a Russian language poet, when it comes to the English language versions. At least, that's my view. There are two Brodsky's, not yet one. (Undated, JBP, S.I, GC, Weissbort, Daniel, Incoming 1972–96, undated, Box17, Folder 439)

Later, Weissbort came to terms with Brodsky's approach to translation to an extent. Translating the poem 'Lagoon', he and Brodsky constructively discussed several drafts of the poem. On 9 October (no year), Weissbort sent a short letter with his translation after he had incorporated some of Brodsky's suggestions to his first version:

> I have followed a number of your suggestions but in here IX have dropped *solokha* altogether – it just doesn't work in English to my mind, the reference being lost entirely. [. . .] There are a number of places where the translation is very inadequate, so perhaps we can go over it together some time, preferably some drunken time, maybe in New York before your reading. (9 October, JBP, S.I, GC, Weissbort, Daniel, Incoming 1972–96, undated, Box 17, Folder 440)

In addition to the poet's interventions, Weissbort's translations were scrutinized by another of Brodsky's translators, Kline. In an undated letter to Brodsky, Weissbort wrote that Kline had complimented him on Weissbort's translation but yet criticized his half-rhyme: '"whole – wheel" might not be so good, as wheel does not immediately suggest a TV turning knob'. Weissbort apologized and 'confessed' that he did not realize what Brodsky had meant. Weissbort clearly forgave Brodsky for his treatment of Weissbort's translations because on 22 September (no year), he suggested that they should jointly buy a house in Maine or get 'some university in England to set up a translation poetry centre' and 'a course in contemporary Russian poetry' (Box 17, Folder 440). He quickly added that he was being 'romantic', which made the whole statement ironic. Weissbort's letters often had a self-deprecating undertone. At Brodsky's request, Weissbort translated more poems. As they carried on working together, Brodsky became more sensitive to Weissbort's feelings. On 3 December 1979, Brodsky wrote to Weissbort to apologize and ask him not to be 'mad at him' for having made changes to the galleys of his translations:

> Dear Danny,
>
> here are 'On Love' and 'Autumn in Norenskaya' reworked by Derek Walcott and my humble self. Knowing your attitude toward this kind of evolutions, I was dead set to avoid them in the first place; but then I saw the galleys. [. . .] What I mean, for example, is that all the poems that deal with love – 'Six Years Later', 'Funeral of Bobò', 'To E.R.', etc. – are in iambic pentameter and rhymed. I just thought that the pattern should be sustained even though nobody will pay any attention to it. And also I remembered that you were saying that you would render them differently if you were to translate them today.
>
> As for the 'Autumn' poem, we've just tightened it up a bit, and made this rhyme business a bit more detectable. Still, I want both of them appear under your name, and this is what this letter is all about. [. . .] Please don't get mad at me. It's not vanity that makes me do all these things, and I'd much rather sit and do other things. But these poems, you see, they are old, and there is no modernist element in them which somehow appears in the unrhymed version. There is certain air of ominousness, of inevitability to them, and this air disappears when the last word in a poem is 'unattainable'. (3 December 1979, JBP S.I, GC, Weissbort, Daniel, Outgoing, 1977–93, Box 17, Folder 441)

Brodsky and his publishers wanted to see consistency in his English poems, a recognized and unswerving voice and tone throughout his volumes or across his collections, while his translators aimed to do the best with a specific text or a few texts in the context of their own translation work. The tension between the poet and his translators was therefore inevitable and not only down to Brodsky's specific approach to poetic translation but also down to the context in which translation was taking place.

Brodsky's letter to Weissbort on 3 December 1979 from New York established the poet's view on poetic translation and more. Brodsky regretted that his 'simple alterations' of Weissbort's translations had hurt him so much and had been surprised by the gravity of his reaction:

> I failed to comprehend the degree of your identification with the work you've done. It's merely because I used to treat any translation including those done by me, as something utterly provisional. I.E., to say the least, as something that can always be improved. Or worsened, you may say. [. . .]
>
> If I got to rework some translation in this forthcoming collection (not yours only, but also Rigsbee's, Kline's, Myers's and others, although I imagine that for you it's of no consequence, and rightly so), it's not because I got to aspire for a higher spot on the local Parnassus, but because I've been given the galleys and found enough time to read them. What I found was often disagreeable and objectionable. That, in itself, wasn't a big surprise. What has surprised me really is that some of them could be easily remedied (or worsened, as you may say again). And here we are getting to the hub of the whole problem. It's not that I believe meters and rhymes being sacred, but I'd rather look trite than slack. [. . .] I think the cited above principle holds equally well with writing in English as it does with things done in Russian. And I felt that by now, once I was capable to acknowledge [*sic*] the pitfalls, I have an additional responsibility – that to the English language. Pathetic as it may sound, I feel that way; and besides, where and to whom may I turn for help. [. . .] it took me these seven years to realise that I am on my own not only in terms of accuracy of these translations, but also in the sense of their linguistic dignity.

Later in the letter, Brodsky explained that he had not questioned Weissbort's technique but claimed that it had lacked 'the sense of the inevitability of the statement'. It did not help much that Brodsky considered some of his translators' attitude to poetry 'cowardly' meaning that they did not care for translating the poetic form faithfully. By using the word 'cowardly', charged with moral undertones, he turned the conversation about a technique of poetic translation to a moral judgement. Some statements in Brodsky's letter appear contradictory and even arrogant; for example, 'If anything really upsets me, it is not the distortion of this or that passage but a really cavalier disrespect for the English language. I repeat: I don't care for mistakes so much, I don't care that my line doesn't scan well. But the point is that it's not <u>my line</u>: it's <u>the line in English</u>' (JBP, S.I, GC, Weissbort, Daniel, Outgoing, 1977–93, Box 17, Folder 441). Even though the poet attempted to sound humble by stating his insignificance in comparison with the authority of the English language, he actually ended up sounding arrogant because he presumed that he knew better what his lines should sound like than his native English translators, some of whom were poets in their own right.

Weissbort's views reflected the more contemporary, post-Venuti, understanding of the role played by the translator, according to which translators own their texts, with their names visible, and their role in the production of a new text should be appreciated. Unfamiliar with translation studies theories, Brodsky held a more traditional view, considering translation as a practice secondary to writing the original.

David McDuff

McDuff is an award-winning professional literary translator who translated from Russian, German, Icelandic, Finnish, Swedish, Norwegian and Danish languages. He rendered from Russian into English Marina Tsvetaeva's *Selected Poems* (Tsvetaeva 1987). McDuff was on friendly terms with Brodsky, and they had friends in common. In his correspondence with the poet, he talked about his personal life, work and, inevitably, his translations of Brodsky's poems. He completed several English versions of Brodsky's poems, including 'Strophes' ('Strofy'), which was published in his translation in *Stand* (UK) in 1979–80. Subsequently this translation was revised by Brodsky for further publications. McDuff also translated 'The Thames at Chelsey' ('Temza v Chelsea') but Brodsky chose to publish David Rigsbee's translation, which appeared in *The New Yorker* on 28 November 1977.

McDuff's letters reveal that he was also in contact with other friends and translators of Brodsky's with whom he discussed the poems he was translating at the time, and not only Brodsky's. For instance, McDuff mentioned that he had sought Diana Myers's help with understanding Tsvetaeva's 'Popytka komnaty' in his letter of 6 May 1982. It was not the only time he contacted the Myers for advice. In an earlier letter, of 5 January 1976, he mentioned that Weissbort had been in touch with him by correspondence, adding that his translations had been sent to Max Hayward who, 'apparently', 'had to approve them' (JBP, S.I, GC, McDuff, David, 1975–85, Box 10, Folder 255).

These instances demonstrate that Brodsky's translators consulted each other as well as the poet himself. However, they were not always fully supportive of each other's approaches to translation. Sometimes they clashed in public debates, as seen from a debate between McDuff and Weissbort about Elaine Feinstein's translations of Marina Tsvetaeva's poems (Tsvetaeva 1981). In his review, McDuff criticized Feinstein's translations for their lack of formal poetic fidelity. Weissbort felt it necessary 'to at least suggest an alternative approach to the absolutist one proposed by McDuff, alias Brodsky', describing McDuff as Brodsky's follower who believed 'in the sanctity of [poetic] form'. McDuff's reply to Weissbort was published in the same issue:

> *Rhyme and rhythm* are all-important in Tsvetayeva's poetic universe – they are what holds it together. In my view, no translator has the 'right' (I use inverted commas, since in art democratic principles don't apply) to traduce the central value of these formal elements of Tsvetayeva's work. Ms. Feinstein's substitution of her own aesthetics for those of Tsvetayeva seems to me such a betrayal. (McDuff 1982)

Weissbort's arguments about poetic translation with Brodsky are echoed in the above reply by McDuff to Brodsky. It shows that these debates about translation and especially poetic translation were taking place widely in the public discourse. Arguably, it was due to Brodsky and his vehement view on the translation of poetry that provoked this wave of debates about the form in poetry.

Peter Viereck

Peter Viereck was a poet and professor of history at Mount Holyoke College. In 1949, he won the annual Pulitzer Prize for Poetry for the collection *Terror and Decorum: Poems 1940–48* (Viereck 1948). Viereck met Brodsky in Leningrad in 1962 and then again in 1969, as Viereck recollected in a letter of 13 August 1979. Subsequently, they had an exchange via a graduate student of Viereck's (Labinger 2000). The two poets were in touch again after Brodsky had settled in the United States. In 1973, Viereck invited Brodsky to give a talk to students as part of Viereck's history course 'Totalitarianism and the Intellectual'. A letter from Colby Chapman of 10 October 1973 is evidence of how much students enjoyed meeting Brodsky, referring to him as 'a poet, a Russian and above all, a sensitive human being' (JBP, S.I, GC, Viereck, Peter, Incoming, 1975–95, Box 16, Folder 419). Shortly after the talk, on 23 October 1973, Viereck sent his 'Recommendation of the poet and teacher Joseph Brodsky for one-year five-college appointment under the distinguished visitor Program'. He described Brodsky's 'creative personality' as 'ornery and unacademic': the "university" he graduated from is the slave-labor camps of Siberia'.[7] He added that he was 'a difficult poet and a man of the strongest opinions (all-out anti-Fascist, anti-Stalinist, anti-totalitarian)'. Viereck's main argument for having him at the five colleges was that he was 'inspiring' and 'patient', 'sympathetic to students, responsive to their questions, a born teacher and with an excellent (though sometimes mispronounced) grasp of English' (JBP, S.I, GC, Viereck, Peter, Incoming, 1975–95, Box 16, Folder 419). Six years later, Viereck congratulated Brodsky on his tenure and took this opportunity to express his admiration (letter of 13 August 1979). After that, they swapped roles. It was Viereck who needed Brodsky's recommendations and support for his 'scribblings', which would be 'ammunition' to publish his 'unsellable' work, as Viereck wrote in a letter of 18 August 1979.

Viereck and Brodsky shared similar views on formal poetry. For both, form was an integral part of the poem. Viereck expanded on the importance of rhyme and metre in his talk 'Strict Form in Poetry: Would Jacob Wrestle with a

---

7. Despite being an academic and teaching a course on the Second World War, Stalin–Hitler alliance, Viereck referred to Brodsky's internal banishment in Norenskaia, Arkhangel'sk, which is in the North of European Russia as a Siberian labour camp. Since Viereck was a historian, I wonder whether he used the expression Siberian labor camps to make it more emphatic and recognizable by American university managers.

Flabby Angel?' which was described in an article published in 'The News', Bryn Mawr and Haverford Colleges on 22 April 1977 (see also Viereck 1978):

> But to Viereck, form is not artificial, but biological. Metrical poetry communicates on a non-verbal level, with muscle. This biological metaphor is the basis for Viereck's attack on free verse. Free verse is 'stillborn', and merely 'articulates', whereas formal verse 'incarnates'.
>
> Free verse lacks the recurrence of all flesh. Iambic meter, on the other hand, is akin to all the natural rhythms of the human body, and by approximating these rhythms, enables us to experience the poem more fully, more enjoyably.
>
> [. . .] the iamb is inhale and exhale of breathing, the systole and diastole of heart, the ebb and flow of tide. Moreover, rhyme is a vital link which ties this denotative meaning. Rhyme forms rings of suggestion around the referential meaning, which is in turn orchestrated by meter.
>
> The entire effect of a rhythmic and metrical poem, then, is to free the reader's imagination to fully experience its meaning. [. . .] iambic rhythm is a universal phenomenon and because it is recognized by all, becomes objective. [. . .] In 'Lids', Viereck developed an 'original' rhyme scheme involving not only the last syllable in a line but the first. The scheme he calls 'criss-cross rhyme', and the less the reader is aware of it, he says, the better. The effect is one of a suggestive rhythmic echo. (JBP, S1, GC, Viereck, Peter, Incoming, 1975–1995, Box 16, Folder 421)

This passage reveals that Viereck was just as passionate about the use of rhythm and rhyme as Brodsky, despite differences in their theories. Viereck shared his views with Brodsky and encouraged him to write a piece on 'how much Russian prosody resembled English prosody', as both poets believed (Box 16, Folder 418). Even when the two poets agreed on fundamental principles, that is, the importance of keeping formal qualities of a poem intact in translation, they still had disagreements about detail. Sometimes Viereck noticed an occasional misspelling in Brodsky's texts. For example, he slightly teased his Russian friend for misspelling 'witch' in a letter to Viereck: 'which hunt'. On some other occasions, Viereck made corrections in Brodsky's texts and explained them. For example, for a 'short-lined but long poem of rapidly oscillating moods and paradoxes', which moved 'rapidly', Viereck suggested using unvoiced consonants and short vowels instead of voiced consonants and long 'oo-vowels'. In another case, Viereck suggested replacing 'deadwood needless word "Merely"' at the end of a poem for 'Nothing at all' so that the poem would finish 'with a bang', not 'a whimper'. Expecting that Brodsky would object to this because this change would 'violate the three-beat rhythm' and to make his case stronger Viereck referred to Auden who had such 'variations in his [. . .] "Shield of Achilles" and Heym in the transl. [. . .] of "With the ships of passage"' (23 December 1979, JBP, S.I, GC, Viereck, Peter, Incoming, 1975–95, Box 16, Folder 418).

According to Stephanie Kamath, Viereck's granddaughter, the first poem from *Terror and Decorum* titled 'Poet' was reworked by Viereck after Brodsky's death to serve as a memorial to Brodsky. Under the title 'Not Worms', the poem is the fourth part of a section dedicated to Brodsky in Viereck (2005: 66–78). The other component of this section, under the title 'For Brodsky', won the New England Poetry Club best poem of 1998 prize. Viereck's tribute was posthumously included in Valentina Polukhina's Russian collection of Brodsky remembrances *By Those Who Remember Me* (Iz nezabyvshikh menia) (Polukhina 2015).

In response to Viereck's request to write an introduction to Viereck's book of poetry *Tide and Continuities* (Viereck 1995), Brodsky dedicated a poem to his friend. This poem is written strictly in the poetic form promoted by Viereck, as described earlier. The typed-up 1993 version of this poem is available at the archive. In this poem, Brodsky also explicitly refers to Viereck's *New and Selected Poems, 1932-1967*, a collection which *Tide and Continuities* in many ways both recalls and reworks. The context of these volumes explains much of the structure and references in Brodsky's poem, not only the explicitly cited first section of 'Hospital' poems but more indirect allusions, for example, to the gods and to Viereck as a speaking tree. The tree imagery is particularly relevant to Viereck's 'I Alone Am Moving', a poem Brodsky referenced in his 1970 communication with Viereck to portray his situation in Russia.

An introduction for a book
of poetry must have a look
of poetry. I thought a lyric
befits this work by Peter Viereck,
perhaps the greatest rhymer of
the modern period, a prof
of history at Mount Holyoke college
famed for its feminists and foliage.
. . . .
He is a solitary tree
himself, both immobile and free
to ponder what's above and rake it
with naked branches and the naked
eye; he essentially is
finality that clearly sees
infinity: his own comeuppance.
He's presence that observes his absence.

Joseph Brodsky, May 1993 (JBP, S. II, Poetry, IP, Introduction to Peter Viereck's
    First and Last Poems, drafts, 1993, Box 59, Folder 1200)

Jonathan Aaron

Jonathan Aaron is an American poet and professor emeritus in the Department of Writing, Literature and Publishing at Emerson College. He published three collections of poems: *Second Sight* (Aaron 1982), *Corridor* (Aaron 1992) and *Journey to the Lost City* (Aaron 2006). In *Collected Poems* by Brodsky, there are four poems translated by Jonathan Aaron with the author: 'Axiom' (see Chapter 3), 'Homage to Chekhov' (first appeared in *The New Yorker* on 7 August 1995), 'After Us' and 'Robinsonade' (both poems first published in *Queens Quarterly* in 102/2, Summer 1995).

Aaron considered Brodsky a close friend whose letters would 'warm his freezing fingers' (13 October 1975, JBP, S.I, GC, Aaron, Jonathan, 1975–87, undated, Box 1, Folder 10). Brodsky evidently valued Aaron's views on poetry and his advice. Brodsky's acceptance of nearly all of Aaron's corrections and suggestions in Brodsky's draft translation of 'Axiom' is a proof of this. Kjellberg consulted Aaron when she needed the support of a native speaker and a poet to help her convince Brodsky in something that he was unwilling to agree on, as she mentioned it in an interview with Rulyova in New York in 2018. In her letter of 20 March 1990, she sent Aaron 'the version of Joseph's Hardy piece' with her comments on it, letting him know what her reactions were to the text. She wanted him 'to agree or disagree' with her editing comments on this essay, adding that she was 'not bound to them by conviction or ego' and she did not want them 'to be working at cross purposes' (20 March 1994, JBP, S.I, Ann Kjellberg Correspondence, GC, 1994, March, Box 32, Folder 695). This shows that Brodsky's voice in English was curated collaboratively: Kjellberg was not only reading and editing his texts on her own but also contacting other readers to ensure that, metaphorically speaking, they were on the same page.

Harry Thomas

Harry Thomas is an author and translator. He has published numerous books, including *Some Complicity: Poems and Translations*, *The Truth of Two*, *Poems about Trees* (an anthology), *The Occasional Demon: Thirty-Six Poems by Primo Levi* and *Haiku*. Harry Thomas was the editor of *Selected Poems of Thomas Hardy* (Penguin, 1993) and *Montale in English* (Penguin, 2002). His poems, translations, essays and reviews have appeared in dozens of magazines. He is editor-in-chief of Handsel Books, an imprint of Other Press, and an affiliate of W. W. Norton between 2001 and 2011. Thomas translated Brodsky's long poem *Gorbunov and Gorchakov*, which first appeared in *The Paris Review*, 93, in autumn 1984, and was subsequently published in the collection *To Urania* (Penguin 1987). Thomas's version was revised by Brodsky and Kjellberg before it was reprinted in *Collected Poems*. (Prior to these translations, the poem was published in Carl Proffer's translation by Ardis (see Chapter 2).) While Kjellberg was helping Brodsky to have the poems for the collection *To Urania* ready, she contacted Thomas to prepare him for potential interventions by Brodsky; this is what she wrote to Harry Thomas:

> I should warn you that, as Joseph has become more confident of his English, he has revised his translations more and more dramatically. His current translators have become grudgingly resigned to this, we feel that it is a good thing for the book as a whole – to modify the patchwork quality of these many-handed translations and express more coherently Joseph's poetic voice. I hope this seems reasonable to you and doesn't strike you as an intrusion. You will of course be consulted as to all changes. (Letter by Kjellberg to Thomas, 15 July 1987, FSGI, M&AD, NYPB, Brodsky, To Urania)

In his gracious response, Harry Thomas failed 'to see the presumption in Joseph's taking a hand in the translation of his own work' (Letter from 27 July 1087, FSGI, M&AD, NYPB, Brodsky, *To Urania*). Brodsky kept a close eye on the translation until the moment of publication and often made corrections in the galleys. In his letter of 5 May 1988, Thomas responded to the alterations that Brodsky had sent to Thomas in the galleys of *Gorbunov and Gorchakov* by saying that he 'adored 90% of the revisions' that Brodsky made: '"Ibid" and "deshabille" and three dozen other such instances of improvement really are splendid improvements'. He also admitted that he came to like Brodsky's 'device of truncating lines by making them nine syllable trochaics where they were 10 syllable iambics'. Thomas found them particularly successful 'with a feminine ending', adding that no English poet had ever 'employed this device so steadily, as more than a once-in-a-poem variation'. Thomas's appreciation of the use of this poetic device was dampened by the unidiomatic use of the English language: he could not approve Brodsky's introducing the idea of 'he said' as an object, 'not merely a pronoun-verb construction'; he continued to criticize latest Brodsky's changes for lacking 'the rhythmical directness and punch of the earlier version' and for surrendering at times 'idiomatic English for the sake of vividness and the exigencies of form' (5 May 1988, JBP, S.I, Anne Kjellberg Correspondence, General Correspondence, 1988, Box 23, Folder 608).

Thomas also translated Brodsky's poem 'Odysseus to Telemachus', which was sent to Brodsky (JBP, S.I, GC, Thomas, Harry, 1980–90, undated, Box 15, Folder 396). However, Thomas's translation was not included in Brodsky's collections. Instead, Brodsky used Kline's translation of this poem in all publications. Despite disagreements, Thomas was fond of Brodsky and his work. As a sign of appreciation, he dedicated Brodsky his book of translations *The Truth of Two*. Thomas and Brodsky became friends. Thomas recollects that Brodsky was always very kind and even loving to him and his family. They met on various occasions, including some readings of Brodsky's poetry.

Thomas's letters to Brodsky are sharp and witty. On 10 December 1980, he began his letter by making a reference to a piece about Brodsky entitled 'He's

Lonely Too . . .' in *Harper's Bizarre*, as he jokingly calls *Harper's Bazaar* (JBP, S.I, GC, Thomas, Harry, 1980–90, undated, Box 15, Folder 396). He gently mocked his Russian friend for having been written about in a fashion magazine.

Howard Moss

On the Poetry Foundation website, Howard Moss is warmly described as 'an American man of letters': a poet, a dramatist and a critic[8].. However, he was best known as the poetry editor of *The New Yorker*, where he worked for nearly forty years. He promoted several young American poets including Richard Wilbur, Sylvia Plath and Mark Strand. He supported Brodsky and encouraged him to publish his poems in *The New Yorker*.

Between 1976 and 1986, Moss corresponded with Brodsky on behalf of *The New Yorker*'s editorial office. The first poem *The New Yorker* accepted was 'The Butterfly' translated by Kline in 1975. Moss confirmed this in a letter to Kline on 19 April 1975. After that, *The New Yorker* published many poems by Brodsky and declined at least one. It was the poem 'December in Florence', explaining that they did not have time to deal with its unidiomatic use of English (2 January 1980, JBP, S.I, GC, New Yorker, 1976–94, undated, Box 10, Folder 284). This comment hints at the fact that Brodsky's translations could be rather time-consuming for the editor to perfect the translation and make it suitable for publication. Moss closely followed the editorial process. For example, he sent Brodsky queries regarding the poem 'Kelomyakki', whose title was corrected to 'Kellomäki'. In his queries, Moss questioned the phrase 'one's things scattered everywhere' (in stanza 3) as 'little mannered' in English (letter by Moss to Brodsky on 16 October 1986, JBP, S.I, Ann Kjellberg Correspondence, General Correspondence, 1986, Box 23, Folder 594). Moss also translated Brodsky's poem 'I sit by the Window', which was published in *The New Yorker* on 4 June 1979.

Moss's role in finalizing Brodsky's poems in English for their publication in *The New Yorker* was crucial. He was a perfectionist who would make sure that the English versions were just right before publishing them. In his letter of 9 December 1977, he apologized for the delay in returning his translation of 'Torso', explaining that he still had some reservations about the poem. But even after prolonged deliberation, mistakes were sometimes unavoidable. In the same letter, he noted that as soon as 'The Thames at Chelsea' was published Barry Rubin called to say that he had identified some inaccuracies. Moss noted that after Rubin had described one of them, Moss asked him not to mention the others because he could not bear it (JBP, S.I, GC, New Yorker, 1976–94, undated, Box 10, Folder 284, Box 10, Folder 284).

8. https://www.poetryfoundation.org/poets/howard-moss

Moss had considerable power to persuade Brodsky to make changes by giving him variants and always asking for his final approval. For example, Moss gave variants for lines 3 and 4 in stanza 5 of the poem 'I Sit by the Window', explaining that there were such strong sexual connotations that it seemed to him that Brodsky should replace them for something else (10 October 1978, Box 10, Folder 264). In one case, at least, he proposed a tentative title to an untitled poem (letter of 4 October 1978). Moss dedicated Brodsky a poem 'The Summer Thunder', which finishes with two lines: 'But the one true floor of history still standing, / I think it will bear you' (JBP, S.I GC, Moss, Howard, 1978–83, Box 10, Folder 266). After he left *The New Yorker*, he was replaced by Alice Quinn.

Paul Graves

Paul Graves was a co-translator (with Carol Ueland) of the book of poems by Aleksandr Kushner *Apollo in the Snow: Selected Poems 1960-87*, for which Brodsky wrote an introduction (Kushner 1991). On 22 March 1987, when Graves was working on his English versions of Kushner's texts, he wrote to Brodsky that only as he was translating these poems was he 'becoming worthy even to read them'. He lamented the fact that it was such a slow process that it would require him three lives to become 'a fit audience' of the Russian poets Baratynsky, Mandelshtam, Tsvetaeva and Brodsky, whose books he sometimes 'labored in' (22 March 1987, JBP, S.I, GC, Graves, Paul, 1985–95, Box 6, Folder 158).

He translated 'Seven Strophes' (first appeared in *Western Humanities Review* in 1988), 'Cappadocia' (with Brodsky, first appeared in *The Times Literary Supplement* on 23 December 1994) and 'Isaac and Abraham', which he mentioned in a letter of 4 April 1995. While he was still working on the latter, he asked Brodsky for his 'imprimatur in just a couple of places where the liberties necessary to carry on the wordplay (or letterplay)' took him 'beyond the usual translator's bounds', referring to lines 311, 319–20, and 497–8 (4 April 1995, JBP, S.I, GC, Graves, Paul, 1985–95, Box 6, Folder 158). This shows that Graves sought not only Brodsky's approval but his help in a few tricky parts of the poem. Like many other translators, he collaborated with Brodsky in the process of translation, exchanging letters and notes.

Volunteer translators

Apart from the formally commissioned translators and the translators who were approached either by the poet, his editor, publishers or by his translators directly, there was a relatively small group of translators who rendered Brodsky's poems without asking for his permission. Most of them were students of Russian language or literature. They usually enjoyed Brodsky's poems and wanted to translate them in order to understand them better. One of them was Mark Hutcheson who wrote to Brodsky on 22 May 1988 prior to the International Writers' Conference in Dublin in June 1988. Hutcheson completed a dissertation on Brodsky's 'Roman Elegies' at Trinity College, Dublin, and translated some of Brodsky's poems into English, which he enclosed with his dissertation. He also attached his article on Brodsky's translations 'Za gorodishkom zlobnym ego' ('Beyond His Malicious Village') published in GRAPH, *Literary Review*, No.4, Dublin, spring 1988 (JBP, S.I, Ann Kjellberg Correspondence, General Correspondence, 1988, Box 23, Folder 613). Hutcheson was critical of Bethell's translations and appreciative of Kline's renderings. While he commented on the patchy quality of *A Part of Speech*, he appreciated the versions by Wilbur, Rigsbee, Hecht and Walcott (JBP, S.I, Ann Kjellberg Correspondence, General Correspondence, 1988, Box 23, Folder 613). Brodsky kindly declined the offer to publish Hutcheson's translations because the poems already had 'formal renderings in English' (8 May 1988, Box 23, Folder 613).

Christopher Fortune also offered to translate some of Brodsky's poems. Fortune was affiliated with the Department of Slavonic Studies at the University of Victoria in British Columbia, Canada and must have had higher hopes for his renderings of some Brodsky's poems. In his letter of 15 March 1982, he resent his translations to Brodsky for the second time since in 1981 (JBP, S.I, GC, 'Fis'-'For', General, 1972–95, Box 5, Folder 129). He was hoping to publish them in *The Malahat Review*.

Naomi Teplow, an Israeli student who taught herself Russian, literally translated the poem 'Isaak i Avraam' after she came across the Russian original in a postgraduate class at UC Berkeley in 1995, as stated in her letter of 5 March 1995 (JBP, Box 59, Folder 1201, S.II, Poetry, Individual Poems, Isaak i Avraam, English translation by Naomi Teplow, draft, 1995). As a student of Calligraphy and Illumination artist, she just wanted to understand the poem. She explains in her email to Rulyova:

> The class I was taking part in (as auditor, not an official student), was about The Binding of Isaac as it appeared in different literatures and languages. At that time, I was absolutely crazy about Brodsky, both his essays and his poetry, and when I found that poem in one of his books that I had at home, and there was no available translation for it, I decided to translate it myself, for that class. My Russian was not that good, so I consulted with some native Russian people, and they helped me a lot, but mostly, I worked on it by myself, and it was very, very hard, but also very, very satisfying and exciting. (Teplow 2020)

Sam Ramer is a historian and a history teacher who personally knew Brodsky and was not a translator but he spoke Russian. He translated a part of 'Mexican Divertismento' for fun. On 18 November 1978, he dropped Brodsky a line, looking forward to seeing him over the forthcoming weekend and have a chat about the poem (18 November 1978, JBP, S. II, Poetry, IP, Meksikanskii divertisment, English Translation by Sam Ramer, draft, 1978, Box 61, Folder 1293). He recollects that he liked the poem and wanted to understand it, like Teplow. He was also curious how Brodsky would render the opening phrase 'Veselyi Meksiko Siti'. Ramer was impressed with Brodsky's quick-witted solution, which he came up with in just a couple of minutes: 'Good old Mexico City' (Ramer 2020).

On 5 July 1990, Carol Rumens who lived in England and translated the poem 'Dorogaia, ia vyshel segodnia', wrote to Brodsky to share her translation with him. She explained that her ability to write in Russian was still 'infantile' and that translating poems was the only way she could bear to teach herself the language. She was apologetic about her mistakes but keen to point out some idiomatic differences between UK English and American English, suggesting that Brodsky's 'formality and irony' were 'closer to the English soul' than American (JBP, S.I GC, 'Roc'-'Rud', General, 1972–94, Box 12, Folder 326).

Michael O'Farrell, a student of Russian poetry at Hampshire College in Amherst, translated a couple of Brodsky's early poems including 'A Slice of Honeymoon' (1963). He also wrote a research paper for a history class given by Professor Viereck on Brodsky's poetry (JBP, S.I, GC, 'Oak'-'Oli', general, 1972–94, Box 11, Folder 290). Viereck gave him some helpful comments and suggested that he should contact the poet if he wanted further comments. He admitted that his translations were amateurish.

* * *

'The translators' accounts discussed in this chapter help us to further understand the translators' motivation to engage in poetic translation. Most of Brodsky's translators loved his poetry and the poet himself. They were mostly driven by their loyalty to the author and their passion for Russian poetry, which they wanted to convey in English. They were prepared to invest a lot of their time and energy in fine-tuning Brodsky's texts in English, accepting the poet's interventions. Amateur translators rendered poems to understand them better, to penetrate their meaning. Their stories of working with Brodsky further explain the complexity of collaboration networks between translators, editors and publishers. Poetic translation is not driven by commercial interests. Brodsky's translators are linked into informal networks centred around the author himself who edits his texts and curates his voice.

CONCLUSION

Poetry is not a form of entertainment and in a certain sense not even a form of art, but it is our anthropological, genetic goal, our evolutionary, linguistic beacon.

Joseph Brodsky (1995)

Authorship in collaborative self-translation: Who is in charge?

This study of Brodsky's self-translation and writing in English contributes to our understanding of authorship in several ways. First, it helps deconstruct the romantic notion of the solo monolingual writer; it reveals a variety and fluidity of self-translating and writing practices, which change depending on various external factors (such as the condition of exile) and internal factors (the poet's decision to become bilingual). Brodsky has moved from solo writing in Russian to collaborative self-translation and multiple authorship in English. The fact that Brodsky was a late bilingual contributed to this change because, in the 1970s, his English was not fluent enough and he needed to have his poems translated by others. Later he co-translated and self-translated his poems with the help of translators, friends and editors. Eventually he started writing in English with less and less editorial help from his collaborators. As a result, his approach to writing in English evolved in the process of cooperation with others.

Although his practice of writing changed when he switched to writing in his second language, his attitude to authorship did not. He transferred his thinking of his Russian texts as *his* to the English versions of his poems, even though they were produced in the process of collaborative translation by others or with others. Considering the translations as *his* poems gave him a licence to make interventions into his translators' versions, which sometimes took place without their prior acknowledgement or agreement. Jonathan Aaron, a co-translator of the poet, summarized the process of arriving at the final English version of a Brodsky poem: 'He and he alone was the judge as to its final form' (Email communication to Rulyova on 5 April 2020). It needs to be noted, however, that neither Brodsky nor many of his collaborators, including Aaron, saw this as the author's ego trip but rather that Brodsky's servitude to language, any language, was more important than anything else, as discussed in Chapter 1.

Brodsky's striking words in the Epigraph to this introduction provide further evidence of the importance he ascribed to poetry and to the poet as a medium of language. Writing in his native Russian, Brodsky was a solo poet accessing language directly through writing.

Difficulties arose when this philosophy of language was applied to the practice of translation, however. Translation is political; it requires translators to make preferences based on informed decisions about their approach to translation. No poem could be transferred in its wholeness; priorities should be identified in translating certain aspects of the text. Translation is also volatile; it follows trends, which determine translators' decisions – for example, whether to translate the metre or not – and change depending on the poetic practices popular at the time of translation in the translating language. Brodsky's esoteric philosophy of language did not allow for translation's volatility and for the fact that he could not access the 'great English language', as he referred to it with admiration, with the same ease as Russian. Brodsky's view of the poet as language's slave or medium would work for a symmetrical bilingual writer like Samuel Beckett, who wrote parallel texts in English and in French; in other words, he was accessing each language directly and independently in parallel; both texts had equal status and value; both were original. Brodsky was a late bilingual, and studying his self-translations allows us to 'go beyond Beckett' (as proposed by Rainier Grutman (2013a)) to advance our knowledge about bilingual writing. In the work of a non-symmetrical bilingual writer, like Brodsky, one language takes priority over the other. Russian was Brodsky's primary language, and English translations followed until the 1990s, when he started writing in English confidently without having to self-translate from Russian. The translations and self-translations of Russian poems remained for Brodsky secondary to their originals and, as a result, versions that could be improved. From this, Brodsky's hierarchical view of translation and translators' networks emerge with the author at the top of this hierarchy. Translators who worked with Brodsky confirm this. For example, Aaron (2020) describes his role as 'strictly secondary' to Brodsky's in the process of collaborative translation.

Brodsky's translators reacted to his proprietorial or 'possessive', to use Isabelle Vanderschelden's term (1998), attitude to the translations of his texts in a variety of ways, depending on their view and practice of translation. At one end of the spectrum were translators and other collaborators whose views could be summarized by Sam Ramer's words, that it was 'an act of blasphemy' to edit Brodsky's texts because although Brodsky's English 'felt a bit rough, on the other hand, some aspects of that roughness were precisely what made Brodsky's voice so unique and ingenious' (Ramer, undated). Ramer is a historian and not a translator; however, his words reflect some professional translators' views too. Alan Myers, a published translator who worked closely with Brodsky for many years, gave the poet permission to do whatever he liked with his translations because he admired Brodsky's poetry and wanted to be of service to his talent. But some years into Myers's working with Brodsky made even Myers feel less enthusiastic about the changes introduced by the poet to his translations. Myers stopped perfecting his translations; instead he started sending Brodsky half-finished translations ('polufabrikaty') because the poet would change them anyway.

At the other end of the spectrum were translators who shared a view that was popular among scholars of translation such as André Lefevere and Susan Bassnett (1990): that translation was a form of rewriting, and therefore translations were authored and owned by translators, not by the author of the ST. Daniel Weissbort, a co-founder and co-editor of the journal *Modern Poetry in Translation*, held this view; so when his translations of Brodsky's poems from the sequence 'A Part of Speech' were changed by the author, Weissbort felt violated and betrayed by the author. Brodsky and his translators found it challenging (although to a different extent in each case) to balance their friendship and good working relationship with Brodsky with their professional integrity as writers, translators and scholars. The ethical and moral aspects of collaborative translation were added to the politics of translation.

Comparing writing with translation, Vladimir Nabokov (1941) remarked that his translation of Alexander Pushkin's *Evgeny Onegin*, unlike Nabokov's novels, possessed 'an ethical side, moral and human elements' and that it reflected 'the compiler's honesty or dishonesty, skill or sloppiness' (Butler 2012). Nabokov referred to the politics of translation in general. In Brodsky's collaborative translation this was amplified by the politics of collaboration. He compiled his own collections of poems in English in which texts were translated by different people, and made judgements regarding which translations would be incorporated into the volume and which should be discarded. Brodsky's judgements were based on largely his mimetic approach to poetic translation, so his ethics followed his aesthetics.

But how did this change from solo writing to collaborative translation feel to the author himself? When his self-translations were corrected, he felt that his English was 'smoothened' by his native English collaborators. On top of that, he was frustrated by translators' inability or reluctance to transfer his rhythm and rhyme schemes to the English versions. Brodsky made interventions even though at times he could not hear his mistakes in English. Many translators pointed to 'real problems' about Brodsky's use of 'colloquial English idioms and syntax', as Anthony Hecht put in a letter to the poet (JBP, GEN MSS 613, Hecht, Anthony, 1976–93, Box 6 Folder 170). At the same time, Hecht, as well as Auden and Spender before, recognized Brodsky's talent despite errors, mistakes and mistranslations. Having read Brodsky's *Less Than One*, he wrote that Brodsky in his prose as well as in his poetry was 'at once witty and tragic', and he had a 'mind of uncanny speed, agility and grace, a mind that both by its sinuosity and clarity represents a vision of wisdom' (JBP, GEN MSS 613, Hecht, Anthony, 1976–93, Box 6, Folder 170). In addition to his extraordinary mind and exceptional poetic talent, it was Brodsky's good humour and sense of camaraderie with his translators that helped sustain his relationships with them throughout years of combative collaboration of the sort Brodsky had with Weissbort.

This analysis of Brodsky's self-translation practices also contributes to the debate about authenticity and authentic voice. Chapters 2 and 3 reveal how in the process of self-translation, Brodsky's idiosyncratic, 'arrant and wilfully provocative' voice with 'the lyric prodigality of invention' (Hoffman 1997: 6–8) emerged and shaped into the voice that has been described as 'authentic' (see discussion in Chapter 2). In this context, 'authentic voice' refers to an author's voice that is recognizable and consistent in the way it is used by the author. This 'authentic', unique and original voice was constructed and curated by the poet collaboratively with his translators and editors, however. This inquiry into Brodsky's translation and writing practices has added to the debate about self-translation by identifying five modes in which the English versions of Brodsky's poems came to exist: (1) borrowing, or 'anthologizing' as a form of collaboration; (2) self-translation as a form of reflection on others' translations; (3) commissioning and intervening, or overt collaborative translation; (4) self-translating from Russian; (5) creative writing in English. Recognizing these stages in a late bilingual author's writing emphasizes that the author's 'authentic' voice is shaped and curated in course of a dynamic process.

Self-translation has been considered a form of retranslation, underpinned by the study of retranslation in the history of poetic translation, as discussed in Chapter 3. Racz (2013) argues that mimetic poetic translation incites retranslation while translating poems *vers libre* does not encourage translators to review prior versions in their search for the successful transferral of the metre and rhyming schemes. In light of this, Brodsky's method of reviewing and rewriting the versions of his translators can be justified by the requirements of mimetic translation, which was seen as 'old fashioned' by some Brodsky's contemporaries, such as Denise Levertov. However, views on poetic translation differ considerably, especially given historical, cultural and linguistic variations. Brodsky's preference for the mimetic approach was usually associated with the Russian tradition of writing and translating poetry, but Brodsky always reminded his critics that his method was characteristic of versification in English, providing examples of metaphysical poets of the past, W. H Auden and others.

No longer invisible translators and texts

Adopting the approach advocated by Anthony Pym (2017) and Jeremy Munday (2014), to study translators and their 'microhistories' before texts, helps show the role played by translators whose contributions were not fully acknowledged in published versions of poems, especially interlinear translators but not only. The process of Brodsky's collaborative translation was often messy and complicated with several translators involved simultaneously or sequentially.

Interlinear versions included lexical and poetic analysis of the ST. Often, poetic versions were based on interlinears but not always. All versions were read by the poet, but translators also had access to other translators' versions at times. Translators were communicating with the poet and each other, sending letters and queries back and forth. Even when Brodsky started to self-translate, the process was still not linear and straightforward, as the poet sent his versions to different readers and editors who returned their feedback. Brodsky considered all the feedback but did not always follow it all. The story of 'Axiom' in Chapter 3 is characteristic of this kind of collaboration. Every form of collaboration led to several translations of each poem before the final one was approved by the author and the publisher. Unpublished English versions were discarded as drafts – with a few exceptions.

Some early translations by others were published without the poet's prior approval in Bethell's volume. Weissbort published his English version of the sequence 'A Part of Speech' before it was revised by the poet. However, in all Brodsky's subsequent volumes, only the translations revised by the author were re-published. Another early poem – *Gorbunov and Gorchakov* – also exists in three published versions: Carl Proffer's translation (published in *Russian Literature Triquarterly* by Ardis in 1971), Harry Thomas's version (which first appeared in *The Paris Review*, 93, in autumn 1984 and then was reprinted in *To Urania* in 1987) and Harry Thomas's translation revised by Brodsky (which was published in Brodsky's *Collected Poems*). All of Brodsky's later poems published in English have been approved by the poet or his editor. The 'authentic' voice of Brodsky in English was curated precisely by publishing only official translations and not allowing other versions to be released under his name. Posthumously, Kjellberg has continued to ensure this policy. This meant that most unauthorized or unfinished translations remain unknown to the reading public. From conversations with Kjellberg, I understand that soon this policy may change, with the publication of other old and new translations of Brodsky's Russian poems allowed. This may well benefit Brodsky's legacy, with the resurgence of interest in his work in English.

Focusing on translators instead of published texts, this book shifts the discourse from Brodsky being the self-translator of his poems (as he is considered by Berlina (2014)) to Brodsky as a co-author in English, advancing Jack Stillinger's (1991) theory of multiple authorship. As translation collaborations are not fixed, each story of co-translation is unique. Unfortunately, there is no perfect system for acknowledging co-translators' contributions. Brodsky commonly changed the authorship of English versions of his poems from the translator '*with* the author' to the translator '*and* the author', sometimes even using these interchangeably. To some extent his decision on how to identify authorship depended on his publishers' recommendation. In one of his letters to Myers, Brodsky explained somewhat apologetically that he would add his name as a co-translator to a poem translated by Myers, despite Brodsky's minimal contribution, because the publishers recommended this (see Chapter 2).

It was a marketing tool to reassure the reader that the TT is a true reflection of the ST and that the translator understood the intention of the ST. Ironically, this strategy supports the more traditional view of translation as a secondary activity to creative writing, something that Lefevere and Bassnett struggle against in the growing field of translation studies.

Translators' microhistories help us understand their motivation and the cognitive process of collaboration with Brodsky by exposing how they thought, acquired knowledge, made judgements and solved problems while trying to interpret his Russian texts or interlinears. Most translators did not fully comprehend Brodsky's poems without clarifications, ideally, with the author, analysis showed. Many private letters in the archive contain long lists of questions from translators to the author. The poets who were approached to create poetic translations from interlinear texts struggled even more trying to understand the texts' nuances. Hecht commissioned an extra interlinear translation by Rice in addition to the one provided by White in order to grasp the meaning and the form of the poem but even then admitted not fully understanding it. Conversations between translators and the poet helped them gain an understanding of the original text and reassured them in their choices. Brodsky's Russian poems presented all his translators, Russian-speaking or not, with many enigmas due to the complexity of his verse in Russian. Equally, translators' insights into the nuances of the use of English were valuable to Brodsky, even though he did not accept all native speakers' suggestions. Brodsky's collaborative self-translation project was a fascinating journey towards writing in English. This study of it has enabled us to analyse his learning curve and learn from the poet and his collaborators directly.

BIBLIOGRAPHY

Aaron, Jonathan (1982), *Second Sight*, New York: Harper & Row.
Aaron, Jonathan (1992), *Corridor*, Middletown, CT: Wesleyan, New England.
Aaron, Jonathan (2006), *Journey to the Lost City*, Port Townsend, WA: Ausable Press.
Aaron, Jonathan (2020), *Email Correspondence with Natasha Rulyova*, 7 April.
Abdo, Diya Mohammed Daoud (2009), 'Textual Migration: Self–Translation and Translation of the Self in Leila Abouzeid's Return to Childhood: The Memoir of a Modern Moroccan Woman and Ruju' "Ila Tufulah"', *Frontiers: A Journal of Women's Studies*, 30(2): 1–42.
Ackerley, Chris (2008), 'Fun de partie: Puns and Paradigms in Endgame', *Samuel Beckett Today–Aujourd'hui*, 19, 1 January: 315–25.
Al-Omar, Nibras A. M. (2012), 'The Self-translator as Cultural Mediator: In Memory of Jabra Ibrahim Jabra', *Asian Social Science*, 8(13): 211–19. Available online: http://www.ccsenet.org/journal/index.php/ass/article/view/21507 (accessed 5 March 2020).
Alphen, Ernst van (1998), 'A Master of Amazement', in Susan Rubin Suleiman (ed.), *Exile and Creativity: Signposts, Travelers, Outsiders, Backward Glances*, 220–38, Durham: Duke University Press.
Anderson, Laura (2020), Email Correspondence with Natasha Rulyova, 13 February.
Anokhina, Olga (2017), 'Vladimir Nabokov and His Translators: Collaboration or Translation under Duress?', in Anthony Cordingley and Céline Frigau Manning (eds), *Collaborative Translation: From the Renaissance to the Digital Age*, 111–29, New York: Bloomsbury Academic.
Auden, W. H. (1973), 'Foreword' to *Joseph Brodsky: Selected Poems*, trans. George L. Kline, 9–11, London: Penguin Books.
Auden, W. H. (1989), *The English Auden: Poems, Essays and Dramatic Writings, 1927-39*, ed. Edward Medelson, London: Faber.
Auden, W. H. and Kline, George L. (1973), 'The Poems of Joseph Brodsky', *The New York Review of Books*, 5 April. Available online: http://www.nybooks.com/articles/1973/04/05/the-poems-of-joseph-brodsky/ (accessed 30 March 2020).
Baer, Brian James (2011), 'Translation Theory and Cold War Politics: Roman Jakobson and Vladimir Nabokov in 1950s America', in Brian James (ed.), *Contexts, Subtexts and Pretexts: Literary Translation in Eastern Europe and Russia*, 171–86, Amsterdam, PA: John Benjamins Publishing Company.
Bassnett, Susan (2013), 'The Self-Translator as Rewriter', in Anthony Cordingley (ed.), *Self-Translation: Brokering Originality in Hybrid Culture*, 13–25, London: Continuum.
Bassnett, Susan (2014), *Translation: The New Critical Idiom*, London and New York: Routledge.
Bassnett, Susan and André (Lefevere), eds (1990), *Translation, History, and Culture*, London: Pinter.

Bayley, John (1981), 'Sophisticated Razzmatazz', *Parnassus: Poetry Review*, Part 9, Spring/Summer: 83–90.

Beam, Alex (2016), *The Feud: Vladimir Nabokov, Edmund Wilson, and the End of a Beautiful Friendship*, New York: Pantheon Books.

Beaujour, Elizabeth (1989), *Alien Tongues: Bilingual Russian Writers of the First Emigration*, Ithaca and London: Cornell University Press.

Benjamin, Walter (1968), 'The Task of the Translator', in *Illuminations*, trans. Harry Zohn, 69–82, New York: Harcourt Brace Jovanovich.

Berlina, Alexandra (2014), *Brodsky Translating Brodsky: Poetry in Self-Translation*, New York and London: Bloomsbury Academic.

Bethea, David M. (1994), *Joseph Brodsky and the Creation of Exile*, Princeton, NJ: Princeton University Press.

Bethea, David M. (1995), 'Brodsky's and Nabokov's Bilingualism(s): Translation, American Poetry and Muttersprache', in Valentina Polukhina (ed.), *Joseph Brodsky: Special Issue, Russian Literature*, 37, 2(3): 157–84.

Bethea, David M. (1998), 'To My Daughter', in Lev Loseff and Valentina Polukhina (eds), *The Art of a Poem*, 240–57, Houndmills, Basingstoke, Hampshire and London: Macmillan.

Birkerts, Sven (1982), 'The Art of Poetry XXVIII: Joseph Brodsky: Interview', *The Paris Review* 24, Spring: 82–126. Reprinted in: (2002), Cynthia L. Haven (ed.), *Joseph Brodsky: Conversations*, 73–4, Jackson: University Press of Mississippi.

Boyden, Michael and De Bleeker, Liesbeth (2013), 'Introduction', *Orbis Litterarum*, 68(3): 177–87. Available online: https://doi.org/10.1111/oli.12021 (accessed 14 March 2020).

Boyden, Michael and Jooken, Lieve, (2013), 'A Privileged Voice? J. Hector St. John de Crevecoeur's "History of Andrew, the Hebridean" in French and Dutch Translation', *Orbis Litterarum*, 68(3): 222–50. Available online: https://lib.ugent.be/catalog/p ug01:4121101 (accessed 14 March 2020).

Boym, Svetlana (1998), 'Estrangement as a Lifestyle: Shklovsky and Brodsky', in Susan Rubin Suleiman (ed.), *Exile and Creativity: Signposts, Travelers, Outsiders, Backward Glances*, 241–62, Durham, NC: Duke University Press.

Brodskii, Iosif (2010), *Kniga interv'iu*, ed. Valentina Polukhina, 5th ed., Moscow: Zakharov.

Brodsky, Joseph (1967), *Elegy to John Donne, and Other Poems*, trans. Nicholas Bethell, London: Longmans.

Brodsky, Joseph (1972), 'Says Poet Brodsky, Ex of the Soviet Union: "A Poet Is a Lonely Traveler, and No One Is His Helper"', trans. Carl R. Proffer, *The New York Times Magazine*, 1 October: 78–9, 82–5.

Brodsky, Joseph (1973a), *Selected Poems*, trans. G. L. Kline, London: Penguin.

Brodsky, Joseph (1973b), 'On Richard Wilbur: Review', trans. Carl R. Proffer, *The American Poetry Review*, 2:1, January/February: 52.

Brodsky, Joseph (1974), 'Beyond Consolation: A Review of Nadezhda Mandel'shtam's *Hope Abandoned*', trans. Barry Rubin, *The New York Review of Books*, 21(1), 7 February: 13–16. Available online: https://www.nybooks.com/articles/1974/02/07/b eyond-consolation/ (accessed 5 March 2020).

Brodsky, Joseph (1978), '"A Part of Speech" by Joseph Brodsky', trans. Daniel Weissbort, *Modern Poetry in Translation*, March.

Brodsky, Joseph (1980), *A Part of Speech*, New York: Farrar, Straus & Giroux.

Brodsky, Joseph (1986), *Less Than One*, New York: Farrar, Straus and Giroux.

Brodsky, Joseph (1987), 'Nobel Lecture', trans. Barry Rubin, 8 December. Available online: http://www.nobelprize.org/nobel_prizes/literature/laureates/1987/brodsky-lecture.html (accessed 5 March 2020).

Brodsky, Joseph (1988a), 'Forword and Biographical Notes', in Alan Myers (ed. and trans.), *An Age Ago: A Selection of Nineteenth Century Russian Poetry*, New York: Farrar, Straus and Giroux.

Brodsky, Joseph (1988b), *To Urania*, New York: Farrar, Straus and Giroux.

Brodsky, Joseph (1989), *Marbles*, New York: Farrar, Straus and Giroux.

Brodsky, Joseph (1992), *Watermark*, New York: Farrar, Straus and Giroux.

Brodsky, Joseph (1995), *On Grief and Reason: Essays*, New York: Farrar, Straus and Giroux.

Brodsky, Joseph (1996), *So Forth*, New York: Farrar, Straus and Giroux.

Brodsky, Joseph (1998), 'Pis'mo Dzheimsu Raisu', in Lev Losev and Petr Vail' (eds), *Trudy i dni*, 21–3, Moscow: Izdatel'stvo Nezavisimaya Gazeta.

Brodsky, Joseph (1999), *Discovery*, New York: Farrar, Straus and Giroux.

Brodsky, Joseph (2000), *Collected Poems in English*, ed. Ann Kjellberg, New York: Farrar, Straus and Giroux.

Brodsky, Joseph (2001), *Nativity Poems*, New York: Farrar, Straus and Giroux.

Brooke-Rose, Christine (1998), 'Exul', in Susan Rubin Suleiman (ed.), *Exile and Creativity: Signposts, Travelers, Outsiders, Backward Glances*, 9–24, Durham: Duke University Press.

Brown, Clarence (1980), 'The Best Russian Poetry Written Today', *The New York Times Book Review*, 7 September: 11, 16, 18. Available online: http://movies2.nytimes.com/books/00/09/17/specials/brodsky-speech.html (accessed 5 March 2020).

Burnett, Leon (1990), 'The Complicity of the Real: Affinities in the Poetics of Brodsky and Mandel'shtam', in Lev Loseff and Valentina Polukhina (eds), *Brodsky's Poetics and Aesthetics*, 12–33, Basingstoke, Hampshire and London: Macmillan.

Burton, Raffel (1974), 'Tongue-Tied', *The New York Review of Books*, 21: 8, 16 May: 10.

Butler, Sarah Funke (2012), 'Document: Nabokov's Notes', *The Paris Review*, 29 February. Available online: https://www.theparisreview.org/blog/2012/02/29/document-nabokov's-notes/ (accessed 7 April 2020).

Carroll, Lewis (1923), *Ania v strane chudes*, trans. Vladimir Nabokov, Berlin: Gamaiun.

Case, Holly A. (2016), 'Brodsky's Method', in *3 Quarks Daily: Science, Art, Philosophy, Politics, Literature*. Available online: https://www.3quarksdaily.com/3quarksdaily/2016/06/brodskys-method.html (accessed 4 March 2020).

Castro, Olga, Mainer, Sergi, and Page, Svetlana (eds) (2017), *Self-Translation and Power: Negotiating Identities in European Multilingual Contexts*, London: Palgrave Macmillan.

Ceccherelli, Andrea, Imposti, Gabriella Elina and Perotto, Monica (eds) (2013), *Autotraduzione e riscrittura*, Bologna: Bononia University Press.

Chénieux-Gendron, Jacqueline (1998), 'Surrealists in Exile: Another Kind of Resistance', in Susan Rubin Suleiman (ed.), *Exile and Creativity: Signposts, Travelers, Outsiders, Backward Glances*, 163–79, Durham: Duke University Press.

Coetzee, John Maxwell (1996), 'Speaking for Language: Review of *On Grief and Reason* by Joseph Brodsky', *The New York Review of Books*, 18(2), 1 February: 28–31.

Cordingley, Anthony (ed.) (2013), *Self-Translation: Brokering Originality in Hybrid Culture*, London: Continuum.

Cronin, A. (1996), *Samuel Beckett: The Last Modernist*, London: Harper Collins.

Crowley, John (2002), *The Translator*, New York: William Morrow & Company.

Davie, Donald (1988), 'The Saturated Line: Review to Urania', *The Times Literary Supplement*, 23–29 December: 1415.
Dietz, Shoshanah (1992), 'The Bitter Air of Exile: Russian Émigré and the Berlin Experience', in James Whitlark and Wendell Aycock (eds), *The Literature of Emigration and Exile*, 43–9, Lubbock, TX: Texas Tech University Press.
Dostoevsky, Fyodor (2008), *Idiot*, trans. Alam Myers, Oxford: Oxford University Press.
Dostoevsky, Fyodor (2009), *The Gentle Creature and Other Stories: White Nights, A Gentle Creature, The Dream of a Ridiculous Man*, trans. Alan Myers, Oxford: Oxford University Press.
Eder, Richard (1980), 'Joseph Brodsky in U.S.: Poet and Language in Exile; Sentenced to Labor Camp Reachable Over Fire Escape Private Relation With Language "Ease" of Poets in Russia "I Would Be Ashamed"', *The New York Times*, 25 March: 2.
Erlich, Victor (1974), 'A Letter in a Bottle: Review of Joseph Brodsky, *Selected Poems*', *Partisan Review*, XLI: 617–21.
Etkind, Efim (1988), *Protsess Iosifa Brodskogo*, 24–8, London: Overseas Publications Interchange.
Falceri, Giorgia (2014), 'Nancy Huston, Self-Translation and a Transnational Poetics', *Ticontre*, Teoria Testo Traduzione [Trento], 2: 51–66. Available online: http://www.ticontre.org/ojs/index.php/t3/article/view/35 (accessed 5 March 2020).
Falceri, Giorgia, Gentes, Eva and Manterola, Elizabete (2017), 'Narrating the Self in Self-Narration', *Ticontre, Teoria Testo Traduzione*, 7, May.
Ferraro, Alessandra and Grutman, Rainier (eds) (2016), *L'autotraduction littéraire: perspectives théoriques*, Paris: Classiques Garnier.
Frame, Donald M. (1983), 'Pleasure and Problems of Translation', *Translation Review*, 13(1): 31–45.
Genis, Aleksand (1998), 'Brodskii v Amerike', in *Iosif Brodskii: Tvorchestvo, lichnost', sud'ba: Itogi trekh konferentsii*, 8–15, Sankt-Peterburg: Zhurnal Zvezda.
Gentes, Eva (ed.) (2017), *Bibliography: Autotraduzione / autotraducción / self-translation XXVIII edition*, 1 April. Available online: www.self-translation.blogspot.com (accessed 8 March 2020).
Gifford, Henry (1978), '*The Language or Loneliness: Review of Konets prekrasnoi epokhi, Stikhotvoreniia 1964–71*, and *Chast' rechi, Stikhotvoreniia 1972–76*', *TLS*, 11 August: 902–3.
Gifford, Henry (1980), 'Idioms in Interfusion', *TLS*, 17 October: 1158.
Gjurčinova, Anastasija (2013), 'Translation and Self-Translation in Today's (Im)migration Literature', *CLCWeb: Comparative Literature and Culture*, 15(7). Available online: http://docs.lib.purdue.edu/clcweb/vol15/iss7/8 (accessed 8 March 2020).
Glad, John (1993), 'Joseph Brodsky: Interview', in John Glad (ed.), *Conversations in Exile: Russian Writers*, 101–13, Durham and London: Duke University Press.
Godard, Barbara (1984), 'Translating and Sexual Difference', in *Resources for Feminist Research*, 13(3): 13–16.
Golubenskii, I. (1963), 'Chto takoe nastoiashchii poet?', *Smena*, 29 March.
Gordin, Iakov (2000), *Pereklichka vo mrake: Iosif Brodskii i ego sobesedniki*, St. Petersburg: Izdatel'stvo 'Pushkinskogo fonda'.
Graffy, Julian (1992), 'Émigré Experience of the West as Related to Soviet Journals', in Arnold McMillin (ed.), *Under Eastern Eyes: the West as reflected in recent Russian émigré writing*, 115–57, Basingstoke: Palgrave Macmillan.

Grutman, Rainier (1998), 'Auto-Translation', in Mona Baker (ed.), *Routledge Encyclopedia of Translation Studies*, 17–20, London and New York: Routledge.
Grutman, Rainier (2013a), 'Beckett and Beyond Putting Self-Translation in Perspective', *Orbis litterarum*, 68(3): 188–206.
Grutman, Rainier (2013b), 'A Sociological Glance at Self-Translation and Self-Translators', in Anthony Cordingley (ed.), *Self-Translation: Brokering Originality in Hybrid Culture*, 63–80, London: Continuum.
Grutman, Rainier (2015), 'L'autotraduction: de la galerie de portraits à la galaxie des langues', *Glottopol*, 25: 14–30. Available online: http://glottopol.univ- rouen.fr/t elecharger/numero_25/gpl25_01grutman.pdf (accessed 8 March 2020).
Hanford, Robin (2000), 'Joseph Brodsky as Critic of Derek Walcott: Vision and the Sea', *Russian Literature*, 47(3–4): 345–56.
Hass, Robert (1980), 'Lost in Translation', *New Republic*, 20 December: 35–7.
Haven, Cynthia (2013), 'Joseph Brodsky's Reading List "to Have a Basic Conversation" – Plus the Shorter One He Gave to Me', in Cynthia Haven's *The Book Haven, Cynthia Haven's Blog for Written Word*. Available online: http://bookhaven.stanford.edu/2013/11/joseph-brodskys-reading-list-to-have-a-basic-conversation-plus-the-shorter-one-he-gave-to-me/ (accessed 4 March 2020).
Heaney, Seamus (1987), 'Brodsky's Nobel: What the Applause Was About', *The New York Times Review*, 8 November: 1.
Heaney, Seamus (1996), 'The Singer of Tales: On Joseph Brodsky', *The New York Times Book Review*, 3 March, 7: 31.
Hecht, Anthony (1993), *The Hidden Law: The Poetry of W. H. Auden*, Cambridge, MA: Harvard University Press.
Hecht, Anthony (1997), 'Introduction' to Joseph Brodsky's *A Part of Speech*, ix–xi, London, New York: Oxford University Press.
Hermans, Theo (1997), 'Translation as Institution', in Mary Snell-Hornbey et al. (eds), *Translation as Intercultural Communication*, 3–20, Amsterdam: John Benjamins.
Hermans, Theo (2007), 'Translation, Irritation and Resonance', in Theo Hermans, Michaela, Wolf and Alexandra Faker (eds), *Constructing a Sociology of Translation*, Benjamins Translation Library 74: 57–75. Available online: https://doi.org/10.1075/btl.74.04her (accessed 8 March 2020).
Hoffman, Michael (1986), 'Measures of a Poet's Mind: A Review of *Less Than One* by Joseph Brodsky', *The Guardian*, 3 October: 11.
Hoffman, Michael (1997), 'On Absenting Oneself: Review of So Forth and On Grief and Reason', *The Times Literary Supplement*, 10 January: 6–8.
Hokenson, Jan Walsh (2013), 'History and Self-translation', in Anthony Cordingley (ed.), *Self-Translation: Brokering Originality in Hybrid Culture*, 39–60, London: Continuum.
Hokenson, Jan Walsh and Munson, Marcella (2007), *The Bilingual Text: History and Theory of Literary Self-Translation*, Manchester: St Jerome Publishing.
Holmes, James S. (1988), 'Forms of Verse Translations and the Translation of Verse Form', in *Translated! Papers on Literary Translation and Translation Studies*, Amsterdam: Rodopi, 23–33.
Horgan, Mervyn (2012), 'Strangers and Strangership',: *The Stranger*, 33(6): 607–22. Available online: https://doi.org/10.1080/07256868.2012.735110 (accessed 9 March 2020).

Iakimchuk, N. (1990), *Kak sudili poeta: Delo I. Brodskogo*, Leningrad: Soiuz kinematografistov RSFSR, Leningradskaia organizatsiia.

Ionin, A., Lerner, I. A. and Medvedev, M. (1963), 'Okololiteraturnyi truten", *Vechernii Leningrad*, 29 November: [n/p].

Ishov, Zakhar (2008), '"Post-horse of Civilisation": Joseph Brodsky Translating Joseph Brodsky: Towards a New Theory of Russian-English Poetry Translation', PhD diss., Institute of English Philology, University of Berlin. Available online: www.dart-europe.eu/full.php?id=597340 (accessed 9 March 2020).

Ishov, Zakhar (2015), 'Brodski i Benjamin – poszukiwanie prawdziwego znaczenia przekładu', *Przekładaniec*, 30. Available online: http://www.ejournals.eu/Przekl adaniec/2015/Numer-30/art/5763/ (accessed 9 March 2020).

Ishov, Zakhar (2017), 'Joseph Brodsky's "December in Florence:" Re-interpreting Exile with the Company of Dante'. *The Australian Slavonic and East European Studies Journal*, 31(1–2): 121–63. Available online: https://www.academia.edu/35502979/J oseph_Brodskys_December_in_Florence_Re-interpreting_exile_with_the_shadow: of_Dante (accessed 9 March 2020).

Ishov, Zakhar (2018), 'The Battlefield of Translation: Joseph Brodsky and Daniel Weissbort', *Wiener Slavistisches Jahrbuch*, N.F. 6: 122–42.

Jimerson, Randall C. (2005), 'Embracing the Power of Archives', 69th Presidential Address at the Society of American Archivists Annual Meeting, 18 August, New Orleans. Available online: https://www2.archivists.org/history/leaders/randall-c-j imerson/embracing-the-power-of-archives (accessed 9 April 2020).

Jung, Verena (2004), 'Writing Germany in Exile: The Bilingual Author as Cultural Mediator: Klaus Mann, Stefan Heym, Rudolf Arnheim and Hannah Arendt: Klaus Mann, Stefan Heym, Rudolf Arnheim and Hannah Arendt', *The Journal of Multilingual and Multicultural Development*, 25(5/6): 529–46.

Kenner, Hugh (1996), 'Between Two Worlds: A Review of on Grief and Reason by Joseph Brodsky', *The New York Times*, 14 April. Available online: https://archive.ny times.com/www.nytimes.com/books/00/09/17/specials/brodsky-grief.html (accessed 20 February 2020).

Keysar, Boaz, Hayakawa, Sayuri, and An, Sun (2012), 'The Foreign-Language Effect: Thinking in a Foreign Tongue Reduces Decision Biases', *Psychological Science*, 18 April: 1–8. Available online: https://pdfs.semanticscholar.org/f6d4/9f9f0022a2fe e290d6737e83a0e5594aef28.pdf?_ga=2.112415623.2017988697.1590436173-268 566561.1590436173 (accessed 24 May 2020).

Khodasevich, Vladislav (1983), *Sobranie sochinenii/Collected Works*, ed. R. Hughes and J. Malmstad, 1, Ann Arbor, MI: Ardis.

Kjellberg, Ann (2020), Shared Google Document with Natasha Rulyova, January–March.

Kline, George L. (1973), 'Note on the Translation', in Joseph Brodsky, *Selected Poems*, London: Penguin Books.

Kline, George L. (1977), 'Working with Brodsky', *The Paintbrush*, 4, 7(8), Spring and Autumn: 25–7.

Kline, George L. (1989), 'Revising Brodsky', in Daniel Weissbort (ed.), *Translating Poetry: The Double Labyrinth: Collection of Essays on Translation*, 95–106, London: Macmillan.

Kline, George L. (1996), 'A History of Brodsky's 'Ostanovka v pustyne' and His *Selected Poems*', *Modern Poetry in Translation*, 10, Winter: 8–19.

Kline, George L. (1999), 'Istoriia dvukh knig', in Lev Losev and Petr Vail' (eds), *Trudy i dni*, 215–28, Moskva: Izdatel'stvo Nezavisimaia Gazeta.

Klots, Yasha (2011), 'The Poetics and Politics of Joseph Brodsky as a Russian Poet-translator', in Brian James Baer (ed.), *Contexts, Subtexts and Pretexts: Literary Translation in Eastern Europe and Russia*, 187–204, Amsterdam, PA: John Benjamins Publishing Company.

Kramsch, Claire (1997), 'The Privilege of the Nonnative Speaker', *PMLA*, 112(3), May: 359–69.

Kushner, Aleksandr (1991), *Apollo in the Snow: Selected Poems 1960-87*, trans. Paul Graves and Carol Ueland, New York: Farrar, Straus and Giroux.

Labinger, Lynette (2000), 'Preface to Lynette Labinger's Conversation with Joseph Brodsky', *Agni* 51, April: 16–20.

Lagarde, Christian (2013), 'Avant-propos: L'autotraduction : terra incognita?', in Christian Lagarde, Helena Tanqueiro and Stéphane Moreno (eds), *L'Autotraduction aux frontières de la langue et de la culture*, 9–22, Limoges: Editions Lambert-Lucas.

Lagarde, Christian (2015), 'Des langues minorées aux "langues mineures": autotraduction littéraire et sociolinguistique, une confrontation productive', *Glotopol*, 25: 'L'autotraduction : une perspective sociolinguistique', January: 2–13.

Lagarde, Christian, Tanqueiro, Helena and Moreno, Stéphane (eds) (2013), *L'Autotraduction aux frontières de la langue et de la culture*, Limoges: Editions Lambert-Lucas.

Lederer, Marianne (ed.) (2006), *Le sens en traduction*, Paris-Caen: Lettres Modernes Minard.

Leitch, Thomas (ed.) (2017), *The Oxford Handbook of Adaptation Studies*, Oxford: Oxford University Press.

Levertov, Denise; Joseph Brodsky and Donald Hall (1973), 'Letters on Poetry and Politics', *The American Poetry Review*, 2(2), March/April: 54–5. Available online: https://www.jstor.org/stable/27774572 (accessed 9 March 2020).

Lezard, Nicholas (2011), 'Less Than One by Joseph Brodsky: Review', *The Guardian*, 11 October. Available online: https://www.theguardian.com/books/2011/oct/11/less-than-one-joseph-brodsky-review (accessed 5 March 2020).

López López-Gay, Patricia (2006), 'Lieu du sens dans l'(auto)traduction littéraire', in Marianne Lederer (ed.), *Le sens en traduction*, Paris-Caen: Lettres Modernes Minard, 215–23.

Losev, Lev (2006), *Iosif Brodskii: Opyt literaturnoi biografii*, Moskva: Molodaia gvardiia.

Losev, Lev and Vail', Petr (eds) (1999), *Trudy i dni*, Moskva: Izdatel'stvo Nezavisimaya Gazeta.

MacFadyen, David (1998), *Brodsky and the Baroque*, Montreal and Kingston, London, Ithaca: McGill-Queen's University Press.

MacFadyen, David (2000), *Brodsky and the Soviet Muse*, Montreal and Kingston, London, Ithaca: McGill-Queen's University Press.

Mackinnon, Lachlan (1996), 'Obituary: Joseph Brodsky', *The Independent*, 30 January. Available online: https://www.google.com/?client=safari (accessed 14 March 2020).

Mackinnon, Lachlan (2001), 'A Break from Dullness: The Virtues of Brodsky's English Verse', *TLS*, 22 June: 9–11.

Mandelshtam, Nadezhda (1999), *Hope against Hope*, London: Harvill Press.

Mandel'shtam, Nadezhda (2001), *Vtoraia kniga vospominanii*, Moscow: Olimp Astrel'.

McDuff, David (1982), 'Battle over Translation: Daniel Weissbort, reply by David McDuff', *The New York Review of Books*, 23 September. Available online: https://www.nybooks.com/articles/1982/09/23/battle-over-translation/ (accessed 2 April 2020).

McGuire, James (1990), 'Beckett, the Translator, and the Metapoem', *World Literature Today [Oklahoma]*, 64(2): 258–63.

Milosz, Czeslaw (1980), 'A Struggle Against Suffocation', *The New York Review of Books*, 14 August: 23–5.

Montini, Sinéad (2007), '*La bataille du filologue*': *Genèse de la poétique bilingüe de Samuel Beckett, 1929–1946*, Amsterdam and New York: Rodopi.

Mooney, Sinead (2002), '"An Atropos All in Black" or Ill Seen Worse Translated: Beckett, Self-Translation and the Discourse of Death', *Samuel Beckett Today / Aujourd'hui: An Annual Bilingual Review / Revue Annuelle Bilingue*, 12: 163–76, Amsterdam: Rodopi.

Mooney, Sinéad (2011), *A Tongue Not Mine: Beckett and Translation*, Oxford: Oxford University Press.

Munday, Jeremy (2014), 'Using Primary Sources to Produce a Microhistory of Translation and Translators: Theoretical and Methodological Concerns', *The Translator*, 20(1): 64–80.

Myers, Alan (trans. and ed.) (1988), *An Age Ago: A Selection of Nineteenth Century Russian Poetry*, New York: Farrar, Straus and Giroux.

Nabokov, Vladimir (1941), 'The Art of Translation', *The New Republic*, 4 August 1941. Available online: http://www.columbia.edu/itc/mealac/pritchett/00ghalib/about/txt_nabokov_translation_1941.html (accessed 3 April 2020).

Nabokov, Vladimir (1969), *Speak, Memory: An Autobiography Revisited*, new ed., London: Penguin.

Naiman, Anatolii (1999), *Slavnyi konets besslavnykh pokolenii*, Moscow: Vagrius.

Nevzgliadova, Elena (1998), 'Peterburgsko-Leningradskaia i Moskovskaia poeticheskie shkoly v russkoi poezii 60kh-70kh godov', in *Iosif Brodskii: Tvorchestvo, lichnost', sud'ba, Itogi trekh konferentsii*, St. Petersburg: Zhurnal Zvezda, 119–23.

Oslon, Jamie (2017), 'Revising "A Part of Speech": Americanness and Self-Translation in Joseph Brodsky's Exile Poetry', *Translation Review*, 97(1): 47–60. Available online: https://www.tandfonline.com/doi/abs/10.1080/07374836.2016.1272378?scroll=top& needAccess=true& journalCode=utrv20 (accessed 9 March 2020).

Oustinoff, Michaël (2001), *Bilinguisme d'écriture et auto-traduction: Julien Green, Samuel Beckett, Vladimir Nabokov*, Paris: L'Harmattan, Collection Critiques Littéraires.

Pavel, Thomas (1998), 'Exile as Romance and as Tragedy', in Susan Rubin Suleiman (ed.), *Exile and Creativity: Signposts, Travelers, Outsiders, Backward Glances*, 25–36, Durham: Duke University Press.

Pavlenko, Aneta (2012), 'Affective Processing in Bilingual Speakers: Disembodied Cognition?', *The International Journal of Psychology*, 47: 405–28. Available online: http://dx.doi.org/10.1080/00207594.2012.743665 (accessed 9 March 2020).

Pavlenko, Aneta (2014), *The Bilingual Mind: And What It Tells Us about Language and Thought*, Cambridge: Cambridge University Press.

Peñalver, Maria Recuenco (2015), 'Encounter with André Brink: Looking on Self-Translation', *Research in African Literatures*, 46(2), Summer: 146–56.

Polukhina, Valentina (1989), *A Poet for Our Time*, Cambridge: Cambridge University Press.
Polukhina, Valentina (1997), *Iosif Brodksii glazami sovremennikov* [Brodsky through the eyes of his contemporaries], St. Petersburg: Zhurnal *Zvezda*.
Polukhina, Valentina (ed.) (2000), *Iosif Brodskii: Bol'shaia kniga interv'iu* [Big book of interviews], Moscow: Zakharov.
Polukhina, Valentina (ed.) (2008), *Brodsky Through the Eyes of His Contemporaries*, 1, Brookline, MA: Academic Press Studies.
Polukhina, Valentina (2012), *Evterpa i Klio Iosifa Brodskogo: Khronologiia zhizni i tvorchestva*, Tomsk: ID SK-S.
Polukhina, Valentina (2015), *Iz nezabyvshikh menia*, Tomsk: Tomskii gosudarstvennyi universitet.
Poole, Steven (2013), 'Why Are We So Obsessed with the Pursuit of Authenticity?', *The New Statesman*, 7 March. Available online: https://www.newstatesman.com/culture/culture/2013/03/why-are-we-so-obsessed-pursuit-authenticity (accessed on 10 April).
Pound, Ezra (2006 [1929]), 'How to Read' (first appeared in the *The New York Herald Tribune*, 'Books', included in *Literary Essays*, [15–40], 285, in Daniel Weissbort and Astradur Eysteinsson (eds), *Translation: Theory and Practice*, Oxford: Oxford University Press.
Prunč, Erich (2007), 'Priests, Princes and Pariahs: Constructing the Professional Field of Translation', in Michaela Wolf and Alexandra Fukari (eds), *Constructing a Sociology of Translation*, 39–56, Amsterdam: Benjamins.
Puccini, Paola (ed.) (2015), 'Regards croisés autour de l'autotraduction', *Interfrancofonies*, Special Issue, 6. Available on: http://interfrancophonies.org/images/pdf/numero-6/Table_des_matires_Interfrancophonies_6_2015.pdf (accessed 7 March 2020).
Pym, Anthony (1998), *Method in Translation History*, Manchester: St Jerome.
Pym, Anthony (2006), 'On the Social and the Cultural in Translation Studies', in Anthony Pym, Miriam Shlesinger and Zuzana Jettmarová (eds), *Sociocultural Aspects of Translating*, Amsterdam: Benjamins, 1–25.
Pym, Anthony (2017), 'Humanizing Translation History', *Hermes: The Journal of Language and Communication in Business*, 22(42), 30 August: 23.
Racz, Gregory (2013), 'No Anxiety of Influence: Ethics in Poetry Retranslation after Analogical Form', *Translation Review*, 85(1): 42–58. Available online: https://doi.org/10.1080/07374836.2013.768150 (accessed 21 March 2020).
Raine, Graig (1996), 'A Reputation Subject to Inflation: Review of *So Forth*: Poems by Joseph Brodsky and *On Grief and Reason*, by Joseph Brodsky', *The Financial Times*, November, XIX: 16–17.
Raine, Craig (2001), 'Joseph Brodsky's English', *The Times Literary Supplement*, 29 June: 17.
Ramer, Sam (undated), 'Iosif Brodskii i amerikanskoie obshchestvo', *Zvezda*. Available online: https://zvezdaspb.ru/index.php?page=8&nput=3278 (accessed 7 April 2020).
Ramer, Sam (2020), Email Correspondence with Natasha Rulyova, 1 February 2020.
Reid, Christopher (1988), 'Great American Disaster', *The London Review of Books*, 8 December: 17–18.
Reid, Robert (1999), 'Belfast Tune', in in Lev Loseff and Valentina Polukhina (eds), *The Art of a Poem*, 191–206, Houndmills, Basingstoke, Hampshire and London: Macmillan.
Rein, Evgenii (1994), 'Iosif', *Voprosy literatury*, 2: 186–96.

Rein, Evgenii (1997), *Mne skuchno bez Dovlatova: Novye stseny iz zhizni moskovskoi bogemy*, St Petersburg: Limbus.
Rice, James L. (1985), *Dostoevsky and the Healing Heart: An Essay in Literary and Medical History*, Ann Arbor, MI: Ardis.
Rice James L. (1998), 'O perepiske s Brodskim', in Petr Vail and Lev Loseff, *Iosif Brodsky: Trudy i dni*, 19–20, Moscow: Nezavisimaia gazeta.
Rice, James L. (2011), *Who Was Dostoevsky? Essays New and Revised*, Oakland, CA: Berkeley Slavic Specialties.
Sardin-Damestoy, Pascale (2002), *Samuel Beckett autotraducteur ou l'art de l'empêchement*, Arras: Artois Presses Université.
Scannell, Vernon (2001), 'Once More, In Russian Vernon Scannell Has His Doubts about Joseph Brodsky Writing in English Collected Poems by Joseph Brodsky', *The Telegraph*, 16 December. Available online: https://www.telegraph.co.uk/culture/4727080/Once-more-in-Russian-Vernon-Scannell-has-his-doubts-about-Joseph-Brodsky-writing-in-English-Collected-Poems-in-English-by-Joseph-Brodsky-Carcanet-14.95-540-pp-12.95-1.99-pandp-0870-155-7222.html (accessed 10 March 2020).
Scammell, Michael (2012), 'Pride and Poetry: A Review of Joseph Brodsky: A Literary Life by Lev Loseff', *The New Republic*, 18 May. Available online: https://newrepublic.com/article/103341/joseph-brodsky-russian-literature-lev-loseff (accessed 19 February 2020).
Schleiermacher, Friedrich (1813), *Über die verschiedenen Methoden des Übersezens*, Lecture 3 of Abhandlungen gelesen in der Königlichen Akademie der Wissenschaften (207–45), in Vol 2 (1838) Zur Philosophie, 149–5 (9 voll. 1835-1846) (reprinted in 4 vols. [1–2, 3–4, 5–6, 7–9]), Berlin: G. Reimer; Part 3 of Friedrich Schleiermacher's sämtliche Werke; trans. Douglas Robinson, 'On the Different Methods of Translating', in Douglas Robinson (ed.), *Western Translation Theory from Herodotus to Nietzsche*, Manchester, UK: St. Jerome Publishing, 225–38..
Schmidt, Michael (1980), 'Time of Cold: Review of *A Part of Speech* by Joseph Brodsky', *The New Statesman*, 17 October: 25.
Sergeev, Andrei (1997), 'O Brodskom', *Znamia*, 4: 139–58.
Sharpe, Jim (1991), 'History from Below', in *New Perspectives on Historical Writing*, ed. Peter Burke, 25–42, Cambridge: Polity Press.
Shraer-Petrov, David (1989), *Druz'ia i teni*, New York: Liberty Publishing House.
Shrayer, Maxim D. (1993), 'Two Poems on the Death of Akhmatova: Dialogues, Private Codes, and the Myth of Akhmatova's Orphans', *Canadian Slavonic Papers/ Revue canadienne des slavistes*, XXXV, 1–2, March–June: 45–64.
Shread, Carolyn (2009), Redefining Translation through Self-Translation: The Case of Nancy Huston, *The French Literature Series*, 36: 51–66.
Siccama, Wilma (1999), 'Beckett's Many Voices: Authorial Control and the Play of Repetition', *Samuel Beckett Today / Aujourd'hui*, 8, Poetry and Other Prose / Poésies Et Autres Proses: 175–88. Available online: https://www.jstor.org/stable/25781288 (accessed 10 March 2020).
Sicher, Efraim (1995), *Jews in Russian Literature after the October Revolution: Writers and Artists between Hope and Apostasy*, Cambridge: Cambridge University Press..
Simeoni, Daniel (2007), 'Between Sociology and History: Method in Context and in Practice', in Michaela Wolf and Alexandra Fukari (eds), *Constructing a Sociology of Translation*, Benjamins Translation Library 74, 187–204, Amsterdam, The Netherlands: John Benjamins.

Simic, Charles (2000), 'Working for the Dictionary: Review of *Collected Poems in English by Joseph Brodsky and Ann Kjellberg*', *The New York Review*, 19 October: 9–12.
Simmel, Georg (2016), 'The Stranger', trans. Ramona Mosse, *The Baffler*, 1 January: 176–9.
Simon, Sherry (2000), 'Introduction', in Sherry Simon and Paul St-Pierre, *Changing the Terms: Translating in the Postcolonial Era*, 9–30, Ottawa, ON: University of Ottawa Press.
Sontag, Susan (2001), 'Joseph Brodsky', in *Where the Stress Falls: Essays*, New York: Farrar, Straus & Giroux, 330–3.
Spender, Stephen (1973), 'Bread of Affliction: Review of *Joseph Brodsky: Selected Poems*', *The New Statesman*, 14 December: 11.
Steiner, George (1975), *After Babel: Aspects of Language and Translation*, Oxford: Oxford University Press.
Steiner, George (1988), 'Poetry from the Shadow-Zone: Review of To Urania by Joesph Brodsky', *The Sunday Times*, 11 September.
Stillinger, Jack (1991), *Multiple Authorship and the Myth of Solitary Genius*, Oxford: Oxford University Press.
Sufaru, Alina (2016), 'On Being "Retroactive and Retrospective": Translingual Self-writing as Heterotopia in Joseph Brodsky's Autobiographical Essays', *Revue française d'études américaines*, 4(149): 175–93.
Teasley, Ellendea Proffer (2017), *Brodsky Among Us a Memoir*, Brookline, MA: Academic Studies Press.
Teplow, Naomi (2020), Email Correspondence with Natasha Rulyova, 1 February.
Thirlwell, Adam (2010), 'The Poet's Head on a Platter', *The New York Review of Books*, 13 May.
Thomas, D. M. (1981), 'On Joseph Brodsky, Czeslaw Milosz and Andrei Voznesensky: Review of a Part of Speech, Bells in Winter, Nostalgia for the Present', *Poetry Review*, 70, 4 March: 47–50.
Thomas, Harry (2013), *Some Complicity: Poems and Translations*, Boston: Un-Gyve Press.
Thomas, Harry (2017), *The Truth of Two*, Boston: Un-Gyve Press.
Tomlinson, Charles (1983), *Poetry and Metamorphosis*, Cambridge: Cambridge University Press.
Tomlinson, Charles (2003), *Metamorphoses*, Manchester, UK: Carcanet Press.
Toury, Gideon (1995), *Descriptive Translation Studies and Beyond*, Amsterdam and Philadelphia: John Benjamins.
Tsui Yan Li, Jessica (2006), 'Politics of Self-Translation: Eileen Chang', *Perspectives: Studies in Translatology*, 14(2): 99–106.
Tsvetaeva, Marina (1981), *Selected Poems of Marina Tsvetaeva*, trans. Elaine Feinstein, Oxford: Oxford University Press.
Tsvetaeva, Marina (1987), *Selected Poems: Marina Tsvetaeva*, trans. D. McDuff, Hexham: Bloodaxe.
Tsvetaeva, Marina (1992), 'The Poet and Time', in A. Livingstone (trans.), *Art in the Light of Conscience: Eight Essays on Poetry* by Marina Tsvetaeva, 87–103, London: Bristol Classical Press.
Ufliand, Vladimir (1991), 'Odin iz vitkov istorii piterskoi kul'tury', *Petropol'*, 3 Al'manakh, 108–15, Leningrad: Private publication.
Vaïl, Petr (1995), *Peresechennaia mestnost'*, Moscow: Nezavisimaia Gazeta.

Vail, Petr and Loseff, Lev (1998), *Iosif Brodsky: Trudy i dni*, Moskva: Nezavisimaia gazeta.
Vail', Petr and Genis, Aleksandr (1990), 'V okrestnostiakh Brodskogo', *Literaturnoe obozrenie*, 8: 23–8.
Van Hulle, Dirk (2007), 'Bilingual Decomposition: The "Perilous Zones" in the Life of Beckett's Texts', *The Journal of Beckett Studies*, 16(1–2): 97–109. Available online: https://www.euppublishing.com/doi/pdfplus/10.3366/jobs.2007.16.1-2.9 (accessed 10 March 2020).
Vanderschelden, Isabelle (1998), 'Authority in Literary Translation: Collaborating with the Author', *Translation Review*, 56(1): 22–31.
Vansina, Jan (2004), 'A Note on Self-Translation', *History in Africa*, 31: 483–90. Available online: https://doi.org/10.1017/S036154130000365X (accessed 10 March 2020).
Venuti, Lawrence (1995), *The Translator's Invisibility*, London: Routledge.
Viereck, Peter (1948), *Terror and Decorum: Poems 1940-48*, New York: Charles Scribner's Sons.
Viereck, Peter (1967) *New and Selected Poems, 1932-1967*, New York: Bobbs-Merrill.
Viereck, Peter (1978), 'Strict Form in Poetry: Would Jacob Wrestle with a Flabby Angel?', *Critical Inquiry* 5.2, Winter: 203–22.
Viereck, Peter (1995), *Tide and Continuities: Last and First Poems, 1995-1938*, Fayetteville: University of Arkansas Press.
Viereck, Peter (2005), *Door*, Higganum, CT: Higganum Hill Books.
Vitale, Tom and Brodsky, Joseph (2014), 'A Conversation with Joseph Brodsky', *Ontario Review*, 23(3). Available online: https://repository.usfca.edu/ontarioreview/vol23/iss1/3 (accessed 20 March 2020).
Volgina, Arina (2006), 'Iosif Brodskii and Joseph Brodsky', *Russian Studies in Literature*, 42(3): 7–20.
Von Flotow-Evans, L. (1997), *Translation and Gender: Translating in the 'Era of Feminism'*, Ottawa, ON: University of Ottawa Press.
Von Flotow-Evans, L. (1997), *Translation and Gender: Translating in the 'Era of Feminism'*, Ottawa, ON: University of Ottawa Press.
Wachtel, Michael (1998), *The Development of Russian Verse: Meter and Its Meanings*, Cambridge: Cambridge University Press.
Wakabayashi, Judy (2011), 'Fictional Representations of Author–Translator Relationships', *Translation Studies*, 4(1): 87–102. Available online:https://doi.org/10.1080/14781700.2011.528684 (accessed 10 March 2020).
Walcott, Derek (1988), 'Magic Industry: Review of Brodsky's To Urania', *The New York Review of Books*, 24 November: 35–9.
Weissbort, Daniel (2004), *From Russian with Love*, Manchester, UK: Anvil Press Poetry.
White, Stephen (2020), Email Correspondence with Natasha Rulyova, 10 March.
Wilson, Ian W. (1999), '"Confusion Too Is Company Up to a Point": Irony, Self-Translation and the Text of Samuel Beckett's "Company/Compagnie"', *The Canadian Review of Comparative Literature/Revue Canadienne de Littérature Comparée*, 26(1), 1 March: 94–106.
Witt, Susanna (2011), 'Between the Lines: Totalitarianism and Translation in the USSR', in Brian James Baer (ed.), *Contexts, Subtexts and Pretexts: Literary Translation in Eastern Europe and Russia*, 149–70, Amsterdam, PA: John Benjamins Publishing Company.

Wolf, Michaela and Fukari, Alexandra (eds) (2007), *Constructing a Sociology of Translation*, Amsterdam: Benjamins.

York, Lorraine Mary (2002), *Rethinking Women's Collaborative Translation: Power, Difference, Property*, Toronto: University of Toronto Press.

Films

Pitkethly, Lawrence (1999), *Joseph Brodsky: A Maddening Space*, New York: New York Center for Visual History.

Rose, Charlie (1996), *Remembering Joseph Brodsky: Three Poets Tomas Venclova, Anthony Hecht, and Mark Strand*, a film, 19 March 1996. Available online: https://charlierose.com/videos/15770 (accessed 9 April 2020).

Wilbur, Richard (2017), *Translating Joseph Brodsky's 'Six Years Later'*, *Web of Stories - Life Stories of Remarkable People*, 11 October. Available online: https://www.youtube.com/watch?v=HEE45m74tb4 (accessed 9 April 2020)

Websites

Collaborative Combative Drawing [https://collaborativecombativedrawing.com/about/].

Joseph Brodsky Fellowship Fund [http://www.josephbrodsky.org/about].

Joseph Brodsky Papers [http://beinecke.library.yale.edu/about/blogs/poetry-beinecke-library/2009/02/11/joseph-brodsky-papers].

INDEX

Aaron, Jonathan   6, 122, 124, 132, 151, 170, 177
Abdo, Diya M.   48
Abouzeid, Leila   48
Academy of American Poets   13
Acmeist tradition   54, 55
aesthetics   3, 4, 7, 27, 29, 46, 163, 179
Age Ago, An   157
Akhmatova, Anna   10, 12, 16, 23, 58, 67
Alice in Wonderland (Carroll)   41
American poetry   61
American Poetry Review, The   154
Anderson, Laura   132, 139
Anglo-American literature   30
Anglo-Saxon communities   31
Anokhina, Olga   51
anti-semitism   9, 10
Apollo in the Snow: Selected Poems 1960-87 (Kushner)   173
Arab women writers   48
archival research   2, 3, 5, 6, 41, 65, 99, 113, 124, 128, 131, 132
Ardis   73, 170, 181
Arendt, Hannah   47
Arnheim, Rudolf   47
'The Arts in the Seventies'   145
Auden, W. H.   4, 12, 13, 20–5, 42, 55, 60, 67, 68, 79, 143, 149, 154, 168, 179, 180
authenticity   3, 43, 48, 61, 180
authentic voice   3, 7, 43, 44, 65, 66, 180, 181
authorial privilege *vs.* vulnerability   46–9, 129
authorship   3, 36, 49, 59, 76, 78, 85, 93, 163, 177–80
'Autotranslation'   38

Baer, Brian James   53
Barańczak, Stanisław'   79
Baratynsky, Yevgeny   133, 173

Baryshnikov, Mikhail   25
Bassnett, Susan   38–9, 43, 44, 179, 182
Bayley, John   57
Beaujour, Elizabeth   19, 33
Beckett, Samuel   3, 40, 44, 45, 50, 58, 178
Beinecke Rare Book and Manuscript Library   1, 6
Benjamin, Walter   54
Berlin, Isaiah   22
Berlina, Alexandra   2, 44, 65, 99, 101, 105, 181
Bethea, David   10, 26, 27, 29
Bethell, Nicholas   13, 36, 66, 67, 174, 181
biculturality   47
bilingualism   31, 32, 37, 40, 42, 43, 46. *See also* symmetrical bilingualism
bilinguals, definition   45
bilingual texts   2, 42–4
bilingual writers   19, 34, 40, 42, 45, 46, 65
bilingual writing   5, 19, 20, 37, 42–4, 65, 128, 178
Blake, Patricia   149
Blake, William   63
Blanchot, Maurice   10
Boas, Franz   42
borrowing/'anthologizing' as form of collaboration   85–98
Bourdieu, Pierre   39
Bowles, Partick   50
Boyden, Michael   46, 47
Boym, Svetlana   10
Brink, Andre   49
Brodsky, Joseph. *See also individual entries*
   and Aaron   170
   approach to self-translation   111, 113–14
   changing translation strategies   65–70
   command of English   14–16, 19, 44, 60, 65, 77–80
   commissioning translators   106, 108–11, 180

creative writing   114–17, 121–2, 180
and debates about his English   56–9
exile   3, 7, 25–8, 41
and Graves   173
and Hecht   143, 145–9
and his bilingual career   3, 7, 37–8, 45, 46, 51, 64, 65, 83
homage to Auden   22–5
and Kline   153–7
as lecturer   16–17
and McDuff   166–7
method of teaching   17–18
as 'mongrel' and self-translator   4, 32–6, 42, 56, 65, 111, 113–14, 181
and Moss   172–3
and Myers   157–60
vs. Nabokov   4–5, 41
offer by US universities   19, 19 n.16
poetic voice   49, 83
relationship with translators   1–2, 4, 5, 7, 51, 133, 178–80
remote control and combative collaboration   70–81
retranslation of poetry   84
and Rice   139–43
in Russia   9–12
Russian poems   52, 66, 79, 128, 132, 181, 182
and Strand   152–3
strangership   61
and Thomas   170–2
and 'unidentified' translator   141–3
and Viereck   167–9
view of language   28–32, 42
view on poetic translation   54–6
and volunteer translators   173–5
and Vorobiov   133–7, 139
and Walcott   151–2
and Weissbort   160–6
in the West   12–22
and White   138–9
and Wilbur   149–51
writing in English   19–20, 124, 128–9, 177
Brodsky, Joseph, works of
'1972' ('*1972 god*')   72, 137, 159
'After Us' ('*Posle nas, razumeetsia, ne potop*')   170

Age Ago: A Selection of Nineteenth Century Russian Poetry, An   74
'Angel' ('*Angel*'')   116
'Anno Domini' ('*Anno Domini*')   137
'Anthem'   124, 128
Autumn in Norenskaia' ('*Osen' v Norenskoi*')   164
'Axiom' ('*Mir sozdan byl iz smeshen'ia griazi, vody, ognia*')   122–4, 170, 181
'Brise Marine' ('*Dorogaia, ia vyshel segodnia iz domu*')   113, 172
From Browning to Our Days   12, 22
'Bust of Tiberius, The' ('*Biust Tiberiia*')   111
'Butterfly, The' ('*Babochka*')   52, 155, 172
'Cappadocia' ('*Kappadokiia*')   172
'Centaurs I-IV' ('*Kentavry I-IV*')   29, 114, 157
'Child of Civilization, The'   23, 26
Collected Poems in English   58, 74, 76, 85, 93, 95, 98, 159, 160, 170, 181
'Collector's Item'   32
'Condition We Call Exile, The'   26, 27
'Daedalus in Sicily' ('*Dedalus v Sitsilii*')   117
'On Death of Friend' ('*Na smert' druga*')   72
'December 24, 1971' ('*24 dekabria 1971 goda*')   160
'December in Florence' ('*Dekabr' vo Florentsii*')   65, 98–106, 151, 155–6, 172
'East Finchley'   157
'Eclogue IV: Winter' ('*Ekloga 4-ia: (zimniaia)*')   105–6, 113, 147
'Eclogue V: Summer' ('*Ekloga 5-ia: (letniaia)*')   106, 108–11, 155, 156
Elegy to John Donne, and Other Poems   13, 66
'Elegy to W. H. Auden'   16
'End of a Beautiful Era, The' ('*Konets prekrasnoi epokhi*')   57
'In England' ('*V Anglii*')   157, 158

'To E.R.' 164
'Funeral of Bobò, The' ('*Pokhorony Bobo*') 150, 164
'Gorbunov and Gorchakov' ('*Gorbunov i Gorchakov*') 73, 170, 171, 181
On Grief and Reason 21, 58, 74
'Hawk's Cry in the Autumn, The' ('*Osennii krik iastreba*') 143
'Homage to Chekhov' ('*Posviashchaetsia Chekhovu*') 170
'Homage to Robert Frost' 74
'Isaac and Abraham' ('*Isaak i Avraam*') 172, 174
Ischia in October (*Iskiia v Oktiabre*) 121–2
'Kellomäki' ('*Kellomyakki*') 113, 172
'Lagoon' ('*Laguna*') 137, 147, 163
Less Than One 19–21, 74, 148, 151, 179
'Letters from the Ming Dynasty' ('*Pis'ma dinastii Min*") 152
'On Love' ('*Liubov*') 164
'Lullaby of Cape Cod' ('*Kolybel'naia Treskovogo Mysa*') 73, 139, 140, 141, 143, 145, 146, 159
Marbles 74
'May 24, 1980' ('*Ia vkhodil vmesto dikogo zveria v kletku*') 33, 113
'Mexican Divertismento' ('*Meksikanskii divertisment*') 160, 174
'To My Daughter' 127–8
Nativity Poems 74
'New Life' ('*Novaia zhizn*') 157
'From nowhere with love' ('*Niotkuda s liubov'iu*') 89, 95
'Odysseus to Telemachus' ('*Oddissei Telemaku*') 78, 157, 171
Part of Speech, A (*Chast' rechi*) 30, 38, 57, 73–6, 85, 87, 88, 90–98, 115, 132, 133, 138, 140, 147, 152, 157, 174
'Part of Speech, A' ('*Chast'* rechi') 54, 73, 75, 76, 85–9, 133, 138, 141, 145, 161, 163, 179, 181
'To Please a Shadow' 20, 23
'Robinsonade' ('*Robinzonada*') 61, 170
'Roman Elegies' ('*Rimskie elegii*") 148, 174
'Second Christmas' ('*Vtoroe Rozhdestvo*') 154
Selected Poems 13, 24, 56, 67–9, 153, 154
'Seven Strophes' ('*Ia byl tol'ko tem, chego*') 172
'Six Years Later' ('*Sem' let spustia*') 149–52, 164
'Slice of Honeymoon, A' ('*Lomtik medovogo mesiatsa*') 172
'So Forth' ('*Konchitsia leto. Nachnetsia sentiabr*") 58, 74, 76, 83, 114
'Soho' ('*Soho*') 157
'Strophes' ('*Strofy*') 166
'Thames at Chelsey, The' ('*Temza v Chelsea*') 166, 172
'Three Knights' ('*Tri rytsaria*') 157
'Torso' ('*Tors*') 172
'Twenty Sonnets to Mary Queen of Scots' ('*Dvadtsat' sonetov k Marii Stiuart*') 70, 73
To Urania 44, 59, 74, 76, 79, 83, 121, 170, 171, 181
'Vertumnus' ('*Vertumn*') 79
Watermark 74
Brodsky Archive 1, 6, 34, 93, 105
Brodsky Translating Brodsky (Berlina) 2
Brooke-Rose, Christine 20
Brown, Clarence 57
Burnett, Leon 27
Burton, Raffel 56

'canonical' self-translator 44
Carroll, Lewis 41
Case, Holly A. 17
censorship 11
Chapman, Colby 167
Chukovskii, Korneyï 12
citizenship 27
Coetzee, John Maxwell 23
collaboration types 49–51

collaborative co-authorship 3, 64, 93, 111, 181
Collaborative Combative Drawing (CCD) 78
collaborative self-translations 5, 62–5, 83, 95, 131, 177–80, 182
collaborative translation 2, 3, 7, 16, 20, 36–8, 66, 83, 128–9, 132, 177–80
collaborative writing 21, 63, 65
Columbia 4 146
combative collaboration 70–81, 161, 180
Conrad, Joseph 58
Constructing a Sociology of Translation (Wolf and Funari) 39
contemporary English poetry 12, 22, 24, 55
'content-derivative' approach 52
Corridor (Aaron) 170
covert collaborative translation 65, 93, 105, 106, 111, 129
Crevecoeur, J. Hector St John de 46–7
criss-cross rhyme 168
Cronin, A. 50
Crowley, John 51
'cultural turn' in translation studies 38–41, 44, 54

Davie, Donald 58
Dietz, Shoshanah 27, 28
disembodied cognition 32
Divine Comedy (Dante) 100
Donne, John 4, 10, 30
Dostoevsky, Fyodor 139, 140, 157
Duncan, John D. 80
Duras, Marguerite 49

early bilinguals 40
Eder, Richard 30
editing 2, 50, 114, 124
Eileen Chang 46
Eliot, T. S. 21, 24, 135
emotions 30, 32
Encyclopaedia of Translation Studies (Grutman) 38
endogenous authors 40
English, Maurice 99, 105, 156
English language 30, 46, 62, 165

English poetry 16, 21, 34, 55, 57–60, 62, 105, 128, 152, 153
English *vs.* Russian language 29–34, 42, 54
Enlightenment 42
Erlich, Victor 56
estrangement 10
ethics 3, 4, 26, 27, 29, 83, 84, 163, 179
ethnicity 10
Etkind, Efim 11
Evening Leningrad, The 11
Evgeniy Onegin (Pushkin) 4, 5, 51, 52, 179
evil, concept of 30–2, 42
exogenous bilingual writers. *See* immigrant writers
experiences 30–2

Faust, Leslie 74
Feinstein, Elaine 166
female gender 40
feminist translators 39–40
Fernea, Elizabeth 48
first-stage translation 140–1, 152, 160
Fisher, Roy 24
For Brodsky (Viereck) 169
foreignizing approach 62
'Forget-me-not' (*Nyezabudka*) 151
'form-derivative' approach 52
Fortune, Christopher 174
Fourth Eclogue (Virgil) 147
Frame, Donald 84
From Russian with Love (Weissbort) 76, 161
Frost, Robert 21, 60, 133
Frydman, Anne 71, 72, 106, 132, 160
FSG 70, 72–4, 85, 132, 133, 137, 140
Fuller, Jamie 154
Funari, Alexandra 39

Genis, Aleksandr 23
Gifford, Henry 57
Ginsberg, Allen 61
Gjellerup, Karl Adolph 40
Gjurčinova, Anastasija 50
Glickstein, Gloria 17
Godard, Barbara 40
'Good old Mexico City' (Ramer) 175

Gordin, Yakov 11, 12, 25
Graves, Paul 6, 132, 173
'Great American Disaster' (Reid) 57–8
Greetings, Young and Unfamiliar Tribe (Pushkin) 135–6
Grutman, Rainier 3, 38, 40, 41, 45, 50
Gumilev, Nikolai 53

habitus 39
Haiku (Thomas) 170
Hall, Donald 154
Hamann, Johann Georg 42
Hanak, Chris 6, 132
Hardy, Thomas 21, 26
Harper's Bazaar 172
Hass, Robert 57
Haven, Cynthia 153
Hayward, Max 166
Haywood, Max 149
Heaney, Seamus 21, 46, 57, 74
Hecht, Anthony 6, 71–3, 76, 106, 132, 137, 139–41, 143, 145–9, 154, 174, 179
Hecht, Helen 132
Herder, Johann Gottfried von 42
heterogeneous lexicon 24
Heym, Stefan 47, 72
Hidden Law: the Poetry of W. H. Auden, The (Hecht) 143
'History of Andrew, the Hebridean'(Crevecoeur) 46
Hoffman, Michael 59
Hokenson, Jan 42, 43, 45, 64
Holmes, James S. 52
Horgan, Mervyn 60
'humanizing translation history' 39
Humboldt, Wilhelm von 42
humorous poems 16
Huston, Nancy 38, 45
Hutcheson, Mark 7, 132, 174

'I Alone Am Moving' (Viereck) 169
iambic rhythm 168
idiosyncratic behaviour 2, 7, 11, 34, 56, 80, 180
immigrant writers 40, 41, 50
implicit collaborative writing 65
Independent, The (Mackinnon) 59

infidelities 43, 45
'In Memory of W. B. Yeats' (Auden) 12, 22
intellectual independence 25
intercultural space 4, 39
interlinear translation 2, 36, 65, 70 n.4, 72, 76, 83, 85, 89, 93, 99, 105, 106, 113, 133, 135, 137–43, 147, 152, 156, 159, 160, 182
interlinear translators 71–3, 75, 106, 128, 129, 131, 132, 180
International Writers' Conference 174
Iowa Review, The 137
Ishov, Zakhar 2, 26, 44, 53, 65, 68, 70 n.4, 86, 99

Jack, Bill 17
Jakobson, Roman 52
Jangfeldt, Bengt 79
Jews ("*yevrei*") 9
Jimerson, Randall C. 6
Joke, The (Kundera) 49
Jooken, Lieve 46, 47
Joseph Brodsky: A Literary Life (Loseff) 25
Joseph Brodsky: A Maddening Space (1999) 12, 25, 28
Joseph Brodsky Fellowship Fund 135
Joseph Brodsky's Auto-Translations (Rulyova) 1
'Joseph Brodsky's "December in Florence" Re-interpreting Exile with the Shadow of Dante'(Ishov) 26
Journey to the Lost City (Aaron) 170
Jung, Verena 47

Kamath, Stephanie Viereck Gibbs 7, 132, 169
Kenner, Hugh 21
Kenyon Review, The 159
Kjellberg, Ann 2, 6, 36, 60, 66, 75, 76, 78–81, 83, 94, 95, 113, 117, 121–2, 124, 128, 133, 137, 170–1, 181
Kline, George L. 5, 12, 13, 24, 56, 66–73, 75–6, 78, 99, 105, 106, 108–11, 132, 145, 153–7, 163, 171, 172, 174
Kundera, Milan 49
Kushner, Aleksandr 11, 133, 143, 173

language   22–3, 27–32, 42, 178
late bilinguals   3, 21, 22, 31–3, 36, 47, 60, 177, 178, 180
Lefevere, André   38, 43, 44, 179, 182
"Letters 22"   19, 20
Levertov, Denise   55, 180
Leyris, Pierre   50
Lezard, Nicholas   21
Li, Jessica Tsui Yan   46
Lilin, Nikolai   50
linguistic citizenship   30
linguistic disobedience   26
linguistic minority writers   40
linguistic relativity   42
logopoeia   52
Loseff, Lev   10, 25, 133
Lost in Translation (Hass)   57
Lowell, Robert   4, 99, 105, 151
Lullaby of Birdland   140

McDuff, David   132, 166–7
McFadyen, David   157
McKane, Juliet   7, 132
McKane, Richard   13, 67, 132
Mackinnon, Lachlan   58, 59
Malahat Review, The   174
Mandelshtam, Nadezhda   4, 10, 11, 16, 61, 101, 151, 173
Mandelshtam, Osip   10, 26, 53
Mann, Klaus   47
Marshak, Samuil   12
masculine/feminine rhyme scheme   94–5
medieval Europe   42
Meiselas, Nancy   6, 70, 72, 73, 75, 145, 150, 159
melopoeia   52
Merwin, W. S.   53, 54
'metempsychosis'   24
metrical poetry   57, 168
metrical traditions   4, 52, 55, 56, 60, 84, 89, 156
migrant writers   47
Milosz, Czeslaw   10, 25, 40
mimetic approach   4, 5, 23, 35, 52–6, 61, 78, 90, 98, 161, 179
mimetic translation   23, 44, 53, 56, 84, 110, 180

Mistral, Frederic   40
modernity   42
Modern Poetry in Translation   73, 85, 93, 95, 98, 160, 161, 179
Monatale in English (Thomas)   170
mongrelization   32
monolingual writing   42–3
Mooney, Sinead   45
Moss, Howard   75, 77, 132, 172–3
Mount Holyoke College   17
multiple authorship   3, 7, 37, 62–5, 98, 128, 177, 181
Munday, Jeremy   3, 41, 131, 180
Munson, Marcella   42, 43, 45, 64
Myers, Alan   68, 85, 87, 88, 90, 93–5, 100–1, 105, 111, 132, 141, 145, 157–60, 178, 179, 181
Myers, Diana   157, 158, 166
Myers, Marty   17, 56, 74, 76, 98

Nabokov, Vladimir   1, 4, 41, 51–4, 58, 106, 139, 179
nationality   9, 9–10 n.1
national language   28, 30, 42
national literary discourse   47
native speaker's privilege   47
New and Selected Poems (Viereck)   169
New England Poetry Club   169
New Yorker, The   75, 77, 105, 157, 166, 172, 173
New York Review of Books, The (*NYRB*)   88, 90, 93, 95, 98, 111, 117, 121, 149, 160
New York Times, The   66
New York Times Sunday, The   145
Not Worms (Viereck)   169

Occasional Demon: Thirty-Six Poems by Primo Levi, The (Thomas)   170
October Revolution (1917)   41
Ode to Felitsa (Derzhavin)   138
O'Farrell, Michael   172
Al-Omar, Nibras A. M.   46
organic translation   16, 84
ostracism   10
overt collaborative translation   65, 83, 93, 106, 108–11

parasitic lifestyle   11
Paris Review, The   170, 181
Parker, Charlie   140
Partridge, Monica   17
patriotism   27
Pavel, Thomas   25
Pavlenko, Aneta   42
Paz, Octavio   50
Péron, Alfred   50
Pervukhin, Eric   156
Peterkiewicz, Jerzy   20
phanopoeia   52
Picken, Margo   114, 116
Pirandello, Luigi   40
plagiarism   64
Plath, Sylvia   172
'Plato Elaborated'(Moss)   75
Platonov, Andrei   31
Poems about Trees (Thomas)   170
Poems of the Caribbean (Walcott)   151
Poet (Viereck)   169
'The Poet and Time'(Tsvetaeva)   27
poetic language   42, 55, 62, 66
poetic rendering   2, 4, 5, 52, 53, 56, 69, 110, 122, 132, 137, 139–43, 147, 155, 156
poetic translation   4, 5, 15, 16, 23, 70 n.4, 73, 76, 78, 85, 90, 98, 100, 106, 131, 157, 159–61, 164, 165, 167, 175, 180, 182
   ethics of   83, 84, 179
   mimetic approach to   52–6
poetic translators   70 n.4, 71, 72, 75, 76, 128, 129, 132, 133
Politburo ruling   9
politics   25–7, 48, 178, 179
Polukhina, Valentina   7, 16, 22, 24, 132, 169
Poole, Steven   43
'Popytka komnaty' (Tsvetaeva)   166
'post-colonial' writers   40, 41
Pound, Ezra   21, 24, 52
Proffer, Carl   12–16, 18, 70, 73, 78, 150, 181
prosody   23, 78, 133, 168
Pushkin, Alexander   4, 5, 51–3, 64, 135–6, 139, 152, 179
Pym, Anthony   3, 4, 39, 41, 63, 180

Queen's Quarterly   124
Quinn, Alice   173

Racz, Gregory   84
Raine, Craig Anthony   46, 58, 59
Ramer, Sam   7, 132, 174, 178
Rasputin, Valentin   157
Recuenco Peñalver, María   49
Reid, Christopher   46, 57
Reid, Robert   58
relativist view   42–3
Renaissance   42
retranslation   3, 7, 83–4, 90, 95, 98–106, 128, 180
Return to Childhood: The Memoir of a Modern Moroccan Woman (Abouzeid)   48
rewriting   38, 39, 43, 44, 180
rhymes/rhyming   4, 15, 16, 23, 34, 53, 55, 56, 60, 68, 84, 128, 135, 138, 155, 156, 159, 166, 168
   in *December in Florence*   98–106
   in *Part of Speech, A*   85, 89, 90, 93–5
rhythm   16, 34, 135, 159, 168
Rice, James   76, 132, 139–43, 145, 182
Rigsbee, David   70, 166, 174
romanticism   42, 64, 155
Rose, Charlie   143
Rousseau, Jean-Jacque   42
Rubin, Barry   4, 71–6, 99, 152, 172
Rulyova, Natasha   19 n.16, 139, 170, 174
Rumens, Carol   175
Russel, John   145
Russia   42
   culture   64
   identity   28
   poems   52–5, 57, 62, 66, 85, 128, 132, 152, 181, 182
   poetic tradition   55, 62, 64
Russian Review, The   66

Sallivan   141–3, 145
Sapir, Edward   42
Sartre, Jean Paul   12
Scammell, Michael   25
Scannell, Vernon   58
Schleiermacher, Friedrich   42
Schmidt, Michael   30, 57
Schtilts, Veronique   79

Schwartz, Rhoda   149
Scully, James   70, 154
Second Sight (Aaron)   170
Selected Poems (Tsvetaeva)   166
Selected Poems of Thomas Hardy
    (Thomas)   170
self-translation   2–5, 7, 16, 20, 33–7,
    42, 48, 56, 65–6, 76, 79, 89–90, 93,
    105, 106, 111, 113–14, 132, 141,
    143, 177, 178, 180
  as form of linguistic *strangership*
    59–62
  French   47
  reasons for studying   43–6
  redefining   38–41
  as retranslation   98–106
  types of collaboration   49–51
self-translators   46, 48, 85
  privileged status of   47
  study of   43
  types of   40
semantics   23
'Semi-Literary Drone, A'   11
September 1, 1939 (Auden)   21
Sergeev, Andrei   26, 29
'Seven Years Later'. *See* Brodsky, Joseph,
    works of, 'Six Years Later' (*'Sem'
    let spustia'*)
Sharpe, Jim   131
Siccama, Wilma   44–5
Sicher, Efraim   27
Simic, Charles   58
Simmel, Georg   4, 37, 37 n.1, 60
Simon, Leslie   85, 88–90
Singer, Isaac Bashevis   40
singular text (ST)   4, 35, 39, 49,
    56, 66, 78, 83, 84, 131, 181,
    182
skopos theory   46
Smena   11
social parasitism   11
'social turn' in translation studies   2, 7,
    37–41, 63
Society of American Archivists, The   6
sociolinguistic theories   40
sociological theories   39
Some Complicity: Poems and Translations
    (Thomas)   170
Sontag, Susan   58

'The Sound of the Tide'   151
Spender, Stephen   16, 56, 69, 154, 179
Stale Mates (Eileen Chang)   46
Stalin, Joseph   9
Steiner, George   59, 84
stereotypes   48
Stevens, Wallace   21
Stillinger, Jack   3, 37, 62, 63, 65,
    106, 181
Story of Goryukhino Village, A (Pushkin)
    139
Strand, Mark   71, 72, 132, 152–3,
    158, 172
strangership   4, 7, 21, 32, 37, 37 n.1,
    59–62, 153
Straus, Roger W.   74
Sufaru, Alina   28, 32
Summer Thunder, The (Moss)   173
Supreme Soviet of the RSFSR   11
symmetrical bilingualism   45
symmetrical bilingual writers   44, 46

Tagore, Rabindranath   40
target texts (TTs)   49, 50, 54, 78, 84,
    85, 182
Teasley, Ellendea Proffer   12–14, 16
Telegraph, The   58
Teplow, Naomi   7, 174, 175
Terror and Decorum: Poems 1940–48
    (Viereck)   167, 169
Thomas, D. M.   57
Thomas, Harry   7, 19 n.16, 78, 132,
    170–2, 181
Tide and Continuities (Viereck)   169
Times Literary Supplement, The   128
Tomlinson, Charles   24, 84
Toury, Gideon   61
'tragicomedy'   27
translation   35, 36, 41, 43, 44, 49, 53,
    61, 62, 66, 69, 76, 83, 85, 95, 111,
    132, 163, 178. *See also* poetic
    translation; self-translation
  moral aspect of   5, 46, 179
  politics of   48, 179
  studies   3, 33, 37–40, 63, 165–6, 182
translationese   4, 49, 58, 59, 79
Translation: Theory and Practice
    (Weissbort)   54
translator identity   39

translators' 'microhistories' 3, 7, 131, 180, 182
translingual practice 47
Truth of Two, The (Thomas) 170, 171
Tsvetaeva, Marina 27, 152, 166, 173

Ueland, Carol 173
Ufliand, Vladimir 15
unauthorized translations 36
United States 12, 13, 16, 19, 25, 37, 38, 47, 48, 55, 64, 67, 133, 135, 167
universalist view 42–3
University of Michigan 13, 16, 21, 138
University of Oregon 139
Updike, John 154
'Using Primary Sources to Produce a Microhistory of Translation and Translators: Theoretical and Methodological Concerns' (Munday) 41

Van Alphen, Ernst 10
Vanderschelden, Isabelle 49, 178
Vansina, Jan 46
Venuti, Lawrence 39, 54, 62
verse libre 55
Vestnik 137
Vienna, Austria 12, 13
Viereck, Peter 7, 17, 71, 72, 132, 167–9, 167 n.6, 175
Vigdorova, Frida 11
Virgil 147
Virgil (Dryden) 84
Vitale, Tom 100
Volgina, Arina 65

volunteer translators 173–5
Von Flotow-Evans, Luise 40
Vorobiov, Masha 36, 71, 72, 106, 113, 114, 132–7, 139, 147
Voznesensky, Andrey 149

Wachtel, Michael 52
Wakabayashi, Judy 51
Walcott, Derek 25, 44, 46, 58, 74, 75, 83, 132, 151–2, 162–4, 174
Weissbort, Ben 132
Weissbort, Daniel 54, 68, 70, 71, 73, 76–8, 85, 88, 90, 93, 95, 98, 100, 101, 132, 137, 141, 154, 157, 160–7, 179, 181
Western monolingualism 43
Westsijn, W. G. 20
'What Is a Real Poet?' 11
W. H. Auden: A Tribute (Spender) 16
White, Stephen 7, 71, 72, 76, 85, 89, 93, 95, 98, 106, 132, 138–9, 145, 182
Wigzell, Faith 16
Wilbur, Richard Purdy 5, 55, 70–2, 132, 149–51, 154, 172, 174
Wilson, Edmund 5, 45
Witt, Susanna 132
Wolf, Michaela 39

Yale University 1
Yeats, W. B. 21
York, Lorraine Mary 65

'Za gorodishkom zlobnym ego' ('Beyond His Malicious Village,' Hutcheson) 174

www.ingramcontent.com/pod-product-compliance
Lightning Source LLC
Chambersburg PA
CBHW072235290426
44111CB00012B/2109